the ultimate guide to

CRYSTALS

the beginner's guide to **THE HEALING ENERGY** of 100 crystals & stones

RACHEL HANCOCK

FAIR WINDS

the ultimate guide to

CRYSTALS

Inspiring | Educating | Creating | Entertaining

Brimming with creative inspiration, how-to projects, and useful information to enrich your everyday life, Quarto.com is a favorite destination for those pursuing their interests and passions.

© 2022 Quarto Publishing Group USA Inc.
Text © 2022 Rachel Hancock
Photography © 2022 Quarto Publishing Group USA Inc
First Published in 2022 by Fair Winds Press, an imprint of The Quarto Group,
100 Cummings Center, Suite 265-D, Beverly, MA 01915, USA.
T (978) 282-9590 F (978) 283-2742 Quarto.com

Fair Winds Press titles are also available at discount for retail, wholesale, promotional, and bulk purchase. For details, contact the Special Sales Manager by email at specialsales@quarto.com or by mail at The Quarto Group, Attn: Special Sales Manager, 100 Cummings Center, Suite 265-D, Beverly, MA 01915, USA.

26 25 24 23 22   1 2 3 4 5

ISBN: 978-0-7603-7661-4

Digital edition published in 2022

eISBN: 978-0-7603-7662-1

Library of Congress Cataloging-in-Publication Data

Names: Hancock, Rachel, author.
Title: The ultimate guide to crystals : the beginners guide to the healing magic of 100 crystals and stones / Rachel Hancock.
Description: Beverly, MA : Fair Winds Press, 2022. | Series: The ultimate guide to... | Includes index. | Summary: "The Ultimate Guide to Crystals is a beginner's guide to crystals from Instagram influencer LovingThyselfRocks (222K) featuring profiles of 100 of the most popular stones plus information on using crystals in ritual and healing"-- Provided by publisher.
Identifiers: LCCN 2021060458 | ISBN 9780760376614 (trade paperback) | ISBN 9780760376621 (ebook)
Subjects: LCSH: Crystals--Miscellanea. | Precious stones--Miscellanea. | Magic.
Classification: LCC BF1442.C78 H36 2022 | DDC 133/.2548--dc23/eng/20211213
LC record available at https://lccn.loc.gov/2021060458

Design: Stacy Wakefield Forte
Cover Images: Rachel and Joel Hancock
Page Layout: Stacy Wakefield Forte
Photography: Rachel and Joel Hancock expect Shutterstock on page 187
Illustration: Shutterstock
Printed in Singapore

The information in this book is for educational purposes only. It is not intended to replace the advice of a physician or medical practitioner. Please see your health-care provider before beginning any new health program.

introduction

Growing up, all I wanted was to be loved. I did everything I could to feel loved by my family, friends, and even enemies.

In high school, I wanted to be loved so badly that I got deathly ill with an eating disorder. I believed that if I was sick, people would finally care for me the way I so desired. And although I recovered physically, I never fully healed mentally and spiritually. I pursued this unhealthy addiction into my early twenties when I had a near-death experience. I pushed myself until my body completely crashed. And I had absolutely no answers from any doctor. I was in and out of the hospital and bedridden for months.

There is something about death that becomes our biggest motivator to live and become well again. I stopped searching for external answers and went within to ask for help, and for the first time, I connected to my spirit. I asked for guidance and told my guides I was ready to do whatever it took to become happy, healthy, and myself again. I promised my spirit that this time was going to be different.

As I prayed, I got an overwhelming sensation of chills up and down my body. It felt as if angels were giving me a hug and telling me everything was going to be all right.

Shortly after this experience, I was guided to see a massage therapist. I was reluctant at first. I didn't believe that a massage could help fix any of my problems, but I decided to give it a try. I was led to a practitioner who wasn't just a massage therapist but also a Reiki energy healer.

Until that point, I had never chosen to care for and love myself first; I only did things for others to feel loved. It was the first moment in my life that I chose *me*, and I began to learn to love myself. During our session, I had my first experience of peace and hope. It was unlike anything I had ever experienced. That day changed my life.

I started doing more things to show love for myself. I began therapy, Kundalini yoga, meditation, daily positive affirmations, journaling, and seeing Lisa monthly. After a few months of gradually beginning to feel better, Lisa told me she believed my energy was ready for a greater shift. That was when I was introduced to crystals.

At the time, I didn't know anything about energy and was just getting started on my spiritual journey. But this session changed my life forever. I had

an out-of-body experience and felt a complete energetic, emotional, and physical release. I was in awe when the session was over, and I felt incredibly full of light and love. I also had a burning desire to learn everything about crystals.

I have always been a sensitive soul, an empath, and intuitive. It wasn't until I began my deep spiritual journey toward loving myself unconditionally that I learned how to take care of, understand, nourish, and love these gifts. And throughout my healing journey, I've found that my gifts and crystals go hand in hand.

As a sensitive soul, I feel energy—my own, others', animals', and the world's—at a heightened state. When I began holding crystals and listening to their energy, I understood it similarly to how I understood my own. I began by intuitively choosing crystals that I needed for whatever I felt was out of balance. Later, I would check to see what the crystals' healing properties were. Every time, I was astonished at how spot-on they were with the energy that I had felt.

As my knowledge of, connection to, and understanding of crystals grew, I felt a calling to help others use crystals to heal their lives too. I started by helping my husband, Joel, with his addiction to alcohol and then my loved ones with their anxiety. To expand my knowledge, I obtained my bachelor's degree in health and physical science with

a minor in psychology, became a Reiki master, and became a certified advanced crystal practitioner. Eventually, Joel and I decided to change the world by sharing our passion for the healing power of crystals, so we started our own company, Lovingthyselfrocks. We named our company after our mission to help others learn to love themselves unconditionally first, before they can love anyone else, just like we have done in our lives.

I am so grateful that Joel and I followed our calling, because we have now helped thousands of amazing souls work with crystals to help bring their bodies back into balance. Hopefully we will help you as well! This book is intended to help you understand crystals in greater detail so you can use them in the most effective and efficient ways. You can come back to it whenever you need help, reassurance, or guidance on which crystals to use and how to use them.

As you gain a greater understanding of crystal healing, I hope you take the time daily to go within and listen to what your body needs and then intuitively select a crystal to use to bring your body back into alignment. We all have different energies; therefore, what I recommend may not always work for you. Remember, I am only a guide—you are the ultimate healer in your own life. I love you and am proud of you. Take it one step at a time. You've got this.

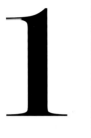

what are crystals?

the science and metaphysics behind crystal healing

CRYSTALS have been prized for their beauty—and used for metaphysical healing purposes—for centuries. They come in many colors, shapes, and sizes, and they can take millions of years to form. Let's examine the science and metaphysics behind crystal healing. The more you understand about crystals, the more effective and efficient they can be in your everyday life.

In the science of crystals, as a crystal begins to form, it goes through an initial stage called nucleation, during which a solution, liquid, or vapor becomes arranged in a crystalline solid structure. Crystals can be formed under pressure, when liquid from a solution evaporates, deep underground, laid in layers, or even as they are dripped into being. Once nucleation has occurred, crystals can grow quite large if they have room and the growth conditions are stable enough. Their internal crystalline arrangement of atoms determines their chemical composition, properties, and color. Most minerals are actually colorless in their pure form, but the way light interacts with different atoms causes impurities in the atomic structure, which creates color.

the science of
crystals

not everything is actually a crystal

This book uses the word *crystals* when describing every crystal, but the reality is that not everything is a crystal. Here are some terms you might encounter as you get to know the world of crystals.

Crystal: A solid material that has an internal crystalline lattice structure. Examples of crystals include clear quartz, rose quartz, and citrine.

Mineral: A naturally occurring solid material with a well-defined chemical composition and fixed structure that may or may not be a crystalline structure. Most minerals, such as quartz (SiO_2), are composed of more than one element. Some minerals contain trace amounts of other elements; for example, amethyst is quartz (SiO_2) with small traces of iron (Fe). This gives amethyst its purple color. Examples of minerals include copper, chrysocolla, fluorite, and kyanite.

Rock: A combination of one or more minerals. Most rocks are made from the most abundant elements on the earth's crust: silicon (Si) and oxygen (O). Examples of rocks include red jasper, unakite jasper, and lapis lazuli.

Gemstone: A cut and polished mineral or crystal that is chosen based on rarity, beauty, and durability. There are only four precious gemstones: diamond, emerald, sapphire, and ruby. These are the rarest, most durable, and most beautiful. Semiprecious gemstones are easier to access on the market and typically less durable. Some examples of these include aquamarine, morganite, watermelon tourmaline, peridot, and topaz.

Stone: Any member of the previous categories (crystal, mineral, rock, or gemstone) except for metallic minerals such as pyrite, copper, or hematite.

Fossil: A rock or stone that is the preserved remains of ancient organisms. The most common examples of fossils used in this book are amber, jet, and petrified wood.

Tektite: A gravel-size body made of natural glass in a color such as yellow, black, green, brown, or gray that has been formed following a meteorite crash. The two big examples of tektites used in this book are moldavite and Libyan desert glass.

the 7 crystal lattice systems

A crystal lattice or structure is a three-dimensional symmetrical arrangement of atoms in a crystal. The shape of the crystal lattice determines which crystal lattice system the crystal belongs to, its physical properties, and its appearance. Crystal lattice systems are groupings of crystal structures according to their arrangement of atoms. In general, minerals with the same crystal structure will often exhibit similarly shaped crystals.

Isometric/Cubic: Crystals that have three equal axes and meet at 90-degree, or right, angles. Spiritually, they represent contentment, nonattachment, focus, physical balance, and amplified energies. Examples: pyrite, fluorite, diamond, garnet, lapis lazuli, and sodalite.

Tetragonal: Crystals that have a rectangular crystal structure of three axes that meet at right angles; two axes have equal length and one is longer than the others. Spiritually, they represent manifestation, positive attraction, creativity, self-awareness, emotional balance, and higher consciousness. Examples: rutilated quartz, apophyllite, wulfenite, chalcopyrite, and vesuvianite.

Hexagonal: Crystals that have a hexagonal interior structure with four axes; three of the axes are at 120-degree angles and the fourth is perpendicular to them. Spiritually, they represent awareness, internal exploration, unconditional love, compassion, and positive communication. Examples: emerald, aquamarine, morganite, sugilite, and blue apatite.

Trigonal/Rhombohedral: Crystals that have a threefold symmetry where three axes of equal length are at 120-degree angles and the fourth axis is perpendicular to them. Spiritually, they represent energy, amplified intentions, healing, alignment, and wellness. Examples: hematite, pink tourmaline, black tourmaline, green tourmaline, watermelon tourmaline, sapphire, ruby, rose quartz, amethyst, and rhodochrosite.

Orthorhombic: Crystals that have an interior structure of three unequal axes all of which meet at right angles. Spiritually, they represent potential, visionary, purification, motivation, concentration, protection, and mobility. Examples: iolite, peridot, celestite, prehnite, chrysocolla, and thulite.

Monoclinic: Crystals that have a parallelogram-shaped interior structure with three axes. Two axes are at right angles and the third axis is at anything but a right angle. Spiritually, they represent protection, release, future predicting, meditation, purification, and motivation. Examples: malachite, epidote, nephrite jade, kunzite, lepidolite, rainbow moonstone, and selenite.

Triclinic: Crystals that have three axes, none of which meet at right angles. Spiritually, they represent protection, personal discovery, higher consciousness, spiritual expansion, yin and yang balance, and transformation. Examples: sunstone, larimar, kyanite, rhodonite, turquoise, amazonite, and labradorite.

mohs hardness scale

One of the most common ways to identify different minerals is by measuring the hardness of a stone using the Mohs hardness scale. This method was discovered by a German mineralogist, Friedrich Mohs, in the nineteenth century. It is done by measuring, comparing, and ranking a mineral's hardness on a scale of 1 to 10, with 1 being the softest and 10 being the hardest.

Hardness is important to note when considering whether your stone should be used in a crystal water or elixir and how it should be stored. Avoid putting any mineral softer than a 5 or 6 on the Mohs hardness scale in water or storing it directly next to crystals. The softer the mineral, the more likely it is to scratch or dissolve in water. For example, if you combined selenite and clear quartz in the same bowl, with selenite being a 2 on the Mohs hardness scale and clear quartz being a 7, the selenite would be scratched by the quartz.

Think about hardness when deciding which crystals to store together. They are sorted by hardness here, and each crystal's profile in chapter 7 mentions its hardness as well. But remember, just because a mineral is hard enough to scratch another crystal or surface doesn't mean it is safe to use in water. Please see chapter 7 to double-check whether your crystal is safe in water or safe as an elixir. When in doubt, always choose the indirect method of making a crystal elixir (see page 45).

HARDNESS	MINERALS
1	Talc
2	Amber (2–2.5), Selenite
3	Angelite (3.5), Blue Calcite, Bumblebee Jasper (2.5–5), Celestite (3–3.5), Chrysocolla (2–4), Copper (2.5–3), Honey Calcite, Howlite (3.5), Jet (2.5–4), Lepidolite (2.5–3), Orange Calcite, Vanadinite (3–4)
4	Azurite (3.5–4), Fluorite, Garnierite, Malachite (3.5–4), Rhodochrosite (3.5–4), Septarian (3.5–4), Shungite (3.5–4)
5	Black Obsidian (5–6), Blue Apatite, Charoite (5–6), Eudialyte (5–6), Gold Sheen Obsidian (5–6), Green Opal, Lapis Lazuli (5–5.5), Larimar (4.5–5), Moldavite (5.5–7), Rainbow Obsidian (5–6), Rhodonite (5.5–6), Scolecite (5–5.5), Turquoise (5–6)
6	Amazonite (6–6.5), Black Moonstone (6–6.5), Bloodstone, Blue Chalcedony (6–7), Blue Lace Agate (6.5–7), Epidote (6–7), Hematite (5.5–6.5), Kyanite (4.5–7), Labradorite (6–6.5), Larvikite (6–6.5), Libyan Desert Glass (6–7), Mookaite Jasper (6–7), Nephrite Jade (6–6.5), Opal (5.5–6.5), Pink Opal (6–7), Prehnite (6–6.5), Pyrite (6–6.5), Rainbow Moonstone (6–6.5), Sardonyx, Serpentine (3–6), Sodalite (5.5–6), Sugilite, Thulite (6–6.5), Unakite Jasper (6–7)
7	Agate (7–7.5), Amethyst, Black Onyx, Black Tourmaline (7–7.5), Carnelian, Citrine, Clear Quartz, Crazy Lace Agate (6.5–7), Fire Agate (6–7), Fire Quartz, Flower Agate (6.5–7), Garnet (6.5–7.5), Golden Healer, Green Aventurine (6.5–7), Green Tourmaline (7–7.5), Herkimer Diamond, Iolite (7–7.5), Kambaba Jasper (6.5–7), Kunzite (6.5–7), Lemurian, Moss Agate (6.5–7), Ocean Jasper (6.5–7), Orca Agate (6.5–7), Peridot (6.5–7), Petrified Wood (7–8), Pink Amethyst, Pink Tourmaline (7–7.5), Red Jasper (6.5–7), Rose Quartz, Rutilated Quartz, Shiva Lingam, Smoky Quartz, Spirit Quartz, Sunstone (6–6.5), Super 7, Tiger's Eye, Watermelon Tourmaline (7–7.5)
8	Aquamarine (7.5–8), Emerald (7.5–8), Morganite (7.5–8)
9	Ruby, Sapphire
10	Diamond

metaphysics of
crystal energy

Perhaps you are open to using crystals for healing purposes, but you wonder how they can help bring your body into balance and alignment. For starters, there is one thing that the entire universe has in common: We are all energy. We are energy, crystals are energy, and at a subatomic level, crystals can work with our energetic body to bring it back into balance.

Crystals are a solid matter composed of atoms, molecules, and ions that come together to form a crystal lattice. This crystal lattice is in a perfect stable structure, unlike us humans. It is believed that a crystal's perfect molecular blueprint has subtle energetic vibrations that, when crystals are placed on your body, cause your body to initiate a process called entrainment. Entrainment is when your energetic body mimics the energy of a crystal—so the perfect energy of the crystal helps bring your body back into balance. This is why crystals can also be used on animals and plants.

It's similar to how negative or positive energy affects your overall well-being. When you're around positive, optimistic, like-minded people, you feel joy, love, and happiness. But when you're around negative, hateful, jealous people, you feel depressed, angry, and drained. One vibrational system is affecting the other through the process of entrainment.

Each crystal has a different mineral composition that forms a specific crystal lattice. Just like our bodies will crave certain foods based on vitamins and minerals we are lacking, our energy field will crave certain vibrational frequencies when we are out of balance. A great example of this is lepidolite. You may be drawn to lepidolite because you're struggling with extreme anxiety or stress.

Ammonite fossil on clear quartz

Lepidolite's chemical composition is $K(Li,Al)3(Al,Si,Rb)4O10(F,OH)2$, with one of the main components being lithium (Li). Lithium is a main ingredient used in anti-anxiety medication because it limits the amount of norepinephrine (stimulation activity in the brain) that the body can process. When using lepidolite, our energetic body goes through entrainment by mimicking the energy of the lepidolite crystal to help calm the body and bring it back into balance.

As you may know, our mind is powerful. Since birth, our mind has been storing and programming information for 24 hours a day. There are two parts of our brain: our conscious mind, which only processes one thought at a time and never stores information, and our unconscious mind, which is the storehouse for all of our thoughts, emotions, dreams, reactions, and traumas. The unconscious mind doesn't understand the difference between reality and imagination, but it affects 95 percent of our daily conscious awareness and actions. This means that throughout your entire life, you have been living your reality based on the unconscious influence of your parents, loved ones, social media, television, culture, and even enemies. This programming distorts our reality and view of our authentic self.

Over time, we store negative emotions, thoughts, and traumas in our unconscious mind, and they eventually become trapped and can develop into physical pain, illnesses, or even diseases.

When using crystals, you are working with the Law of Resonance, which is when a vibrating system or an external force causes another system to vibrate with increased amplitude at certain frequencies. When you resonate with crystals, you can bring unconscious stuck energy (emotions, traumas, negative thoughts) to the surface and finally let go of everything that no longer serves you so you can vibrate at your most authentic, highest vibrational, loving self.

tapping into the entrainment process with clear quartz

Your body will entrain to the energy of whatever crystal you use, but for this practice I want you to test out the waters by using two clear quartz points. Place one clear quartz point in your receiving hand (typically your nondominant hand) with the termination, the point, facing upward toward your elbow and the other clear quartz point on your sending hand (typically your right hand) with the termination facing downward toward your fingertips. Then close your eyes and visualize a white beaming light traveling in from your receiving hand, up through your arm, through your whole chest, and out your sending hand. By doing this exercise, you will also tap into your body's piezoelectric crystals to bring your body back into balance and alignment.

your
crystalline body

We are human crystals. That's right, our body contains both piezoelectric crystals and liquid crystals, which both play a significant role in our body by sending and receiving energy signals from the universe. Piezoelectricity crystals are crystals whose energy is generated with sparks of light when pressure is applied. We have piezoelectric crystals in our teeth, bones, intestines, ligaments, collagen, cartilage, amino acids, trachea, muscle fibers, and tendons. Piezoelectricity generates electrical charges that are carried throughout the body to communicate from one cell to the next.

Liquid crystals are in a state between liquid and a solid. Marcel Vogel, a scientist who researched them for decades, found that the molecules in quartz (SiO_2) and water (H_2O) are naturally in sync with one another, which initiates a positive change at the subcellular level in our body. Liquid crystals are responsible for our cellular membranes, cytoskeletal proteins, muscular proteins, fatty tissues, white blood cells, collagen, and DNA. Our liquid crystalline body is a major reason why we can connect with mother earth's crystals. The crystalline structure of the earth's minerals is recognized by our body, which entrains with them to produce more balance in our bodies.

major and trace minerals found in the human body

Major and trace minerals are important for maintaining a healthy body. They help keep your bones, heart, muscles, and brain working properly. We can use these same major and trace minerals in our bodies for healing on an energetic level.

MAJOR MINERALS

Calcium (Ca) aids in maintaining healthy bones, muscles, nervous system, blood, heart, kidneys, immune system, and blood pressure. Spiritually, calcium helps us calm the mind, set boundaries, stop negative habits or addictions, reduce fear, and understand our emotions.

Crystal examples: fluorite, calcite, selenite, and aragonite

Potassium (K) aids in maintaining healthy muscle contractions, pancreas, spleen, thyroid, fluid balance, endocrine system, and nerve contractions. Spiritually, potassium helps release stagnant energies, boost self-confidence, release anger and stress, and stimulate intuition.

Crystal examples: lepidolite, rainbow moonstone, amazonite, and pink tourmaline

Chloride (Cl) aids in maintaining healthy fluid balance, GI tract, ears, hair, nails, eyes, kidneys, spleen, and endocrine system. Spiritually, chloride helps release stress, purify the mind and body, calm the mind, and promote positivity.

Crystal examples: sodalite and chlorapatite

Phosphorus (P) aids in maintaining healthy bones, teeth, cells, lungs, heart, and endocrine system. Spiritually, phosphorus helps restore vitality, reduce irritability and anger, and increase higher consciousness and intuition.

Crystal examples: blue apatite, turquoise, variscite, and lazulite.

Magnesium (Mg) aids in maintaining healthy bones, nervous system, adrenal glands, medulla, and blood vessels. Spiritually, magnesium helps bring emotional balance, heal the heart, and reduce stress and fears.

Crystal examples: peridot, serpentine, and nephrite jade

Sulfur (S) aids in maintaining a healthy endocrine system, digestive system, and detoxification of the body. Spiritually, sulfur helps us conquer our fears, confront our shadow self, and release negative attachments.

Crystal examples: sulfur, bumblebee jasper, pyrite, selenite, and angelite

TRACE MINERALS

Chromium (Cr) aids in maintaining a healthy pancreas, cholesterol, hormones, and blood sugar. Spiritually, chromium helps stimulate your intuition, gain deeper insight of your best self, and open the heart chakra.

Crystal examples: emerald, diopside, and garnet

Copper (Cu) aids in maintaining a healthy circulatory system, blood, skin, spleen, and iron metabolism. Spiritually, copper helps magnify energies, provide protection from negative energy, provide emotional relief, and strengthen personal power.

Crystal examples: copper, chrysocolla, malachite, azurite, and turquoise

Fluoride (F) aids in maintaining healthy ears, digestive system, bones, teeth, eyes, kidneys, adrenals, skeletal system, skin, and nervous system. Spiritually, fluoride helps you connect spiritually, release limiting beliefs, focus, and stimulate and expand the mind.

Crystal examples: fluorite, cryolite, and fluorapatite

Iron (Fe) aids in maintaining healthy red blood cells, oxygen, immune system, heart, circulatory system, and reproductive organs. Spiritually, iron helps calm the mind, provides protection from negative energy, boosts confidence and personal power, and helps you connect within.

Crystal examples: pyrite, amethyst, hematite, and hypersthene

Manganese (Mn) aids in maintaining healthy adrenal glands, immune system, kidneys, lungs, brain, nervous system, and heart. Spiritually, manganese helps reduce anxiety, provide emotional balance, spark creativity, stay grounded, and stimulate intuition.

Crystal examples: rhodochrosite, rhodonite, garnet, morganite, and smithsonite

Sodium (Na) aids in maintaining healthy blood circulation, spleen, digestive system, and kidneys. Spiritually, sodium helps bring alignment, releases stuck emotions, wards off negative energy, and cleanses the mind, body, and spirit.

Crystal examples: larimar, charoite, sodalite, and halite

Zinc (Zn) aids in maintaining a healthy immune system, liver, pancreas, blood, hair, nails, immune system, reproductive system, skin, and hormones. Spiritually, zinc helps boost spirits, spark creativity, increase overall energy, boost courage, and ignite spiritual transformation.

Crystal examples: hemimorphite, smithsonite, and sphalerite

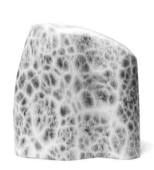

10 fun crystal healing
history facts

Crystals have been prized historically throughout the entire world. Below are some fun facts on how and when crystals have been used metaphysically to instill healing and protection.

1. Quartz has been used by humans since ancient times. To enhance fertility, women in Scotland would put it in water and bathe their feet in it. Celts used quartz to see visions of the past and future.

2. Buddhists from India, Nepal, and Tibet used sapphire to promote a peace of mind, spiritual devotion, serenity, enhanced meditation, higher awareness, and joy.

3. Cleopatra crushed up lapis lazuli and used it as eyeshadow. It was believed to represent eternal life.

4. Back in 4000 BCE, Egyptians crushed malachite into powder and used it as cosmetics to enhance their clairvoyant intuition.

5. In Babylon in 4000 BCE, carnelian was worn as an amulet to protect against loose teeth, bleeding gums, tumors, internal bleeding, and respiratory diseases.

6. Amethyst (*amethystos*) is named after the ancient Greeks, who believed it prevented drunkenness—that is what *amethystos* translates to. They would carve amethyst into drinking goblets, fill them with water to look like wine, and keep it next to them while they drank wine to prevent intoxication.

7. Amethyst was also worn by Roman soldiers, who used it as protection during battle; Roman women wore it to ensure their loved one stayed faithful.

8. Hematite comes from the Greek word *haima*, which translates to "blood." The Romans used it for treating blood disorders, the eyes, and burns.

9. Ruby was first utilized by people in India and Tibet during the Stone Age. Tibetans used it to increase sperm production, and people from India used it to reunite lovers who had been separated.

10. During the Paleolithic period, amber was worn to ward off evil spirits and cure diseases.

2 | where do you begin?

crystal basics and how to use them

WHEN YOU START your crystal healing journey, deciding which crystals to use to aid specific aspects of your life, mind, or body can be overwhelming. If you're anything like me, you just want them all, but that isn't realistic for most of us. Instead, start off slow and steady, so you can care for, love, and understand the energy of each of your crystals and the impact it makes on your overall well-being. We must walk before we run. This chapter is about how to choose the right crystal for you, how to connect with your crystal, the steps to take once you get your crystal, and other great beginner information I wish I had when I began my crystal healing journey.

choosing a crystal

Shopping for crystals is exciting yet overwhelming. There can be so many choices! You may ask yourself, where do I even begin? Here's how to let your intuition guide you to the perfect crystals for you.

using your intuition

Using your intuition is the best way to decide which crystal is best for you. How you select your crystal can vary based on how you are shopping. But whether you're shopping in a crystal shop or online, make sure to ground yourself first by taking a short walk outside barefoot, doing a 10-minute meditation, or closing your eyes and gently tapping your thymus for 20 to 30 seconds.

While shopping, be aware of which crystal really draws you in. It may be a certain color, shape, or type of crystal. This awareness will give you a greater understanding of which crystal(s) to choose. If you are in a crystal shop, set the crystals that you're drawn to out in front of you. Quickly and firmly rub your palms together for 20 to 30 seconds, or until you feel a sense of heat rising. Slowly hover your nondominant hand over each crystal, with your palm facing the crystal. As you scan each crystal, ask your intuition to tell you whether the crystal is right for you. You may feel heat, a tingly sensation, a loud yes from the universe, or another message from your intuition.

If you want more confirmation, you can use a crystal pendulum to give you a direct yes or no answer. (See page 197 for directions on how to use a pendulum.) Once you have picked your crystal(s), use the crystal directory in this book to give you even more confirmation on why you were drawn to one or several crystals.

If you are shopping online, you can set crystals aside by placing them in your shopping cart. As you go over the cart, ask your intuition to tell you whether each crystal is right for you. If the online listing is one where you cannot individually select your crystal and you want to be pickier, try messaging the seller to see if they can show you options to select from.

what to do when
you get a new crystal

Here are a few easy steps to take when you bring your new crystal home.

cleanse it

Ensure that your crystal is free of any stored-up energy residue before using it. Crystals absorb all energy, good and bad, so they may take on energy from a previous owner, a crystal shop, or their travels. To cleanse your crystal, put it in the sunlight, in the moonlight, under water, or next to sound vibration, or pass it through the smoke of sage, palo santo, or incense. How often you need to cleanse your crystal after the first use depends on how often you will be working with it and for how long. For further detail on how to properly cleanse your crystal, see chapter 3.

charge it

Just as humans cannot function properly without sleep (because it helps our body and brain repair, restore, and re-energize), crystals cannot function optimally without charging. It helps the crystal operate at its highest vibration. Just as you care for your body, you should care for your crystal.

To charge your crystal, put it in the sunlight, in the moonlight, under a copper pyramid, under water, next to sound vibration, or submerged in dried flowers or herbs. How often you need to charge your crystal after the first use depends on how often you will be working with it and for how long. For further detail on how to properly charge your crystal, see chapter 3.

attune to its energy

When you first come in contact with your crystal, you naturally begin to attune to its energy, which causes subtle changes in your energy field. By tuning into your crystal's energy, you will be able to raise your vibrations and understand your crystal on a deeper level.

Begin by grounding and centering yourself. You can do this by closing your eyes and gently tapping your thymus for 20 to 30 seconds or by doing a 3-minute meditation. Then quickly and firmly rub your palms together for 20 to 30 seconds or until you feel heat rising. Pick up your crystal and become aware of its energy. How does it feel to touch? How does it feel when it's on your body? How does it make you feel?

You may want to keep a crystal journal next to you so you can take note of your crystal's energy. You may come to find that it's not the right time just yet to be working with it—or that it's exactly what you need in your life at this time. By understanding your crystal's energy, you will be able to be more intuitively guided as to when to use and not use it, when it needs to be cleansed or charged, and how it's affecting your energy and overall well-being.

set intentions

Each crystal's unique structure is believed to store energy, ideas, and memories. And each crystal has multiple healing properties, so by setting your intentions before using it, you can program it to work for a specific healing, goal, or intention. You are simultaneously programming yourself by focusing on exactly what you want to heal or achieve. To set your intentions, hold your crystal up to your third-eye chakra level with both hands, close your eyes, and focus on the crystal. As you do, envision your intention and repeat the affirmation "Crystal, please assist me with __." Fill in the blank with your specific intention. Repeat this affirmation several times until you feel that the crystal's energy is programmed. This should make you feel good and warm.

place it with intention

Finally, intentionally place your crystal somewhere in your home, in a crystal layout on your body (skin contact is preferable for better results), somewhere it will be taken with you, or on a crystal grid.

Displaying your crystals with intention

top 15 crystals
for beginners

Yes, you can technically start out with any crystals you'd like, but below are my top 15 recommendations. Think of these crystals as a starter kit that will always be beneficial. I have multiples of each because they serve so many different purposes. I have them all over my house, especially my meditation area, I wear them as everyday jewelry, and I have some especially for crystal grids.

1. **CLEAR QUARTZ**
    Everyone should have clear quartz in their crystal collection. It is known as the master healer because it can be programmed to be used on any physical, mental, emotional, or spiritual ailment that you want to work on. It amplifies the energy of any crystal, human,

or intention. It speeds up manifestation, infuses the body with divine light, helps restore the body's health and wellness, and brings the body back into balance. Clear quartz is compatible with any crystal and can be used alongside it to amplify its healing properties.

2. **ROSE QUARTZ**
    Rose quartz is one of the very first crystals I purchased for my crystal journey. Its gentle, subtle energies make it perfect to use for anyone. Rose quartz bathes you in unconditional love for yourself and others. It helps open the heart back up to love again. It promotes forgiveness, compassion, empathy, joy, and generosity. Rose quartz can be used

to enhance loving positive affirmations and nourish the soul during your daily meditation.

3. **AMETHYST**

Amethyst was the first crystal in my crystal collection—it was a gift from my husband. It's one of the most versatile crystals to be used daily in your home, car, jewelry, pocket, wallet, or meditation. Amethyst helps enhance your meditation, boost intuition, reduce stress and anxiety, promote peaceful sleep, and overcome bad habits or addictions. If you are a sensitive soul who tends to absorb people's energy, Amethyst will help provide an energy protection field around you to keep you feeling positive and balanced.

4. **SELENITE**

Selenite is most known by the crystal community for cleansing and charging other crystals because of its ability to cleanse itself and its ability to absorb and release negative energy. Selenite also helps clear energetic blockages, reduce pain and inflammation in the body, promote peace of mind, and provide access to past and future lives. It is known for cleansing, protecting, and expanding the auric field.

5. **CARNELIAN**

Carnelian has a fun wavy energy that will help you bring some pep to your step! It is known for increasing physical energy, libido, vitality, and strength. It's my number one recommendation for women trying to get pregnant, as it can increase fertility. Emotionally, carnelian helps you set boundaries with others, encourages positive relationships, and boosts feelings of self-confidence. Carnelian can help spark creativity, making it amazing for artists or those in business trying to cultivate unique ideas.

6. **LEPIDOLITE**

Lepidolite is my number one recommendation for most of my loved ones and clients. That is because of its amazing ability to help reduce anxiety, depression, stress, worry, nervousness, and fear. It's a great stone to have in your pocket at all times as a "crystal first aid kit" to help calm the mind, body, and spirit when needed. I personally never leave my house without it. Lepidolite also helps promote positive thoughts, balance emotions, induce peaceful sleep, encourage independence, and release emotional traumas.

7. **LABRADORITE**

Labradorite is a very popular crystal for its gorgeous flashy appearance and its incredible ability to shield from negative energy. As a sensitive soul myself, I highly recommend it to all my loved ones and clients for protection against all surrounding negative energies. Labradorite is also known as the stone of transformation, helping you get through major changes in your life, such as moving or getting a new job. Labradorite helps provide insight into the root cause of physical symptoms, increases imagination, promotes psychic connection, and helps overcome fearful thinking.

8. **BLACK TOURMALINE**

Black tourmaline is most often used for its amazing ability to help protect you from negative energy and EMFs (electromagnetic fields). You can keep a small raw piece or wear it as jewelry daily to provide you with an energy shield of protection. Black tourmaline also helps encourage spiritual growth, remove toxins from the body, dive deep into self-discovery, and ground yourself to become present in the moment.

9. **CITRINE**

Citrine is most often used for manifesting wealth and abundance in your life. It's a very high vibrational crystal that can raise your vibrations quickly. It's seen often as heat-treated amethyst clusters; natural citrine can be pretty expensive and has pristine energy (see page 88). Citrine also helps increase self-confidence, provide stomach relief, boost stamina and energy, release old limiting beliefs, strengthen personal power, and find a deep sense of purpose in life.

10. FLUORITE

Fluorite is one of the most well-known crystals. Not only is it beautiful in every color (purple, green, blue, yellow, pink, red, orange, white, brown, and black) but it also has a very vibrant energy that will keep you stimulated and connected spiritually. Fluorite is my number one recommendation for students because of its amazing ability to promote focus, concentration, and mental clarity. Fluorite also helps stimulate intuition, renews all seven chakras, stabilizes emotions, enhances meditation, protects and stabilizes the aura, and sparks creativity.

11. CELESTITE

In general, I have found we humans are most often attracted to blue and pink crystals because of our strong desire to feel at peace and loved. Celestite is no exception and is my top recommendation for keeping in nearly every room in your home. It brings soothing and gentle vibrations that will help quiet the mind, calm the nervous system, and put the day's stress and worries to the side, promoting overall peace and harmony. Celestite also aids in spiritual connection and awakening, helps you speak your truth, and promotes a peaceful night's rest.

12. SMOKY QUARTZ

Daily life's stressors can make you feel ungrounded, spacy, dizzy, and anxious. Smoky quartz has incredible vibrations that help you reconnect to the earth's healing vibrations, bringing you back into the present moment and allowing you to feel more grounded, balanced, and clear-headed. Smoky quartz also works to reduce negative thoughts, pain, harmful radiation, irrational fears, and anger. I highly suggest either keeping a small pocket stone with you or wearing it as jewelry at all times.

13. HOWLITE

Howlite has one of the gentlest and most soothing energies. It is great for those who are more sensitive to energy, such as empaths and lightworkers, because it brings in soft, subtle energies that aren't over-whelming. Howlite pairs well with lepidolite when you are placing the intention of reducing anxiety or stress and promoting peace and harmony. Howlite also helps deepen your meditation, encourages emotional expression, and aids in a peaceful night's rest.

14. PYRITE

Pyrite is most well known by its nickname, "fool's gold," because of its appearance—it looks like gold. If you want to attract more wealth, good luck, success, and abundance to your life, pyrite will help magnify those manifestations and speed up the process. It's best to keep pyrite in your wallet or office space to increase the vibrations and magnify your universal attraction to all your greatest dreams and aspirations. Pyrite helps strengthen and balance the solar plexus chakra. It also works to support a healthy digestive system, increase self-worth, and increase motivation.

15. SUNSTONE

Sunstone is my number one recommendation for those who are struggling with depression. I find sunstone to be a great pick-me-up on days when you feel tired, sad, lonely, or unmotivated. It can also be worn daily to promote a constant reminder that all is well in your world and that after every storm the sun always shines. It can also provide you with the motivation to get out of bed and accomplish activities that bring you joy, gratitude, and enjoyment in life again. Sunstone also sparks creativity, boosts self-confidence, and helps improve overall health and well-being.

For further detail on each of these, see chapter 7.

soothing vibrational crystals

Some crystals are gentler, and others have a very high vibrational pull. This topic is especially important for sensitive souls and empaths—as a beginner, you should start off with a more gentle and soothing crystal, so you don't feel overwhelmed and overworked, and possibly withdraw from crystals because it feels too much for you.

For example, moldavite, one of the highest vibrational tektites, is so high vibration that almost anyone can feel its energy, no matter how sensitive they are. And it shouldn't be taken lightly. It's known for giving people a "moldavite flush"—a huge opening of the heart chakra that can cause a flush in the face, anxiety, lightheadedness, dizziness, an overwhelming sensation of emotional release, and even the feeling of being lifted out of your body. This is because moldavite and the other high vibrational crystals mentioned below excite and speed up your vibrations at a rapid pace.

Your body needs to become acclimated to these high vibrations. To do so, slowly introduce your body to a crystal's vibrations. Start with 1 minute and see how its energy feels for you. Then up it to 2 to 3 minutes the next day or whenever you're ready. It took me three weeks to be able to meditate with moldavite for 10 minutes, but some people can wear it all day immediately. This is why attuning to its energy is such an important step when getting your crystal. Please listen to your body, but don't be afraid to get uncomfortable. Change doesn't come from comfort. We want to release what no longer serves our best selves—but only through love and care.

Here are ten high vibrational and ten soothing vibrational crystals, stones, and tektites to consider for your crystal healing journey.

HIGH VIBRATIONAL CRYSTALS, STONES, AND TEKTITES

1. Moldavite
2. Herkimer diamond
3. Libyan desert glass
4. Super 7
5. Malachite
6. Lemurian
7. Clear quartz
8. Kunzite
9. Selenite
10. Citrine

SOOTHING VIBRATIONAL CRYSTALS AND STONES

1. Rose quartz
2. Amethyst
3. Blue calcite
4. Blue lace agate
5. Celestite
6. Howlite
7. Lepidolite
8. Pink opal
9. Red jasper
10. Kambaba jasper

crystal precautions

Just because crystals are natural doesn't mean it's safe to go about using them any way you'd like. Here are some safety concerns to keep in mind.

- Not all crystals are safe to put in water, and some contain toxic or hazardous minerals that shouldn't be ingested. If you aren't sure whether your crystal is safe, it's best to avoid putting it in water, especially water to be ingested.

- Do not push the process and overwhelm your system with too many crystals at once. Honor your intuition. If you are having negative side effects, completely stop using your crystals for a time. You may be using too many different crystals and causing your energy system to become overwhelmed and overworked.

- Not all crystals are safe to put outside in the sunlight for a prolonged period. Some can crack, break, fade, or even start a fire! Some of the most photosensitive crystals are beryls, quartz, and calcites. You can always place any crystal outside for 5 to 10 minutes, but if you're unsure, don't go any longer than that.

- Be mindful of which crystals you are using. Not all crystals have a soft gentle energy (see page 27). You don't want to be overwhelmed, overworked, or possibly convinced to withdraw from crystals because the energy is too much for you. Listen to your intuition. Typically, choose soothing and gentle vibrational crystals to ease into the crystals' energy.

- Crystals that amplify energy, such as clear quartz, can bring in positive energy and remove negative energy from the body if placed correctly. However, it can also amplify or exacerbate physical symptoms if not used correctly. When in doubt, use this book to guide you.

oh no, my crystal broke! now what?

Throughout your crystal journey, you may break a crystal or two. If you crack, break, or chip a crystal, it does not lose its healing properties, but there are a couple of spiritual meanings behind a broken crystal. One is that the crystal has done its work. When it breaks, it's letting you know that it's time to move on from that crystal. And if it's a protective crystal such as amethyst, black obsidian, or black tourmaline, it could have broken while protecting you from intense negative energy. Regardless of the meaning, it's up to you to decide what to do with it next. Let your intuition guide you as to whether you glue it back together, cleanse and charge it, gift it, or do anything else that best serves you.

not all crystals

are what they say they are

Unfortunately, not all crystals on the market are natural, and some aren't even what they claim to be. This can be confusing. For instance, there is a man-made opal on the market called opalite. When something is man-made, there is no natural crystalline structure to provide the healing vibrations you are hoping to receive. This happens most frequently with extremely rare crystals that have a high dollar value.

Look for terms such as:

- **Heat-treated.** Heat-treated crystals are heated at extremely high temperatures, causing inclusions, chemical elements, and other impurities to reform and affect the hue of the stone. This is typically done to intensify the color, making it look more vibrant and valuable. It is most seen in "citrine" that is really heat-treated amethyst. Other commonly heat-treated crystals are morganite, aquamarine, fluorite, tanzanite, sapphire, tourmaline, kunzite, topaz, and smoky quartz.

- **Man-made, artificial, or synthetic.** Man-made stones are made in a laboratory. Synthetic stones are made to look almost identical to the natural stone and even have their crystalline structure, composition, and properties. This is typically done with sapphire, emerald, ruby, citrine, and other valuable gemstones. One of the best ways to tell whether it's real or fake, because they end up looking so similar, is the price. If the price is too good to be true, that's because it typically is. Artificial stones, which don't have any minerals from nature, have completely different crystalline structures, compositions, and properties from those of the stone they are mimicking. You see this in the market as man-made glass such as opalite, goldstone, and cherry quartz.

- **Dyed.** Dyeing crystals is typically done to intensify their color, making them look more vibrant and appealing. Frequently dyed crystals include turquoise, howlite, amethyst, and agate. The biggest problem with dyeing crystals, besides not having them in their natural color, is that if you are unaware that a stone is dyed and you use it in a crystal bath, water, or tonic, it could potentially be hazardous. Amethyst is safe to place in water, but dyed amethyst is not. The chemical composition of the crystal is not altered, so the metaphysical properties remain the same.

- **Aura-treated.** Aura-treated crystals are coated with the metals titanium and niobium to form a vibrant rainbow finish on top of the crystal. This is typically done with clear quartz, spirit quartz, rose quartz, and kyanite; however, I have seen this treatment done to almost every crystal on the market. The biggest concern with aura-treated crystals is that if you are unaware that it is treated and you use it in a crystal bath, water, or tonic, it could potentially be hazardous. For instance, clear quartz is safe to place in the water, but aura-treated clear quartz is not.

3 | caring for your crystals

cleansing, charging, and storing your crystals

AS AN EMPATH, I take the cake for absorbing other people's energies like a sponge! Or at least I did until I learned about crystals. Crystals absorb all energy, good and bad. Regardless of whether you have utilized the precious stone, a friend or family member has, or you went to a shop to pick another one up, it needs love and care. Before you use your crystal(s), make sure they are cleared of any energy residue and recharged to bring you or a loved one the healing needed. It's important that you first clear the energy of the crystal and then charge it. Think of your crystal like us humans— we can take as many showers as we want to be cleansed from all the debris from our day, but we cannot survive very long if we don't have a good night's rest.

your crystal

You can tell a crystal needs to be cleansed when:

- The energy feels dull, empty, or lifeless.
- You or a loved one just used it.
- Seems less effective when you are using it.

Here is a general rule of thumb for how often you should be cleansing and charging your crystals.

- **Multiple times a day**: if you are a crystal healer and are using them on clients all day.
- **Daily**: if you are wearing them all day or sleeping with them at night.
- **Weekly**: if you are doing short meditations with them or keeping them in your purse or car.
- **Monthly**: if you have them dispersed in your home for feng shui.

cleansing methods

Here are a few effective ways to cleanse your crystals.

sunlight

Place your crystal(s) out in direct sunlight for 1 to 2 hours. All crystals are safe for a quick 5 minute cleanse, but some crystals can become damaged or hazardous if left in the sunlight for too long. See chapter 7 to check whether your crystal is safe for prolonged sunlight exposure.

moonlight

Place your crystal(s) out in direct moonlight overnight. Check below for specific cleansing intentions depending on which phase the moon is in. If you live in a place where you cannot take your crystals into direct moonlight, place them on your windowsill.

water

Place your crystal(s) in a bowl of water from a natural body of water (such as a lake, river, or ocean) or lightly sea-salted water. Keep them in the bowl for 1 to 5 minutes and then rinse them with regular tap water. Leave them out to air-dry. Note: Not all crystals are safe in water. Some can crack, break, dissolve, or expose you to toxic chemicals if ingested through an elixir. Make sure to double-check chapter 7 to see whether your crystal is safe in water.

sound vibration

Sound waves pass through the crystal and release energy stored within it. Place your crystal next to a sound vibrational tool, such as a sound bowl, tingsha, bell, tuning fork, gong, or crystal pyramid. Play the instrument for a couple of minutes.

selenite or clear quartz

Place your crystal(s) on a selenite or clear quartz plate or bowl. You can cleanse your crystal(s) by your bedside overnight or leave them to charge throughout the day. I would recommend leaving them to cleanse for at least 4 to 6 hours.

energetic intentional breath

For this method, you can use Reiki or intentional visualization. Place the crystal in your hand. As you breathe in, visualize your hand filling up with pure bright light and expanding that light into the crystal. As you breathe out, visualize any stagnant, negative, or stuck energy releasing from the crystal. Continue this breathing technique until you intuitively feel the crystal has been cleansed.

sage, palo santo, or incense

Light your sage, palo santo, or incense and pass the crystal(s) through the smoke for 30 seconds to a few minutes. One way you will know whether the clearing work is done is that the smoke will move to one side of the crystal instead of all over.

storing crystals

Ultimately you want to use your inner guidance when choosing where you want to display crystals in your home. See page 47 for a discussion of the feng shui of where to energetically place your crystals in your home. However, something important to consider when storing your crystals are:

- Is the crystal okay in prolonged sun exposure? If it's not, you will want to avoid putting it in direct sunlight from your windowsill or outside in your garden.
- Is your crystal soft? If it's a 5 or below on the Mohs hardness scale, I would make sure it isn't touching any other crystals, so it doesn't scratch, and is in a safe place where it cannot fall, because if it does it will more than likely chip or break.
- If you choose to put your crystal in a container, make sure that it won't damage it. The safest containers are made of wood, cotton, silk, or anything soft to the touch.
- Keep your most precious crystals in a safe place where they won't be touched by others.

charging methods

Here are a few good ways to charge your crystals after you have cleansed them.

sunlight

Place your crystal(s) out in direct sunlight for 1 to 2 hours. Note: All crystals are safe for a quick 5-minute charge, but some crystals can crack, break, change color, or even start a fire if left in the sunlight for too long. Make sure to double-check chapter 7 to see whether that your crystal is safe in prolonged sunlight exposure.

moonlight

Place your crystal(s) out in direct moonlight overnight. Check below for specific charging intentions depending on which phase the moon is in. If you live in an apartment or a place where you cannot take your crystals into direct moonlight, place them on your windowsill.

copper pyramids

Copper pyramids represent enhanced energy, preservation, purification, protection, and spiritual connection. Place your crystal(s) in the center of your pyramid for at least 6 hours. Keep a pyramid near your bedside for a nightly charging station.

sound vibration

Sound waves pass through the crystal, restore its energy, and put it back into balance. Place your crystal next to a sound vibrational tool, such as a sound bowl, tingsha, bell, tuning fork, gong, or crystal pyramid. Play the instrument for a couple of minutes.

selenite or clear quartz

Place your crystal(s) on a selenite or clear quartz plate or bowl. You can charge your crystal(s) by your bedside overnight or leave them to charge throughout the day. I recommend leaving it to charge for at least 4 to 6 hours. This process can be done simultaneously with the cleansing process.

clear quartz grid

Place six clear quartz points around your crystal, facing inward toward it. You can use fewer or more quartz points depending what your intentions are; see the numerology section in chapter 4 to help decide how many. I recommend leaving it to charge for at least 4 to 6 hours.

dried herbs, seeds, leaves, or flowers

Place your crystal in a bowl and fill it with your choice of dried herbs, seeds, leaves, flowers, or even a combination of them all. Make sure the crystal is completely covered and leave it overnight to charge.

snow

Place your crystal outside and completely cover it with snow. Make sure you mark the place you have chosen so it doesn't get lost. Leave it overnight to charge. Snow brings the intentions of peace and serenity to the crystal. This method is great for those who live up north and may not get as many sunny days. Note: Not all crystals are safe in water. Some can crack, break, dissolve, or expose you to toxic chemicals if ingested through an elixir. Make sure to double-check chapter 7 to see whether your crystal is safe in water.

storm

Place your crystal outside during a storm somewhere it has direct connection to mother nature. I recommend leaving it to charge for at least 2 to 3 hours. Storms bring the intentions of excitement, renewal, and balance to the crystal. This method is great for those who live in a place with a lot of storms and may not get as many sunny days. If you don't feel comfortable bringing your crystal out in the storm, your windowsill will suffice. Note: Not all crystals are safe in water. Some can crack, break, dissolve, or expose you to toxic chemicals if ingested through an elixir. Make sure to double-check chapter 7 to see whether your crystal is safe in water.

fog

Place your crystal outside in the fog, preferably where it has direct connection to mother nature. I recommend leaving it to charge overnight. Fog brings the intentions of protection and overcoming obstacles to the crystal. This method is great for those who live in a place that may not get as many sunny days. If you don't have access to bringing your crystal out in the fog, your windowsill will suffice.

moon phases

& their cleansing and charging intentions

Different phases of the moon bring different intentions to your cleansing and charging.

- **New moon:** new beginnings, clear intentions, new opportunities, self-reflection, self-care, and renewal
- **Waxing crescent:** planning, preparing, positive energy, amplified manifestations, inner wisdom, personal strength, optimism, and communication
- **First quarter:** supporting intentions, love and romance, determination, commitment, overall health and wellness, and courage
- **Waxing gibbous:** moving forward, cultivating intentions, taking action, acceptance, surrender, creativity, tranquility, and commitment

- **Full moon:** amplified intentions, abundance, manifestation, heightened intuition, transformation, personal power, protection, and flow
- **Waning gibbous:** letting go of what doesn't serve you, setting boundaries, gratitude, nurturing, and reflection
- **Last quarter:** compassion, release, enjoying accomplishments, independence, success, blossoming, and epiphany
- **Waning crescent:** solitude, relaxation, rest, solidification, preparation for new intentions to be set, stillness, release, and reflection

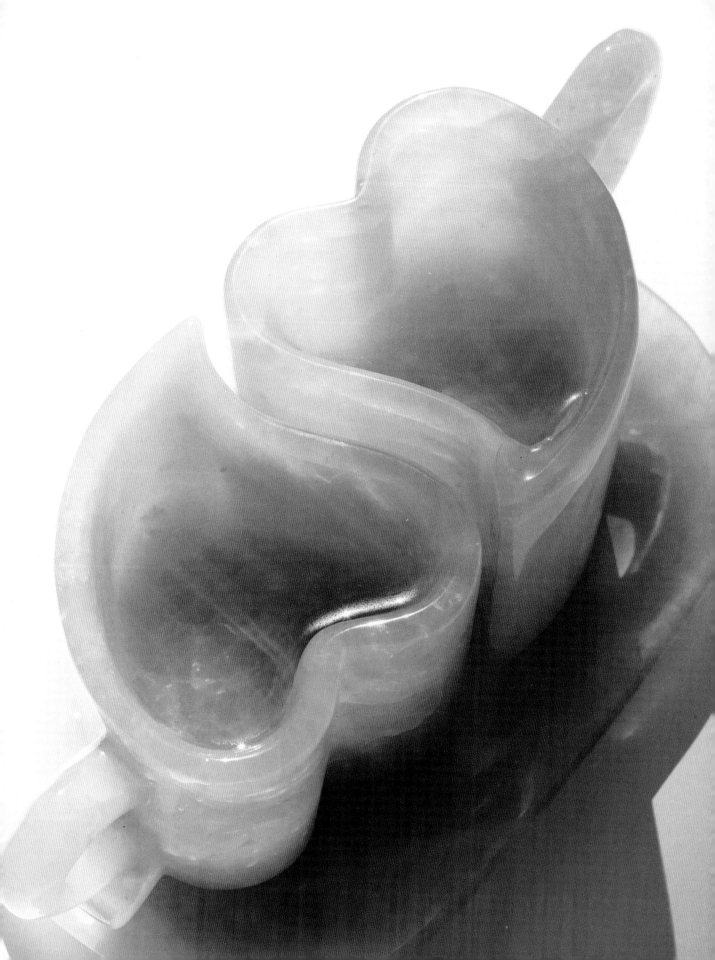

4 | nine ways to use your crystals

crystal grids, reiki, yoga, oracle or tarot cards, astrology, crystal water or elixirs, baths, meditation, and crystal feng shui

CRYSTALS CAN BE used alongside many of your spiritual practices to enhance the energy, healing, and intention. This chapter explores nine different ways to use your crystals: crystal grids, reiki, yoga, oracle or tarot cards, astrology, crystal water or elixirs, baths, meditation, and crystal feng shui. You may find you absolutely love all of these methods or only one. Give them all a try to ignite change in your energy and life.

one
crystal grids

A crystal grid is an intentional arrangement of crystals placed using sacred geometry and numerology to manifest a specific goal, desire, outcome, or intention. Here's how to set one up.

1. **SET YOUR INTENTION.**
   Make sure this intention is as specific as possible. Let the universe know exactly what you're asking for. You can even write your intention out on a piece of paper and set it in the middle of your crystal grid.

2. **CHOOSE THE GRID.**
   There are different materials and geometric shapes that can enhance the energy and intentions of your grid. If you don't have a grid, you can always make one on a bare surface. You can also use feng shui (see page 47) to determine which area in your home best enhances your intentions.

3. **CHOOSE, CLEANSE, AND CHARGE YOUR CRYSTALS.**
   Before you place the crystals on your grid, it's important that all your crystals are cleansed and charged. You want them to radiate the most vibrant energy! When choosing your crystals, make sure to select one central stone and several supporting stones.

4. **PLACE THE FIRST CRYSTAL IN THE CENTER OF YOUR GRID.**
   This crystal should be the largest, and it should be aligned with your overall intention. Typically, crystal points or pyramids work best for this area of your grid so they can direct and amplify your intentions straight out into the universe.

5. **PLACE YOUR SUPPORTING CRYSTALS ON YOUR GRID.**
   These crystals surround your central crystal and further define your intention. The number of crystals that you add to your grid will depend on the complexity of your intention, numerology, and sacred geometry. Typically, you want to choose the same type and size of crystal when placing them around your grid.

6. **ADD OTHER ELEMENTS TO YOUR GRID.**
   This step is optional but great for adding personal touches and enhancing your intention. You could include photos, affirmations, herbs, feathers, flowers, candles, oracle cards, or anything else that has a spiritual representation to you that you believe will support and enhance your intention.

7. **ACTIVATE YOUR GRID.**
   Use a cleansed and charged clear quartz point or selenite wand. Starting from the outside of the grid, draw an invisible line between each crystal, connecting the dots, all the way to the central crystal. As you connect the crystals, imagine a white light unifying their energies. Another way to activate your crystal grid is by using the clear quartz point or selenite wand to circle the grid three times, either clockwise to send energy outward or counterclockwise to bring energy into you around the crystal grid. You can repeat this activation as often as you'd like to maintain the grid's high vibrational frequency.

numerology: the spiritual meanings of numbers

When selecting supporting crystals for your crystal grid, you can amplify your intentions by using numerology. Below is the number of supporting crystals to use based on your intention. For instance, if your main intention is to attract more abundance, you may want your supporting intention to be to manifest more wealth. You could then place eight citrine tumbled stones surrounding your central crystal on your grid, because the number eight spiritually represents manifestation.

1. Independence, new beginnings, unity, confidence, power, inspiration, solidary, self, and anchoring

2. Balance, polarity, grace, partnership, equality, harmony, and teamwork

3. Communication, mind/body/spirit balance, serenity, engaging, and joy

4. Grounding, completion, stability, four elements (earth, water, fire, air), protection, security, and contentment

5. Freedom, curiosity, change, empowerment, creative, and innovative

6. Harmony, manifestation, self-improvement, healing, love, service, and movement

7. Luck, intuition, spirituality, personal growth, solitude, and wisdom

8. Expansive, achievement, eternity, strength, manifestation, goals, and abundance

9. Closure, completion, self-reflection, transition, transformation, and wisdom

sacred geometry: the language of the universe

Once you decide on your main intention for a crystal grid, choose a shape from sacred geometry that supports it to be the base of your grid. For instance, if your main intention is to provide support through a large transition in your life, then you may choose a hexagon (spiritual transformation) or seed of life (new beginnings). See Sacred Geometry Symbols chart on the next page.

crystal grid examples

Here are some examples of how this comes together.

INTENTION: MANIFESTING PROSPERITY AND ABUNDANCE

Center crystal and intention: 1 clear quartz point, power

Supporting crystal and intention: 8 pyrite tumbles, abundance

Supporting crystal and intention: 6 citrine tumbles, manifestation

Supporting crystal and intention: 5 green aventurine tumbles, change

Supporting crystal and intention: 8 double-terminated herkimer diamond, expansiveness and magnification

Numerology: 1, 5, 6, 8

Sacred Geometry: Flower of life

SACRED GEOMETRY SYMBOLS

TRIANGLE	△	change, empowerment, amplification, serenity, trinity, creation, manifestation
CIRCLE	○	unity, completion, boundaries, oneness, cycles of life
SQUARE	▢	balance, equality, stability, foundation, safety, practicality, grounding
SPIRAL	◉	as above so below, evolution, raising consciousness, rapid change, energy flow
CROSS	✚	union of heaven and earth, stability, balance, protection
PENTAGON	⬟	protection, luck, five elements (earth, water, fire, air, spirit)
HEXAGON	⬣	expansion, harmony, spiritual transformation, balance, grounding
HEART	♡	emotional balance, love, passion, romance, compassion, joy
VESICA PISCIS		divine femininity, universal creation, birth, womb
TRIQUETRA		sacred trinities and life cycles
SEED OF LIFE		manifestation, new beginnings, creation
FLOWER OF LIFE		blueprint of creation, manifestation, activation, healing
TREE OF LIFE		divine love, oneness, knowledge, personal development, strength
FRUIT OF LIFE		transition, purity, unity
METATRON'S CUBE		positivity, balance of feminine and masculine energies, personal power, empowerment, harmony, protection
SRI YANTRA		connection between universe and humanity, energy, shakti

INTENTION: SELF-LOVE

Supporting crystal and intention: 6 rose quartz tumbles, love

Supporting crystal and intention: 6 lemurian, healing

Supporting crystal and intention: 6 raw morganite, self-improvement

Numerology: 6

Sacred Geometry: Spiral

INTENTION: CALMING THE MIND

Center crystal and intention: 1 raw blue lace gate, unity

Supporting crystal and intention: 2 aquamarine points, harmony

Supporting crystal and intention: 2 lepidolite tumbles, balance

Supporting crystal and intention: 4 raw black tourmaline, grounding

Numerology: 1, 2, 4

Sacred Geometry: Hexagon

INTENTION: PROTECTION FROM NEGATIVE ENERGY

Center crystal and intention: 1 amethyst cluster, self

Supporting crystal and intention: 4 raw black tourmaline, protection

Supporting crystal and intention: 4 selenite tumbles, protection

Numerology: 1, 4

Sacred Geometry: Cross

INTENTION: JOY

Center crystal and intention: 1 sunstone, confidence and self

Supporting crystal and intention: 3 citrine tumbles, joy

Supporting crystal and intention: 2 ocean jasper tumbles, harmony

Numerology: 1, 2, 3

Sacred Geometry: Heart

long-distance healing

Long-distance healing is the art of sending healing energy to loved ones remotely. Your loved one doesn't need to be near you to receive energy healing from your crystals. But please only do this if you get permission from the recipient.

The best way I have found to work with crystals and long-distance healing is through crystal grids. Here's how to set one up.

1. **Pick an element for your loved one.**
   Choose a physical representation of the loved one to whom you want to send long-distance healing. For example, it can be a photo, drawing, or anything that best represents the loved one. Set this in the middle of your crystal grid.

2. **Set your intention.**
   This can be intuitive or an intention that your loved one has recommended. Make this intention as specific as possible. You want to let the universe know exactly what you're asking for. You can even write your intention out on a piece of paper and set it in the middle of your crystal grid.

3. **Choose the grid.**
   Different materials and geometric shapes can enhance the energy and intentions of your grid in different ways. However, you can always make your grid on a bare surface.

4. **Choose, cleanse, and charge your crystals.**
Before you place the crystals on your grid, be sure that all of your crystals are cleansed and charged. You want them to radiate the most vibrant energy! When choosing your crystals, select one central stone and several supporting stones.

5. **Place the first crystal in the center of your grid.**
This crystal should be the largest, and it should be aligned with your overall intention. Typically, crystal points or pyramids work best, as they can direct and amplify your intentions straight out into the universe.

6. **Place your supporting crystals on your grid.**
These crystals surround your central crystal and further define your intention. The number of crystals that you add to your grid will depend on the complexity of your intention, numerology, and sacred geometry. Typically, you want to choose the same type and size of crystal to be supporting crystals.

7. **Add other elements to your grid.**
This step is optional but great for adding personal touches and enhancing your intention and connection to the loved one you're working on. You could include photos, affirmations, herbs, feathers, flowers, candles, oracle cards, or anything else that has a spiritual representation that you believe will support and enhance your intention.

8. **Activate your grid.**
Use a cleansed and charged clear quartz point or selenite wand. Starting from the outside of the grid, draw an invisible line between each crystal, connecting the dots, all the way to the central crystal or representation that you chose for your loved one. As you connect the crystals, imagine a white light unifying their energies. One you have finished, use the clear quartz or selenite crystal to circle the grid three times to send energy outward and toward your loved one. You can repeat this activation as often as you'd like to maintain its high vibrational frequency. Keep this grid activated for a minimum of 24 hours.

Instead of a crystal grid, you can also use a body representation: Place crystals on specific parts of a layout of their body just like you would if they were with you in person.

two
reiki

Whether you are a Reiki master or about to go to your first Reiki session, crystals can enhance your healing process. Reiki is a healing modality in which a practitioner uses specific symbols to send universal light from themselves to the patient through the palms of their hands.

The first time I was introduced to crystals was during a Reiki session with Lisa Toney. I was very ill at the time, with little life force in me. It wasn't until I had been to several sessions with Lisa that she felt called to use crystals. During my next session, I had a complete out-of-body experience. Personally, I've noticed the most positive change in my overall health when I combine Reiki and crystals. This could be the case for you as well.

If you're a Reiki master who works with clients, you can add crystals to the session by intuitively placing a crystal layout on the patient's body based on their goals and intentions. You can then choose to leave them on their body during the session or add to the energy by using a clear quartz point, energetically "drawing" the Reiki symbols over each crystal. Another way you can use crystals in your Reiki session is by choosing the symbol and crystal with intention. For instance, if you are working on emotional healing with the client, you could use the Sei He Ki symbol, infuse that symbol into a rose quartz, and then place it on the client's heart chakra.

three

yoga

Yoga in Sanskrit means "union," and yoga unifies physical poses, meditation, and breathwork to help you become your best self. Typically, when we do our yoga practice, we have an intention behind it. It may be to find inner peace, to find balance, to relieve anxiety, to reduce pain, or to get better sleep. When you incorporate crystals into your yoga practice, you strengthen your intentions and bring positive energy into your space and body.

Choose a crystal that goes with your intentions. For instance, if you want to relieve anxiety, you may want to use a lepidolite or blue lace agate. The simplest way to add crystals to your yoga practice is to place them on or nearby your mat. You can also hold a crystal in your hand or place it lightly on top of one of your chakras during Savasana, toward the end of your yoga practice.

four

oracle or tarot cards

Oracle and tarot cards are used to gain insight into the past, present, and future, as well as to provide insight on any questions you may have. When you use crystals in your oracle or tarot readings, the crystals can give you more context to your answers from the cards.

To do this, first choose your cards intuitively. This can be one card or multiple cards, depending on the complexity of your question. Then, without looking, intuitively choose a crystal and place it on the card. First look up the meaning of your card and then find the meaning of your crystal to give you greater context around what the card is referring to.

five

astrology

Astrology is the study of the movements of distant cosmic objects, such as stars and planets, and their influence on our lives. Crystals based on your zodiac sign can be worn or used daily to help balance your energies.

Here are some crystals that correspond with zodiac signs.

♈ *aries* *march 21–april 19*

Personality traits: adventurous, competitive, energetic, confident, courageous, bold, impulsive, quick tempered, ambitious, spontaneous, impatient

Crystals: tiger's eye, bloodstone, eudialyte, fire agate, garnet, green tourmaline, honey calcite, jet, kambaba jasper, ruby, shiva lingam

♉ *taurus* *april 20–may 20*

Personality traits: dependable, homebody, dislikes change, resentful, determined, loving, creative, sensual, go-getter, protective, patient

Crystals: black onyx, copper, emerald, eudialyte, green aventurine, jet, kunzite, kyanite, malachite, morganite, moss agate, nephrite jade, peridot, petrified wood, rhodochrosite, rhodonite, rose quartz, rutilated quartz, selenite, septarian, serpentine, smoky quartz, thulite, unakite jasper

♊ *gemini* *may 21–june 20*

Personality traits: expressive, curious, charismatic, know-it-all, inconsistent, youthful, funny, versatile, kind, smart, witty, childlike, gentle, open-minded

Crystals: agate, azurite, blue apatite, blue lace agate, celestite, crazy lace agate, epidote, fire agate, flower agate, howlite, jet, lemurian, lepidolite, Libyan desert glass, orca agate, pyrite, rainbow moonstone, rose quartz, rutilated quartz, serpentine, thulite, watermelon tourmaline

♋ *cancer* *june 21–july 22*

Personality traits: emotional, sensitive, loving, sympathetic, protective, empath, cautious, clingy, intuitive, compassionate, imaginative, nurturing

Crystals: black moonstone, blue calcite, bumblebee jasper, celestite, citrine, honey calcite, howlite, iolite, kyanite, larimar, lepidolite, morganite, orange calcite, pink opal, rainbow moonstone, rainbow obsidian, rhodochrosite, selenite, shiva lingam, shungite

♌ *leo* *july 23–aug 22*

Personality traits: enthusiastic, outgoing, dramatic, loving, intolerant, bossy, creative, leader, big heart, confident, giving, strong, brave, self-motivated, stubborn

Crystals: amber, bumblebee jasper, carnelian, clear quartz, garnierite, golden healer, honey calcite, kunzite, labradorite, orange calcite, peridot, petrified wood, pyrite, red jasper, ruby, rutilated quartz, septarian, sunstone

♍ *virgo* *aug 23–sept 22*

Personality traits: loyal, practical, introvert, humble, logical, perfectionist, hardworking, creative, reliable, modest, easily frustrated, picky, responsible

Crystals: amazonite, blue sapphire, carnelian, clear quartz, crazy lace emerald, eudialyte, flower agate, garnierite, green aventurine, howlite, lepidolite, Libyan desert glass, malachite, mookaite jasper, moss agate, nephrite jade, ocean jasper, opal, peridot, petrified wood, red jasper, sardonyx, septarian, serpentine, smoky quartz, spirit quartz, sodalite, sugilite, vanadinite, watermelon tourmaline

♎ *libra* sept 23–oct 22

Personality traits: easygoing, romantic, charming, social, clever, idealistic, gullible, indecisive, non-confrontational, cooperative, peaceable

Crystals: black tourmaline, blue chalcedony, crazy lace agate, epidote, green aventurine, green tourmaline, herkimer diamond, lapis lazuli, lepidolite, ocean jasper, opal, pink opal, pink tourmaline, prehnite, rainbow obsidian, sodalite, spirit quartz, sunstone

♏ *scorpio* oct 23–nov 21

Personality traits: intuitive, determined, jealous, compulsive, honest, brave, loyal, passionate, ambitious, secretive, focused, patient, outsider

Crystals: amber, black obsidian, black onyx, black tourmaline, fire quartz, green opal, herkimer diamond, kambaba jasper, kunzite, labradorite, mookaite jasper, ocean jasper, opal, petrified wood, pink opal, red jasper, rhodochrosite, rhodonite, selenite, septarian, serpentine, shiva lingam, shungite, smoky quartz, unakite jasper

♐ *sagittarius* nov 22–dec 21

Personality traits: optimistic, outgoing, energetic, funny, generous, extroverted, irresponsible, restless, independent, family-oriented, blunt, stubborn, too serious

Crystals: charoite, chrysocolla, copper, gold sheen obsidian, iolite, kyanite, labradorite, lapis lazuli, turquoise

♑ *capricorn* dec 22–jan 19

Personality traits: realistic, disciplined, independent, humorous, pessimistic, reserved, ambitious, tenacious, hardworking, organized, stubborn, unforgiving, serious

Crystals: black obsidian, black tourmaline, blue sapphire, emerald, fluorite, garnet, green aventurine, green tourmaline, malachite, moss agate, ocean jasper, petrified wood, prehnite, scolecite, septarian, serpentine, shungite, smoky quartz, spirit quartz, sugilite, unakite jasper

♒ *aquarius* jan 20–feb 18

Personality traits: friendly, honest, loyal, clever, optimistic, outsider, independent, imaginative, unpredictable, detached, friendly, original, condescending

Crystals: amazonite, amethyst, angelite, aquamarine, azurite, blue chalcedony, blue sapphire, garnet, hematite, larvikite, spirit quartz, turquoise

♓ *pisces* feb 19–march 20

Personality traits: sensitive, selfless, intuitive, sympathetic, affectionate, gullible, no boundaries, romantic, compassionate, kind, healer, lazy, moody, selfless

Crystals: amazonite, amethyst, aquamarine, azurite, blue calcite, blue chalcedony, blue lace agate, chaorite, crazy lace agate, fluorite, honey calcite, iolite, kyanite, nephrite jade, pink amethyst, pink opal, rhodochrosite, selenite, spirit quartz

crystal water or elixirs

Crystal water or elixir is another way to use your crystals daily. Crystal water is water infused with crystals and is used immediately upon making it. Meanwhile, crystal elixirs are made using brandy, vodka, apple cider vinegar, or glycerin and can be used over a longer period. You ingest them to transmit the crystals' healing energy to your body. If you are a sensitive soul, this is one of the best ways to reap the crystals' energy benefits because the energy is very subtle; it may take two to four weeks before you notice any results. Think of a crystal water or elixir as a vitamin—you must take it daily for it to consistently work.

Note: If a crystal is radioactive it should never be used in either the direct or indirect method of making crystal elixirs or crystal waters.

preparing your crystal water

1. Choose your crystals.

2. Cleanse and charge your crystals (physically and energetically).

3. Place your crystals in a glass bowl or pitcher filled with distilled water.

4. Place the glass bowl or pitcher filled with crystals in the sun and moonlight for a minimum of 2 hours.

5. Remove the crystals and bottle the water. Keep it refrigerated.

6. Drink within 24 hours. You can ingest this the same as you would regular water throughout your day.

crystal water recipes

Which crystal you choose depends on your intention.

Intention: Self-love
Crystals: rose quartz, ocean jasper, clear quartz
Intention: Grounding
Crystals: red jasper, smoky quartz, black obsidian
Intention: Energy boosting
Crystals: red jasper, sardonyx, rutilated quartz

preparing your crystal elixir

1. Choose your crystals.

2. Cleanse and charge your crystals (physically and energetically).

3. Place your crystals in a glass bowl or pitcher filled with distilled water.

4. Place the glass bowl or pitcher filled with crystals in the sun and moonlight for a minimum of 24 hours. You can let it stand undisturbed for up to seven days.

5. Remove the crystals.

6. Add enough of your desired preservative (brandy, vodka, apple cider vinegar, or glycerin) such that it makes up 25 percent of the total volume.

7. Bottle the elixir. Make sure to label your elixir with the date it was bottled and the intention.

8. Keep it in a dark and cool place for the longest shelf life.

indirect method

Not all crystals can be safely placed directly into water. Please check chapter 7 to be sure yours can. When in doubt, use this indirect method.

1. Choose your crystals.

2. Cleanse and charge your crystals (physically and energetically).

3. Place your crystals in a glass container (jar or bowl), one that is small enough to fit inside of another larger glass container. Make sure there is no water in with the crystals.

4. Place the glass container with the crystals inside of a larger glass container filled with distilled water. This protects the water from toxic or hazardous minerals, but also allows the crystals' energy to transfer to the water.

5. Cover the bowl tightly with a lid, plastic wrap, or cheesecloth.

6. Place it in the sun and moonlight for a minimum of 24 hours. You can let it stand undisturbed for up to seven days.

7. Remove the crystals.

8. Add a 25 percent ratio of your desired preservative (brandy, vodka, apple cider vinegar, or glycerin).

9. Bottle the elixir. Make sure to label your elixir with the date it was bottled and the intention. Keep it in a dark and cool place for the longest shelf life.

shelf life of preservatives

Elixirs last different amounts of time depending on their base:
- **Brandy**: 4–6 months
- **Vodka**: 3–4 months
- **Apple cider vinegar**: 2–3 months
- **Vegetable glycerin**: 2–3 months

crystal elixir dosage

For the first month, internally take in a maximum of six drops daily. They can be dispersed throughout the day. For the following months, internally take in a maximum of three or four drops daily. These can also be dispersed throughout the day. If you don't notice any differences after four weeks, you may need to change your elixir crystal recipe.

crystal elixir recipes

As with crystal water, which crystal you choose for an elixir depends on your intention.

INTENTION: STRESS RELIEF
Crystals: lepidolite, blue lace agate, howlite, smoky quartz
Method: Indirect
Distilled water: 3 cups (710 ml)
Preservative: ¾ cup (180 ml)

INTENTION: DIGESTIVE HEALTH
Crystals: citrine, kambaba jasper, Libyan desert glass, crazy lace agate
Method: Direct
Distilled water: 3 cups (710 ml)
Preservative: ¾ cup (180 ml)

INTENTION: IMMUNE BOOSTING
Crystals: green aventurine, lemurian, mookaite jasper, black tourmaline
Method: Direct
Distilled water: 3 cups (710 ml)
Preservative: ¾ cup (180 ml)

baths

A great form of self-care is simply taking a bath. Baths not only put your mind and body in a state of relaxation, but they also release any negative energy that was absorbed throughout the day. Adding crystals to your bath is an extremely powerful and effective way of receiving crystal healing. Typically, you should also add some type of salt, which cleanses the body of toxins and relaxes the muscles; use oils to smooth the skin, and candles to lighten the mood. It's really an overall win for your mind, body, and soul.

crystal bath setup

Not all crystals can be safely placed directly into water. Please check chapter 7 before choosing to use a particular one for your bath. Here's how to set up a bath.

1. Choose your crystals with intention. You'll want to choose crystals that are larger in size (palm-size or larger) so the vibrations amplify your water. If larger crystals aren't an option, you can always use smaller crystals, but in larger quantities (five or more).

2. Make sure your crystals are cleansed and charged and your intentions are set before the bath.

3. Fill up your tub and add your crystals.

4. Let the crystals soak for 20 minutes.

5. While they are soaking, finish setting up your bath by adding your favorite salts, oils, and/or herbs, and put your candles around the tub.

6. Once your bath is ready, soak in the tub for a minimum of 20 minutes and enjoy your me time.

meditation

Meditation is the practice of mindfulness or being fully aware of what is going on in the present moment. If you have never meditated before, know that it takes practice. When I first started out with meditation, I couldn't even concentrate for a minute, but I practiced, and now time doesn't seem to exist when I meditate; I usually come out of my meditation after about 30 minutes.

You don't have to be a monk to be good at meditation. You just need to be quiet, grounded, and fully present within. I would suggest starting with 3 minutes and working your way up from there. Adding crystals to your meditation raises your vibrations, enhances your intentions, and raises your consciousness. You can choose as many crystals as you'd like when meditating. Sometimes I only use one crystal in each hand; other times I do a full crystal layout on my body. Let your intuition guide you to what serves your energy best for that day. Below is a guided meditation that you are welcome to do with your crystals. If you want more guided meditations, check out chapter 11.

guided meditation for grounding and centering the body

This guided meditation is perfect for smoky quartz and red jasper.

Begin by getting into a comfortable position in a place where you are free from all distractions. Close your eyes and gently tap your thymus to ground yourself. Do this for a few seconds. Then hold your smoky quartz in one hand and your red jasper in the other.

Inhale a smooth, slow breath for four counts, pause for two, and exhale slowly for seven.

Repeat this three times, or until you feel calm. Once you are present and relaxed, bring your breath back to its natural rhythm.

Throughout this meditation, focus on becoming aware of your body. Begin at your feet, wiggling your toes. Slowly move up your body from your toes to your head, breathing into each sensation of your body. Notice the arches of your feet, your heels, your ankles, your shins, knees, legs, hips, belly, back, chest, heart, shoulder, arms, forearms, each finger, your neck, chin, jaw, mouth, nose, ears, eyes, third eye, and head.

Then focus on the crystals in your hands. Visualize a bright red light coming from the crystals into the rest of your body, filling you up, allowing you to feel grounded and connected to the earth's energy.

When you are ready, open your eyes and notice how you feel.

nine

crystal feng shui

Feng shui is a traditional Chinese practice centered on the notion of *chi*, or life-force energy. *Feng shui* translates to "wind and water"; you change the space of your home to go with the flow of wind and water. These intentional placements invite positive chi into your home to achieve balance, harmony, and overall well-being. A feng shui bagua map is used to divide your home into nine areas based on intention. This practice is a great way to determine where to put crystals in your home. You always want to be intentional with your crystals, so they can serve your highest good.

The feng shui bagua map includes the following nine themes.

1. **WEALTH AND PROSPERITY**
   Crystal colors: purple, blue, and red
   Intention: abundance
   Location: southeast area or rear left corner of your home

2. **FAME AND REPUTATION**
   Crystal color: red
   Intention: acclaim
   Location: southern area or rear middle section of your home

3. **LOVE AND MARRIAGE**
Crystal colors: pink, white, and red
Intention: passion
Location: southwest area or rear right corner of your home

4. **FAMILY AND HEALTH**
Crystal colors: green and blue
Intention: support
Location: eastern area or middle left section of your home

5. **BALANCE AND WELL-BEING**
Crystal colors: yellow, orange, and brown
Intention: foundation
Location: center of your home

6. **CHILDREN AND CREATIVITY**
Crystal colors: white, silver, gray, and copper
Intention: playful
Location: western area or middle right section of your home

7. **KNOWLEDGE AND PERSONAL GROWTH**
Crystal colors: black, blue, and green
Intention: wisdom
Location: northeast area or the bottom left corner of your home

8. **CAREER AND LIFE PATH**
Crystal colors: black and dark blue
Intention: job success
Location: northern area or the middle bottom area of your home

9. **HELPFUL PEOPLE AND TRAVEL**
Crystal colors: gray, white, and black
Intention: networking and mentorship
Location: northwest corner or the bottom right corner of your home

feng shui crystal placements in your home

Here are some intentions and crystals to consider for different rooms in your home. See chapter 2 for more on placing a crystal.

FRONT ENTRY

Intentions: safety, warmth, inviting, protection
Crystals: black tourmaline, black obsidian, citrine, selenite, amethyst, morganite, ocean jasper, septarian, sunstone, tiger's eye, charoite, jet, gold sheen obsidian

LIVING ROOM

Intentions: relaxation, social, warmth, expression, wellness, relationships
Crystals: amethyst, rose quartz, clear quartz, aquamarine, angelite, garnierite, kunzite, sodalite, fire quartz, lapis lazuli

KITCHEN

Intentions: social, communication, relationships, uplifting, creativity
Crystals: rose quartz, green aventurine, citrine, sunstone, moss agate, orange calcite, sardonyx, blue apatite, ocean jasper, carnelian

BEDROOM

Intentions: passion, peace, tranquility, rest, love, relaxation
Crystals: rose quartz, lepidolite, howlite, celestite, amethyst, scolecite, angelite, larimar, pink opal, sugilite, blue chalcedony, green opal, blue lace agate, shungite

BATHROOM

Intentions: cleansing, rejuvenating, renewal, peaceful, soothing

Crystals: blue lace agate, rose quartz, shungite, hematite, clear quartz, moonstone, blue chalcedony, blue calcite, larimar

CHILD'S BEDROOM
Intentions: safety, peace, warmth, nurturing, calming, love
Crystals: rose quartz, celestite, howlite, red jasper, angelite, smoky quartz, chrysocolla, septarian, sugilite, kambaba jasper, larimar

OFFICE
Intentions: energy, focus, motivation, success, wealth, abundance, peace
Crystals: moldavite, carnelian, shungite, pyrite, green aventurine, citrine, smoky quartz, fluorite, lepidolite, hematite, orange calcite

Wealth & Prosperity	Fame & Reputation	Love & Marriage
Family & Health	Balance & Wellbeing	Children & Creativity
Knowledge & Personal Growth	Career & Life Path	Helpful People & Travels

Front Entrance

5 | the seven chakras & their corresponding crystals

CHAKRAS ARE THE seven major energy centers that spiral up the spine. They represent our *prana* (life force). Each chakra consists of physical anatomy and emotional and spiritual well-being. Together they contain a universal spiritual life lesson, which evolves into connection to your higher self and spiritual awakening.

When our chakras are in a healthy alignment, they are about 3 to 4 inches (8 to 10 cm) in diameter starting from our physical body and extending into the auric field, the energy field that surrounds our physical body.

Physical symptoms and illnesses can begin to arise when one or more chakras are out of alignment for a period of time. One of the most common ways to get your chakras back into balance is through crystal healing.

Let's look at each of the chakras, symptoms that you might experience when it is overactive or underactive, and a meditation that will help balance it. When a chakra is underactive, this usually signifies that one is experiencing energetic blockages or stagnant energy to a particular chakra. When a chakra is overactive, this usually signifies that one is experiencing too much energetic flow into one area of the body instead of being dispersed evenly throughout the body. When our chakras are balanced, we can achieve optimum health physically, mentally, and spiritually.

root chakra

LOCATION:
base of the spine

COLORS:
red, brown, or black

REPRESENTS:
stability, grounding, group identity, foundation, survival

SYMPTOMS OF AN UNDERACTIVE ROOT CHAKRA:
feeling ungrounded, weak, passive, restless, or unmotivated

SYMPTOMS OF AN OVERACTIVE ROOT CHAKRA:
greed, aggression, controlling behavior, self-centered behavior, addiction, deceitfulness

POSSIBLE PHYSICAL SYMPTOMS:
lower back pain, depression, suppressed immune system, sciatica, inflammation, feet or bone issues, lethargy, varicose veins

SIGNS OF A BALANCED ROOT CHAKRA:
feeling grounded, affectionate, energetic, or confident; physical health; safety; ability to provide for self and family; positive home environment; stability, understanding that all is one

CRYSTALS USED TO BALANCE THE ROOT CHAKRA:
red garnet, red jasper, black obsidian, jet, black tourmaline, hematite, smoky quartz, black moonstone, fire agate, fire quartz, and petrified wood

meditation

This meditation will focus on your roots, allowing you to sink into a deep connection within yourself and mother nature. Before meditating, select two root chakra crystals that call to you. Get into a comfortable position in a place where you are free from all distractions. Hold one root chakra crystal in each hand. Close your eyes and begin.

1. Inhale a smooth, slow breath for four counts, pause for two, and exhale slowly for seven.

2. Repeat this three times or until you feel calm.

3. Once you are present and relaxed, imagine yourself as a tree. Trees are grounded at all times, but sway with the wind (*the flow of life*). Imagine your feet as roots of the tree, grounded into the earth. Then imagine your legs up to your chest as the trunk of the tree. Then imagine your arms, neck, and head as the branches. Lastly, imagine your connection to the world around you as the leaves of the tree.

4. As you begin to sink into this deep connection to yourself and mother nature, direct your focus to the two crystals in your hands. Breathe into their grounding energy.

5. Anytime your mind travels elsewhere, bring your attention back to your crystals. Allow their energy to bring you back into the present moment.

Continue this meditation for as long as your body needs. I highly recommend meditating for a minimum of 3 minutes; 11 minutes is ideal.

AFFIRMATION
I trust the process of life.

sacral chakra

LOCATION:
lower abdomen to belly button

COLOR:
orange

REPRESENTS:
relationships with others, sexuality, pleasure, creativity, personal identity, strength

SYMPTOMS OF AN UNDERACTIVE SACRAL CHAKRA:
shyness, clinginess, feeling overly sensitive or resentful, loss of personal power, playing the role of a victim, guilt, emotional stagnation

SYMPTOMS OF AN OVERACTIVE SACRAL CHAKRA:
overwhelming sensation of constant fear; blaming others; power and control issues; acting manipulative, overindulgent, or selfish; highly reactive

POSSIBLE PHYSICAL SYMPTOMS:
urinary problems, intense PMS symptoms, lower back and pelvic pain, sexual organ imbalances, fertility issues

SIGNS OF A BALANCED SACRAL CHAKRA:
boundaries, acting communicative or intuitive, creativity, empathy, honoring of others, emotional balance, healthy relationships

CRYSTALS USED TO BALANCE THE SACRAL CHAKRA:
carnelian, crazy lace agate, tiger's eye, moonstone, mookaite jasper, orange calcite, sardonyx, shiva lingam, sunstone, and vanadinite

meditation

This meditation will be focused on connecting you to your inner light, which will expand your sacral chakra to bring you feelings of joy and optimism. Before meditating, select two sacral chakra crystals that call to you. Get into a comfortable position, lying down on your back in a place where you are free from all distractions. Place the two sacral chakra crystals on your lower abdomen area and then gently place your hands on top of them. Close your eyes and begin.

1. Inhale a smooth, slow breath for four counts, pause for two, and exhale slowly for seven. Repeat this three times or until you feel calm.

2. Focus your attention and energy on the two sacral chakra crystals you chose. Imagine a beautiful bright orange light expanding from the crystals to the rest of your sacral chakra. This light shines bright like the sun. Allow it to expand beyond your sacral chakra and out into the world. This light brings you joy, creativity, empathy, healthy relationships, and emotional balance.

3. Allow yourself to soak in this beautiful energy.

Continue this meditation for as long as your body needs. I highly recommend meditating for a minimum of 3 minutes; 11 minutes is ideal.

AFFIRMATION
I honor my sacred body.

solar plexus chakra

LOCATION:
abdomen/core

COLORS:
yellow or gold

REPRESENTS:
personal power, self-esteem, manifestations, trust, care for oneself, courage, independence, self-respect, self-care

SYMPTOMS OF AN UNDERACTIVE SOLAR PLEXUS CHAKRA:
depression, lack of self-care or self-worth, anxiety, being extremely sensitive toward others, fear of rejection, insecurities, stress

SYMPTOMS OF AN OVERACTIVE SOLAR PLEXUS CHAKRA:
egotistical, entitled, judgmental, or demanding behavior; overworking; trying to be an overachiever

POSSIBLE PHYSICAL SYMPTOMS:
eating disorders, adrenal dysfunction, digestive issues, intestinal issues, arthritis

SIGNS OF A BALANCED SOLAR PLEXUS CHAKRA:
generosity, courage, self-confidence, joyfulness, respect toward others and oneself, self-love and self-care, personal power and honor, ability to make decisions

CRYSTALS USED TO BALANCE THE SOLAR PLEXUS CHAKRA:
citrine, honey calcite, mookaite jasper, ocean jasper, bumblebee jasper, golden healer, pyrite, Libyan desert glass, septarian

meditation

This meditation will be focused on your core to ignite and strengthen your personal power and the center of your overall well-being. Before meditating, select one solar plexus chakra crystal that calls to you. Get into a comfortable position in a place where you are free from all distractions. Place your solar plexus chakra crystal on your belly and then gently place your hands on top of it. Close your eyes and begin.

1. Inhale a smooth, slow breath for four counts, pause for two, and exhale slowly for seven. Repeat this three times or until you feel relaxed and present.

2. Then focus your attention and energy on the solar plexus chakra crystal you chose. Imagine your crystal as a candle. Its flame starts at a dim light in the core of your power (belly). This flame slowly begins to get brighter and brighter as it expands from the very core of your solar plexus chakra to fill up the entire chakra, bringing it back into balance. Then the candle's flame becomes so bright, it expands from your belly to the rest of the world. This beautiful bright light brings you abundance, self-love, confidence, personal power, and honor.

3. Allow yourself to soak in this beautiful energy.

Continue this meditation for as long as your body needs it. I highly recommend meditating for a minimum of 3 minutes; 11 minutes is ideal.

AFFIRMATION

I love and accept myself for exactly who I am.

heart chakra

LOCATION:
center of the chest through the arms

COLORS:
green or pink

REPRESENTS:
love, the most powerful energy we have

SYMPTOMS OF AN UNDERACTIVE HEART CHAKRA:
inability to make decisions, fears of rejection, feeling unworthy or stagnant, self-centeredness, loneliness, grief, trust issues

SYMPTOMS OF AN OVERACTIVE HEART CHAKRA:
hatred of others or oneself, resentment, apathy, possessiveness, overly dramatic or aggressive behavior, bitterness, and dominance issues

POSSIBLE PHYSICAL SYMPTOMS:
heart failure or attack, lung cancer and dysfunctions, breast cancer, asthma, severe allergies, upper back or arm chronic pain

SIGNS OF A BALANCED HEART CHAKRA:
ability to forgive, compassion, unconditional love, generosity, positive attitude, joyfulness, loving relationships with oneself and others, trust

CRYSTALS USED TO BALANCE THE HEART CHAKRA:
rose quartz, rhodochrosite, rhodonite, pink tourmaline, pink opal, emerald, malachite, bloodstone, epidote, flower agate, kunzite, red or green garnet, green aventurine

meditation

Allowing your heart to receive unconditional love one rose petal at a time will be the focus of this meditation. Before meditating, select a rose quartz crystal. If you do not have rose quartz, use your current favorite pink heart chakra crystal. Get into a comfortable position in a place where you will be free from all distractions. Place your heart chakra crystal on your heart and then gently place your hands on top of it. Close your eyes and begin the meditation.

1. Inhale a smooth, slow breath for four counts, pause for two, and exhale slowly for seven. Repeat this three times or until you feel relaxed and present.

2. Then focus your attention and energy on the pink heart chakra crystal you chose. Imagine your crystal as a rose. As you begin to open your heart to unconditional love, the rose begins to open one petal at a time. As you are focusing on unconditional love, repeat the affirmation *I love myself unconditionally* as each petal opens.

3. This rose slowly begins to develop and expands to the entire heart chakra. The energy from the crystal becomes so bright and expansive that it expands from your heart, out into your arms, through your hands, and into the rest of the world. This beautiful bright light brings you unconditional love, joy, gratitude, and forgiveness.

4. Allow yourself to soak in this beautiful energy.

Continue this meditation for as long as your body needs. I highly recommend meditating for a minimum of 3 minutes; 11 minutes is ideal.

AFFIRMATION
I love myself unconditionally.

throat chakra

LOCATION:
throat through the neck and into the jaw

COLOR:
blue

REPRESENTS:
power of choice, communication, self-expression, peace

SYMPTOMS OF AN UNDERACTIVE THROAT CHAKRA:
shyness, dishonesty, inability to express your truth, flakiness, inability to make decisions, fearfulness

SYMPTOMS OF AN OVERACTIVE THROAT CHAKRA:
acting judgmental, overly talkative, arrogant, or dominant; addictive behavior; controlling issues toward others

POSSIBLE PHYSICAL SYMPTOMS:
thyroid and parathyroid issues, inflammation in the throat, scoliosis, laryngitis, swollen glands

SIGNS OF A BALANCED THROAT CHAKRA:
ability to speak your truth, ability to let go of what should be and honor what is, ability to make decisions for yourself, personal power, feeling a life purpose

CRYSTALS USED TO BALANCE THE THROAT CHAKRA:
blue lace agate, blue chalcedony, angelite, aquamarine, amazonite, blue calcite, celestite, chrysocolla, kyanite, turquoise, sodalite, larimar

meditation

This meditation will be focused on your breath and allowing you to release anything that feels constricting (verbally or physically). Before meditating, select one throat chakra crystal that calls to you. Get into a comfortable position, lying on your back in a place where you are free from all distractions. Place your throat chakra crystal on the back of your neck and then gently place your hands on top of it, so that the front of your throat is open and free. Once you're ready, close your eyes and begin the meditation.

1. For the entire meditation, inhale smooth, slow breaths for four counts, pause for two, and exhale slowly for seven.

2. Allow yourself to just be; be present in the moment.

3. Allow the crystal to fill your entire throat with the gentlest blue light, which allows you to speak your truth, let go, and feel a life purpose. Move this beautiful blue energy with the flow of your breath.

4. Allow yourself to soak in this beautiful energy.

Continue this meditation for as long as your body needs. I highly recommend meditating for a minimum of 3 minutes; 11 minutes is ideal.

AFFIRMATION

I speak my truth with ease and comfort.

third-eye chakra

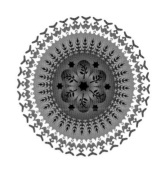

LOCATION:
center of forehead between eyebrows

COLORS:
indigo or purple

REPRESENTS:
wisdom, intuition, self-evaluation, openness, perception

SYMPTOMS OF AN UNDERACTIVE THIRD EYE CHAKRA:
high sensitivity, feeling unworthy and inadequate, lack of discipline, hopelessness, rejection of life

SYMPTOMS OF AN OVERACTIVE THIRD EYE CHAKRA:
pride, manipulativeness, egocentricity, conniving, being impersonal

POSSIBLE PHYSICAL SYMPTOMS:
brain tumor, nervous system dysfunctions, learning disabilities, epilepsy or seizures, blindness, deafness, strokes, memory disorders such as Alzheimer's

SIGNS OF A BALANCED THIRD-EYE CHAKRA:
intuition, ability to take leadership, expanded consciousness, spiritual connection, ability to learn from mistakes, emotional intelligence, enhanced psychic abilities

CRYSTALS USED TO BALANCE THE THIRD-EYE CHAKRA:
amethyst, iolite, azurite, lepidolite, charoite, fluorite, lapis lazuli, larvikite, spirit quartz, labradorite, sugilite

meditation

Allowing your third eye to awaken by traveling through galaxies will be the focus of this meditation. Before meditating, select one third-eye chakra crystal that calls to you. Make sure it has a flat side so it can rest easily in the center of your forehead without falling. Get into a comfortable position, lying on your back in a place where you are free from all distractions. Place the third-eye chakra crystal in the center of your forehead, in between your eyebrows. Close your eyes and begin.

1. Inhale a smooth, slow breath for four counts, pause for two, and exhale slowly for seven. Repeat this three times or until you feel relaxed and present.

2. With your eyes still closed, direct your attention to your third eye. As you continue to breathe slowly, imagine a bright purple light that comes from the crystal out into the galaxies. As this purple light expands deeper into the galaxies, you notice special stars. As you pass by each star, more and more negativity is taken away from your body. As the negativity is melting away from your body, you start seeing a brighter purple light completely cover you in the purest energy, which makes you feel spiritual, conscious, intuitive, and at peace.

3. Allow yourself to soak in this beautiful energy.

Continue this meditation for as long as your body needs. I highly recommend meditating for a minimum of 3 minutes; 11 minutes is ideal.

AFFIRMATION

I trust my intuition to guide me for my highest good.

crown chakra

LOCATION:
top of head

COLORS:
purple or white

REPRESENTS:
divinity, connection to Source, prayer, higher consciousness

SYMPTOMS OF AN UNDERACTIVE CROWN CHAKRA:
feeling ungrounded, inability to trust the process of life, apathy, depression, feeling disconnected to others and higher power, loss of identity

SYMPTOMS OF AN OVERACTIVE CROWN CHAKRA:
self-centeredness, destructiveness, delusion, extreme desire to have power, imbalance, inconsistency

POSSIBLE PHYSICAL SYMPTOMS:
skin inflammation, energy disorders, extreme sensitivity to light or sound, chronic fatigue, depression, psychosis, vertigo, memory loss, nervous system imbalances

SIGNS OF A BALANCED CROWN CHAKRA:
spiritual connection, enlightenment, ability to trust and honor what is, selflessness, faith, devotion

CRYSTALS USED TO BALANCE THE CROWN CHAKRA:
howlite, clear quartz, amethyst, lemurian quartz, scolecite, selenite, moonstone, herkimer diamond, sugilite, super 7

meditation

This meditation will be focused on connecting you to your spirit guides to balance your crown chakra. Before meditating, select three crown chakra crystals that call to you, preferably ones that have points so you can direct energy to expand the crown chakra. Get into a comfortable position, lying on your back in a place where you are free from all distractions. Place the crown chakra crystals on the top of your head, with the points pointed away from your head and in the shape of a crown. Close your eyes and begin.

1. Inhale a smooth slow breath for four counts, pause for two, and exhale slowly for seven. Repeat this five times or until you feel relaxed and present.

2. With your eyes still closed, begin to fill your entire body from your root to your crown chakra with a beautiful white divine light. Once you feel full, imagine yourself as a goddess and all the amazing qualities that come with being a goddess. Then direct your attention toward the three crown chakra crystals in the shape of a crown. Allow the crystals to fill your entire crown chakra with the most abundant white light, allowing you to feel spiritually connected, enlightened, and at peace.

3. Allow yourself to soak in this beautiful energy.

Continue this meditation for as long as your body needs. I highly recommend meditating for a minimum of 3 minutes; 11 minutes is ideal.

AFFIRMATION

I know that all is well in my world.

crystal guide

for balancing all seven chakras

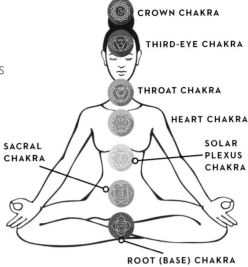

CROWN CHAKRA

THIRD-EYE CHAKRA

THROAT CHAKRA

HEART CHAKRA

SACRAL CHAKRA

SOLAR PLEXUS CHAKRA

ROOT (BASE) CHAKRA

Now that you have a greater understanding of what each chakra is, it's time we put the power of crystal healing into practice! Here is a complete chakra-balancing crystal layout to help you focus on and bring all your chakras back into harmony.

1. Select seven crystals, one that corresponds to each chakra. For example:
   Root chakra: red jasper
   Sacral chakra: carnelian
   Solar plexus chakra: citrine
   Heart chakra: rose quartz
   Throat chakra: blue lace agate
   Third-eye chakra: amethyst
   Crown chakra: howlite

2. Cleanse your sacred space, crystals, and body (see chapter 3).

3. Get into a comfortable position lying down.

4. Place each crystal corresponding to the chakra location on your body, starting at the root chakra and moving up one by one to the crown chakra.

5. Once the crystals are placed on your chakras, close your eyes and place your hands on the root chakra crystal. Then visualize your crown chakra opening as you inhale white light from the Universe/Source. Allow this light to flow through to your root chakra and fill up your crystal with this beautiful white universal light.

6. Expand into this energy for 3 to 5 minutes, or as long as you intuitively feel is enough for you.

7. Continue this process for all seven chakras, going in order from the root chakra to the crown chakra.

8. Try to allow yourself to be in this chakra-balancing layout for 21 to 35 minutes. Allow your intuition to guide you if you need more or less time in each chakra.

9. Once you are finished, remove all the crystals, starting from the crown chakra and moving down to the root chakra. This order will help ease your energy back down gently. You may notice, when the crystals are removed, that the energy is still vibrating heavily; take time to relax and come back to the present moment when you are ready.

10. When you are fully present, it will be a good time to take out your journal and write about your experience: how you felt before, what you feel like now, and how it felt during the crystal chakra layout.

11. Carry a positive affirmation with you throughout your day to bring you back to your chakra balancing. For example, it could be: *I am present, healthy, and balanced.*

6 | crystal shapes and formations

CRYSTALS IN THEIR natural state from the earth are called raw crystals. Some healers choose to work with only raw crystals due to their powerful and direct energy. However, other healers, including myself, believe that when you pair your intentions with a cut, polished, or tumbled crystal shape, the energy emitted from the crystal will amplify your transformations and healing. The shape does not change the energy of the crystal, but instead affects the way that you receive it.

crystal shapes

Here are some shapes you may encounter as you shop for crystals. For reference, please see Crystal Shapes and Formations Visual Glossary on page 218.

raw

A raw crystal is one that is taken with love directly from mother nature. Raw crystals are usually rough, but some form natural points, double termination, or clusters. Their energy is very powerful, strong, and direct. If you are working on manifesting something relatively quickly, a raw crystal may be the choice for you. If you are an empath or sensitive soul, sometimes raw can be a bit strong, so I would suggest starting with a gentler stone like a tumbled or palm stone.

tumbled

A tumbled stone has been placed in a rock tumbler for an extended period of time and comes out small and smooth. Tumbled stones provide a very gentle and subtle energy. Their energy radiates from the center of the stone outward equally in every direction. They are the perfect beginner, pocket, travel, crystal grid, or meditation stones. If you are an empath or sensitive soul, tumbled stones are perfect to use to begin your crystal healing journey.

sphere

A sphere is a crystal that has been carved into a perfectly symmetrical spherical shape and emits energy equally out in every direction. Spheres provide a soothing and complete energy, making them the perfect stone for meditation, enhancing your intuition, grounding you into your well-being, and filling up your cup completely. Spheres can also be used as a massage tool; they release any energy blockages that may be stuck and allow you to feel whole and full again.

point

A crystal point has a flat bottom with faceted sides that join into a perfect point at the terminated end of the crystal. Points provide a powerful energy that can be used to direct the flow and amplify the power of the crystal. They are the perfect stone to use in the center of your crystal grid to focus channeled or intentional healing energy. You can use a point to direct energetic healing by either facing the point toward you to bring in healing energy or away from you to remove any excess or unwanted energy.

double-terminated point

A double-terminated crystal has a perfect point at two terminated ends of the crystal. Their energy does double the work of a regular crystal point. It receives energy from one point and releases energy from the other side. Double-terminated points are excellent tools for balancing the chakras, providing consistent energetic flow, physical alignment, maintaining high energetic vibrations, enhancing your psychic gifts, and interpreting dreams. They are also amazing when used in a crystal grid or physical layout on the human body.

merkaba

A merkaba is an eight-pointed star that is made up of two intersecting tetrahedrons that spin in opposite directions. Merkabas emit equal energy out in eight directions. The word *merkaba* translates from Hebrew to "light" (*mer*), "spirit" (*ka*), and "body" (*ba*). Merkabas provide a balancing energy that makes them the perfect stone for chakra balancing, yin and yang balancing, and aura protection. Merkabas can be used best during a deep meditation, providing a balancing energy of the mind, body, and soul.

worry

A worry stone is completely smooth all around like a palm stone but has an indention on one side for your thumb. Worry stones emit a soft and gentle energy, similarly to a tumbled stone. They are used most often to help relieve stress, anxiety, or worry. The action of rubbing your thumb is associated with reflexology (the action of applying pressure to specific points on the hand and feet). By placing pressure to that exact area on your thumb, you are helping bring your pituitary gland back into balance. Keeping a worry stone on you at all times can be especially beneficial, providing relief even when you are out and about like a first-aid kit.

obelisk

A crystal obelisk has a flat bottom with four sides that join into a perfect pyramidal point at the top of the crystal. Obelisks provide high vibrational energy that can be used to direct the flow and amplify the power of the crystal. They are the perfect stone to use for new beginnings, emotional balance, release of negative energy, enhancing memory, and intuition. You can use an obelisk to direct energetic healing by having the point either faced toward you to bring in healing energy or away from you to remove any excess or unwanted energy.

palm

A palm stone is a flat, smooth stone carved into a circular or oval shape. Palm stones are made to fit in the palm of your hands, making them perfect for meditation. They provide a very gentle and subtle energy. If you are an empath or sensitive soul, palm stones are perfect to use to begin your crystal healing journey. Their energy radiates from the center of the stone outward in every direction. They're amazing stones for using during meditation, crystal layout, relaxation, manifestation, and anytime you want to really be present in the moment.

cabochon

A cabochon has a domed top with a flat bottom and is typically used in jewelry. A cabochon's energy radiates from the center of the stone outward in every direction. Its energy is associated with vitality, protection, healing, prosperity, and peace. Most healers wear their cabochon securely tightened in a piece of jewelry, but it can also be used during a healing crystal layout due to its flat bottom so that the crystal doesn't fall off the body during the session.

pyramid

A pyramid has a flat base with four sides of equal length. Pyramids have fascinated humans since ancient civilization and are a sacred shape that is known to amplify energies, intentions, and vibrations. The base provides grounding for your intentions, while the pivotal point sends out your intentions to the universe. Pyramids help you manifest your intentions, energize the chakras and meridians, enhance your meditation, and transmute negative energy into positive energy. They make great healing tools for meditation, manifestation, distance healing, and crystal grids.

freeform

A freeform crystal has a flat bottom with an irregular round top. A freeform can also be a thick, randomly faceted shape without a flat bottom. Freeforms have a gentle soothing energy that is especially useful when put in a designated room of your home, as the energy will fill that area up fully. Freeforms can be used as the centerpiece on your altar, in your home, for meditation, in crystal grid work, in crystal healing layouts, and to recharge your energy.

vogel wands

A vogel wand is double-terminated with flat sides that come in multiples of twelve, and it is wider on one end and thinner on the other end. The triangles are composed of a back side and a front side with four triangular facets on each side, and they are cut so you can see a Star of David when looking through the triangles. The vogel wand was founded, named, and taught by Marcel Vogel. Vogel wands are typically only cut using crystals in the quartz family. They have one of the highest vibrational pulls, which can be used for intense healing work. Vogels can be used to transmit healing energy from one person to another, transformation, healing emotional trauma, spiritual rebirth, bringing the immune system back into balance, removing negative energy, harmonizing the chakras, and bringing the physical body back into balance. When working on yourself or a loved one, hold the vogel with the widest side facing toward the left of your body and narrower side facing the right side. Then begin to scan your body up and down with the vogel until you feel an area that calls to you to be worked on. Once you know the area, begin to scoop the negative energy that needs to be removed from the wider side of the vogel and release it into the universe to be healed with the narrow side of the vogel. Repeat this process until you feel your or your loved one's body has been cleansed and restored.

egg

An egg has a rounded end with a shorter rounded tip. Eggs provide a gentle, even energy that is directed through the smaller rounded end. They are used for fertility, female energy, miracles, vitality, sexuality, life force, strength, and health. Eggs can be used to scan the aura and detect energetic imbalances within the body. They can also be used as a massage tool, by releasing any energy blockages that may be stuck and allowing you to feel whole and full again. Yoni eggs are specifically made for women to insert into their vagina, which aids in sensuality, vaginal health, boosting libido, passion, and fertility.

cube

A cube has six equal square-shaped faces. Cubes emit energy out in all directions, providing very grounding, stable energy. They can be used for protection, releasing excess energy, for safety and security, regaining focus, removing any tension or stress, reconnection with mother nature, and meditation. When using them for energetic protection, place one cube in each of the four corners of your home.

carved deities

A carved crystal deity is any crystal that is formed into your favorite carved figurine, such as a Buddha or Ganesha. Its energy combines the attributes of the deity with the healing property of the stone it is carved out of. Typically, when choosing a crystal symbol, you will want to choose one that heightens, complements, or balances the energy of the deity. Use these crystal figurines to help you learn lessons that the deities' energies provide, such as prosperity from Lord Ganesha or unconditional love from Kuan Yin. See below for some examples. These crystals are very sacred and should be treated with great honor and respect.

Buddha: enlightenment, protection, meditation. **CRYSTAL PAIRING:** lapis lazuli, black tourmaline, amethyst

Ganesha: fortune, wisdom, overcoming obstacles. **CRYSTAL PAIRING:** green aventurine, sunstone, carnelian

Kuan Yin: unconditional love, empathy, compassion. **CRYSTAL PAIRING:** rose quartz, rhodochrosite, rhodonite

Shakti: strength, power, energy. **CRYSTAL PAIRING:** clear quartz, black obsidian, orange calcite

flame

A flame has a flat-cut base and spirals up to the top of the crystal in the shape of a flame. Flames are associated with the fire element, exuding energy of transformation, passion, love, impulse, strength, motivation, inspiration, and resilience. Flames emit an intense energy starting at the base and spiraling up and out of the top. Place your flame in any space in your home where you want to spark that boost in energy and flow.

bowl

A bowl has a flat bottom with a large indentation in the center, where crystals can be stored. Bowls radiate their energy from the center out. You can use crystal bowls for charging other crystals, a gem water bath (if water-safe), the center of your altar, or a crystal grid. Selenite bowls are most often made not only to store your crystals, but also to charge and cleanse them.

carved animals

A carved crystal animal is any crystal that is formed into your favorite animal, such as a bear or an owl. Its energy combines the attributes of the animal with the healing property of the stone it is carved out of. Typically, when choosing a crystal animal, you will want to choose one that heightens, complements, or balances the energy of the animal. Use these crystal animals to help you learn lessons that the animals' energies provide, such as strength from an elephant or patience from a cat.

- **Elephants:** strength, luck, loyalty. **CRYSTAL PAIRING:** clear quartz, pyrite, emerald
- **Owls:** independence, wisdom, courage. **CRYSTAL PAIRING:** amethyst, sunstone, bloodstone
- **Cats:** patience, curiosity, freedom. **CRYSTAL PAIRING:** petrified wood, tiger's eye, sunstone
- **Dogs:** protector, bravery, caring. **CRYSTAL PAIRING:** black tourmaline, hematite, rose quartz
- **Dolphin:** self-love, affection, playfulness. **CRYSTAL PAIRING:** rose quartz, carnelian, orange calcite
- **Dragon:** success, confidence, fearlessness. **CRYSTAL PAIRING:** green aventurine, citrine, lepidolite

- **Bear**: truthfulness, compassion, determination. **CRYSTAL PAIRING:** red jasper, rhodonite, moss agate
- **Snake**: creation, fertility, transformation. **CRYSTAL PAIRING:** citrine, carnelian, labradorite
- **Turtle**: wisdom, patience, flexibility. **CRYSTAL PAIRING:** sunstone, petrified wood, turquoise

carved symbols

A carved crystal symbol is any crystal that is formed into your favorite symbol, such as a heart or star. Its energy combines the attributes of the symbol with the healing property of the stone. Typically, when choosing a crystal symbol, you will want to choose one that heightens, complements, or balances the energy of the symbol. Use these crystal symbols to help you learn lessons that the symbol energies provide, such as love from a heart or miracles from an angel.

- **Heart**: love, relationships, empathy. **CRYSTAL PAIRING:** rose quartz, carnelian, rhodonite
- **Star**: union, enlightenment, divinity. **CRYSTAL PAIRING:** iolite, lapis lazuli, amethyst
- **Moon**: eternity, manifestation, balance. **CRYSTAL PAIRING:** clear quartz, citrine, shungite
- **Flower**: expansion, growth, rebirth. **CRYSTAL PAIRING:** epidote, ocean jasper, rose quartz
- **Angel**: miracles, messengers, hope. **CRYSTAL PAIRING:** angelite, moonstone, amazonite
- **Skull**: protection, wisdom, fearless. **CRYSTAL PAIRING:** amethyst, sunstone, lepidolite

crystal formations

I could probably dedicate an entire book just to all the crystal formations! But I want you, as a beginner, to understand and be able to identify the most common crystal formations. These 15 formations are commonly found in quartz crystals, but they can sometimes be found in other minerals as well. For reference, please see Crystal Shapes and Formations Visual Glossary on page 218.

geode

You will find geode halves in any crystal store you go into—I'm sure you've seen an amethyst geode! A geode is a complete rock structure with a hollow inside that is crystalized with different minerals. Spiritually, geodes are most often used to amplify your intentions and radiate positive energy throughout your space. Geodes can also be used to deepen your meditation, balance the chi flow of your home, assist with spiritual growth or inner work, and deepen your connection to higher awareness.

cluster

Clusters are most often just a chunk of a geode. They are composed of lots of crystal points that are formed together and emerge at one flat base. Clusters emit energy starting from the base and out through each point in all directions. Spiritually, they bring harmony, boost manifestations, promote positive group energy, and help you connect to like-minded people.

elestial

Elestials have a very distinctive formation. They have a skeletal pattern in which several small multi-terminated crystals grow on top of the sides of a larger crystal or cluster. Elestials are highly vibrational and are named after their strong connection to celestial beings, especially angels. Spiritually, elestials enhance your meditation and intentions, aid in decision making, strengthen your spiritual awakening, and strengthen your connection to higher realms.

etched

Etched crystals have unique exterior markings and intricate patterns that were formed when minerals were eroded by hydrothermal water during their formation. Spiritually, they have stored messages for you, help you tap into your Akashic records, and can connect you with the wisdom of ancient civilization. They can also further assist you in making positive life changes, inner healing, and personal growth and development.

druzy

Druzy crystals are those sparkly crystals that you can spot anywhere because their beauty just takes your breath away. They are a composition of several mini crystals on a rock surface. They emit energy out through each point in all directions. Spiritually, a druzy crystal promotes gratitude, stimulates imagination and creativity, radiates your inner beauty to shine, promotes positive group energy, and reminds you not to sweat the small stuff.

manifestation

Manifestation crystals can be identified when a smaller crystal (typically double-terminated) is totally enclosed inside of a larger crystal. These crystals get their name from their incredible ability to magnify and speed up your manifestations. They can also be used to encourage deep inner healing, increase intuition and spiritual development, and provide spiritual guidance.

key/imprint

A key crystal formation occurs when two crystals grow as one, but then one is separated and leaves a key or imprint on the other crystal as it becomes unattached. Spiritually, they are great amplifiers for speeding up the manifestation process. Key crystals also help you unlock information stored in your subconscious mind, aid in releasing energetic blockages, enhance your meditation and personal growth, and serve as a portal connecting you to higher dimensions/realms.

record keepers

Record keeper crystals can be identified by raised triangles typically found on the faces of a crystal. They are most known for their access to information or data that has been stored in the crystal, such as Akashic records, ancient civilization wisdom, spiritual maps, past lives, and information from your spirit guides. They can also be used to release energetic blockages and facilitate deep healing.

self-healed

Self-healed crystals can be identified by a skeletal formation. When you look from afar, the crystal may appear broken or chipped, but when you get up close, you can see where the original crystal matrix broke off and then healed itself, forming tiny points over the surface. Spiritually, these are most often used when doing inner healing work on yourself. Self-healed crystals also promote self-love and care, compassion toward others, and optimism. They support overall health and well-being and can be especially healing for those caretakers and lightworkers of the world who typically tend to suffer from burnout.

striations

Striations are commonly found forming on lemurian seed quartz. These can be identified by raised horizontal grooves or lines that look like barcodes that run along the sides of the crystal. Spiritually, they are highly vibrational and can be used to speed up healing during the recovery process after an injury or surgery. They are also great for accessing spiritually guided information, Akashic records, and past lives.

window

a window is a crystal with a four-sided diamond shaped "window" located where the face meets the side of the crystal. Spiritually, the window represents a self-reflection, or mirror, of yourself. You can access this information by placing the window portion of your crystal directly onto your third-eye chakra. Windows can also heighten your intuition and psychic abilities and stimulate personal growth and development.

phantom

A phantom formation is where you see faint ghost-like crystal point(s) inside of a larger crystal point. This occurs when a crystal stops growing, is covered with another mineral, and then resumes

growing. Spiritually, it is known to encourage spiritual transformation and personal growth. It also stimulates intuition, activates healing, opens communication to higher realms, releases karma, and enhances spiritual exploration.

inclusions

There is a huge variety of crystals with inclusions. This formation can most often be identified in quartz crystals, where you will see traces of minerals within the crystal. Examples of these include rutile, enhydro, hematite, epidote, chlorite, and tourmaline in quartz. The minerals that are trapped inside of the crystal are amplified by the quartz. Spiritually, they teach us harmony, cooperation, and inner strength.

rainbow

a rainbow is the easiest out of all 15 formations to identify because it's a beautiful rainbow inside of a crystal! It can usually only be seen at an angle. A rainbow is typically formed inside of a crystal due to cracks or fractures, which goes along with the spiritual guidance that there is a rainbow after every storm. Spiritually, rainbows represent hope, optimism, joy, equality, and good luck. They are also seen as the bridge between the spiritual world and the physical world.

asterate star

Asterism is most often seen in rose quartz, but it can also be seen in other minerals, such as ruby, garnet, and sapphire. It can be identified when held in direct light; a four-ray or six-ray star of reflected or refracted light can be seen in the crystal. This is due to needle-like inclusions of rutile or hematite that are aligned perpendicularly to the rays of the star. Spiritually, these crystals bring expansive and healing light to the mind, body, and soul. They also help you dive deep into inner healing.

get to know 100 crystals

a crystal directory

EACH OF THE PROFILES in this chapter features some basic information on a crystal—including physical properties such as hardness (see page 12) and associations such as zodiac sign and element—along with its spiritual, physical, and emotional healing benefits. My hope is that you feel inspired and hopeful about how crystals may benefit your life.

To begin our exploration of crystals, let's look at their colors.

Wave Length in Nanometer

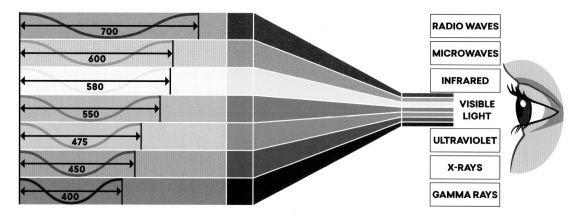

crystals by color

Have you ever noticed that you were really attracted to a certain color at a certain time in your life? Or maybe there's a color that you currently just cannot seem to get enough of. There is a deeper meaning to this besides just the beauty.

We see color through the presence of light, which is known as electromagnetic energy. All colors carry their own unique vibrational energy on the electromagnetic spectrum. Colors arrange themselves in order of decreasing vibrational wavelengths, starting with red at 700 nm (lower frequency) and all the way up to violet at 400 nm (higher frequency).

When we introduce specific light frequencies (i.e., colors) into our electromagnetic field, our aura, this entrains our physical and emotional frequency and encourages good health by putting our body back into balance. This process is called color therapy. Color therapy is not a new concept; it has been used since ancient times and is now used in modern science and holistic healing.

When you combine crystal healing and color therapy by matching the chakra colors (see chapter 5), it allows photons of light to harmonize and facilitate healing. For instance, if you want to start opening yourself up to love again, you would work with the color pink and pair it with a pink stone such as rose quartz or rhodochrosite.

Simply put:

- **Colors we *love*** = Positive reflections of ourselves or comfort in places we are ready to heal
- **Colors we *avoid*** = Energy we have in excess that we may not be ready to heal

Now that you have a deeper understanding of why you are drawn to certain colors, you will have an easier and greater understanding of why you are also drawn to a particular crystal, even without knowing the properties of that crystal. Following are reasons you may be attracted to or avoiding certain colors and their corresponding crystals to work with in crystal or color therapy.

red

When attracted to red, you may be reflecting—or ready to heal and grow in—the following areas: grounding, safety, stability, motivation, energy, strength, health, independence, survival, vitality, action, achievement, passion, centering.

When you are avoiding red, you may not be ready to heal in one of the following areas: condescension, greed, addiction, instability, controlling, weakness, depression, self-centeredness, anger, deceit, egotism, perfection, aggression, lack of grounding.

RED CRYSTALS INCLUDE:

- Fire quartz   78
- Red jasper   79
- Fire agate   80
- Garnet   81

orange

When attracted to orange, you may be reflecting—or ready to heal and grow in—the following areas: sexual energy, vitality, fertility, attraction, success, joy, creativity, relationships, warmth, optimism, expansion, selflessness, vigilance, passion.

When you are avoiding orange, you may not be ready to heal in one of the following areas: sexuality, selfishness, reactiveness, fearfulness, aggression, apathy, meanness, manipulation, blaming others, resentfulness, confusion, delusion, controlling, tension.

ORANGE CRYSTALS INCLUDE:

- Orange calcite   82
- Sunstone   83
- Carnelian   84
- Sardonyx   85
- Vanadinite   86

yellow

When attracted to yellow, you may be reflecting—or ready to heal and grow in the following areas: abundance, clarity, gratitude, self-love, self-esteem, fortune, happiness, manifestation, worthiness, courage, confidence, willpower, humor, expression.

When you are avoiding yellow, you may not be ready to heal in one of the following areas: overachieving, jealousy, entitlement, conceit, anxiety, hatred, depression, demanding, fearfulness, loathing, judgment, insecurities, rudeness, unworthiness.

YELLOW CRYSTALS INCLUDE:

- Bumblebee jasper   87
- Citrine   88
- Golden healer   89
- Libyan desert glass   90
- Crazy lace agate   91
- Honey calcite   92
- Septarian   93
- Amber   94
- Mookaite jasper   95

Bumblebee Jasper

green

When attracted to green, you may be reflecting—or ready to heal and grow in—the following areas: compassion, love, empathy, kindness, emotional healing, nature, prosperity, forgiveness, hope, self-love, harmony, generosity, wealth, renewal.

When you are avoiding green, you may not be ready to heal in one of the following areas: possessiveness, tension, greed, aggression, materialism, apathy, drama, dominance, selfishness, misery, resentment, inconsiderateness, bitterness, hatred.

GREEN CRYSTALS INCLUDE:

- Unakite jasper   96
- Nephrite jade   97
- Malachite   98
- Bloodstone   99
- Emerald   100
- Green aventurine   101
- Garnierite   102
- Green tourmaline   103
- Kambaba jasper   104
- Moss agate   105
- Moldavite   106
- Peridot   107
- Serpentine   108
- Prehnite   109
- Green opal   110
- Epidote   111
- Ocean jasper   112

blue

When attracted to blue, you may be reflecting—or ready to heal and grow in—the following areas: communication, peace, calm, harmony, purification, grace, relaxation, comprehension, focus, patience, wisdom, serenity, loyalty, trust.

When you are avoiding blue, you may not be ready to heal in one of the following areas: unfaithfulness, strictness, arrogance, dominance, unforgiving, rigidity, controlling, untrustworthiness, toxicity, spite, depression, addiction, aloofness, passivity.

BLUE CRYSTALS INCLUDE:

- Agate   113
- Blue lace agate   114
- Larimar   115
- Turquoise   116
- Angelite   117
- Aquamarine   118
- Blue calcite   119
- Celestite   120
- Chrysocolla   121
- Amazonite   122
- Blue chalcedony   123

purple

When attracted to purple, you may be reflecting—or ready to heal and grow in—the following areas: spirituality, intuition, wisdom, inspiration, imagination, insight, sensitivity, imagination, destiny, foresight, connection, awakening, renewal, meditation.

When you are avoiding purple, you may not be ready to heal in one of the following areas: manipulation, aloofness, pride, delusion, egotism, bossiness, impracticality, conniving, cynicism, apathy, impersonality, judgment, corruption, disconnection.

PURPLE CRYSTALS INCLUDE:

- Amethyst   124
- Sugilite   125
- Super 7   126
- Spirit quartz   127
- Fluorite   128
- Lepidolite   129
- Chaorite   130

pink

When attracted to pink, you may be reflecting—or ready to heal and grow in—the following areas: unconditional love, family, self-love, nurturing, forgiveness, feelings, romance, relationships, gentleness, affection, openness, kindness, joy, empathy.

When you are avoiding pink, you may not be ready to heal in one of the following areas: over-emotion, naivety, drama, weakness, immaturity, neediness, resentfulness, aggression, apathy, hatred, powerlessness, dominance, bitterness.

PINK CRYSTALS INCLUDE:

Morganite

BLACK CRYSTALS INCLUDE:

black

When attracted to black, you may be reflecting—or ready to heal and grow in—the following areas: protection, safety, release, journey, grounding, creation, exploration, transformation, power, security, revelation, banishing, daring, discovery.

When you are avoiding black, you may not be ready to heal in one of the following areas: self-centeredness, emptiness, ungrounding, aggression, negativity, pessimism, conservativeness, withholding, anger, avoidance, secretiveness, depression, seriousness, controlling.

white

When attracted to white, you may be reflecting—or ready to heal and grow in—the following areas: new beginnings, intuition, divinity, cleansing, awareness, radiance, spirituality, enlightenment, unity, harmony, awakening, connection, simplicity, wholeness.

When you are avoiding white, you may not be ready to heal in one of the following areas: frustration, loss, distance, isolation, inconsistency, unfaithfulness, depression, withdrawl, emptiness, caution, delusion, lack of balance, apathy, boredom.

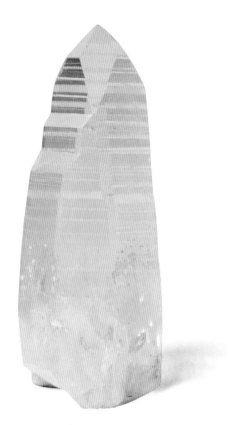

Lemurian

self-centeredness, fearfulness, conceitedness, demanding, judgment, anxiety, depression, untrustworthiness, entitlement, egotism, pessimism, insecurity, falseness.

GOLD CRYSTALS INCLUDE:

silver

When attracted to silver, you may be reflecting—or ready to heal and grow in—the following areas: equilibrium, intuition, rebirth, purifying, resourcefulness, grace, justice, intuition, victory, optimism, soothing, dreams, purity, strategy.

When you are avoiding silver, you may not be ready to heal in one of the following areas: lack of balance, dullness, lifelessness, pessimism, indecisiveness, neutrality, blandness, carelessness, loneliness, rigidity, deception, insincerity, impurity, apathy.

SILVER CRYSTALS INCLUDE:

brown

When attracted to brown, you may be reflecting—or ready to heal and grow in—the following areas: grounding, loyalty, safety, alignment, blessings, solitude, practicality, independence, comfort, discovery, centering, concentration, care, abundance.

When you are avoiding brown, you may not be ready to heal in one of the following areas: materialism, frugality, stagnancy, lack of grounding, carelessness, dullness, predictability, untrustworthiness, seriousness, stinginess, controlling, rowdiness, instability, dependence.

WHITE CRYSTALS INCLUDE:

gold

When attracted to gold, you may be reflecting—or ready to heal and grow in—the following areas: abundance, luck, fortune, positivity, manifestation, courage, authority, confidence, power, justice, purification, worthiness, prosperity, optimism.

When you are avoiding gold, you may not be ready to heal in one of the following areas:

copper

When attracted to copper, you may be reflecting—or ready to heal and grow in—the following areas: purification, success, balance, passion, abundance, career, amplification, relationships, energy, power, optimism, self-esteem, love, potential.

When you are avoiding copper, you may not be ready to heal in one of the following areas: restrictions, fearfulness, powerlessness, pessimism, unworthiness, reactivity, selfishness, closure, apathy, lethargy, delusion, lack of grounding, resentfulness, meanness.

indigo

When attracted to indigo, you may be reflecting—or ready to heal and grow in—the following areas: awakening, insight, intuition, faith, channeling, truth, meditation, awareness, foresight, expansion, spirituality, enlightenment, virtue, conscious.

When you are avoiding indigo, you may not be ready to heal in one of the following areas: judgment, fearfulness, untruthfulness, disconnection, addiction, pride, inconsiderate, impracticality, bossiness, conformity, containment, depression, intolerance, unfaithfulness.

rainbow

When attracted to all of the colors of the rainbow, you may be reflecting—or ready to heal and grow in—the following areas: hope, enlightenment, wealth and success, spiritually, new beginnings, change, transformation, all seven chakras, connection, optimism, joy.

When you are avoiding all the colors of the rainbow, you may not be ready to heal in one of the following areas: all seven chakras, depression, fear, guilt, universal energy and life force, spirituality, anger, despair, loneliness, misery.

Azurite

fire quartz

Grounding | Love | Calm | Present | Radiance

Fire quartz has the following spiritual, physical, and emotional healing properties.

spiritual healing

- Activates the energy centers within the spiritual body.
- Dispels negative energy and replaces it with positive energy.
- Helps ground you with earth's healing vibrations.
- Helps facilitate healing of past wounds spiritually, mentally, and physically.
- Combines the properties of hematite and quartz, making it a highly vibrational yet very grounding stone.

physical healing

- Helps reduce panic attacks, anxiety, and hysteria.
- Stimulates the mind and boosts memory.
- Stimulates the body's physical vitality and energy.
- Supports a healthy nervous system.
- Accelerates the body's natural healing process.

emotional healing

- Increases feelings of self-esteem, self-confidence, and self-worth.
- Allows you to feel free and accept a happy and abundant life.
- Aids in the expression and acceptance of unconditional love.
- Promotes stillness and peace.
- Stimulates focus and mental clarity to the emotional state.

Life is meant to be filled with joy and abundance. To get back to your natural state of being, wear fire quartz as jewelry (skin contact) daily.

COLORS	red and white
HARDNESS	7
CHAKRAS	root, sacral, and solar plexus
ZODIAC SIGN	Scorpio
ELEMENT	fire
CRYSTAL PAIRINGS	fire agate, golden healer, red jasper, or ocean jasper
PRECAUTIONS	Do not put fire quartz in direct sunlight; the colors will begin to fade.
AFFIRMATION	I accept, love, and honor myself for exactly who I am.

red jasper

Grounding | Strength | Energy | Fulfillment | Mental Stability

Red jasper has the following spiritual, physical, and emotional healing properties.

spiritual healing

- Deepens your meditation and raises your Kundalini energy.
- Assists you in setting boundaries.
- Gives you a sense of stability, safety, security, and grounding.
- Increases your life force (*prana*).
- Provides a protective energy shield from negative energy and danger.

physical healing

- Can help replenish your muscles after a workout.
- Boosts physical energy, stamina, vitality, and strength.
- Aids in speeding up recovery after an illness or surgery.
- Can detoxify the liver, circulatory system, and bile ducts.
- Supports a healthy heart.

emotional healing

- Helps you maintain your mental stability.
- Works to release feelings of irritability, guilt, shame, or regret.
- Helps soothe upset feelings and calm your emotions.
- Helps bring more joy to your life by letting you become more present in the moment.
- Increases willpower and mental strength.

Rub or hold a Red Jasper stone to become more centered, to be more grounded, and to find a sense of safety and security within.

COLOR	red
HARDNESS	6.5–7
CHAKRA	root
ZODIAC SIGNA	Leo, Virgo, Scorpio, and Taurus
ELEMENT	earth
CRYSTAL PAIRINGS	agate, crazy lace agate, fire quartz, garnet, mookaite jasper, petrified wood, smoky quartz, or sardonyx
PRECAUTIONS	none
AFFIRMATION	I am rooted into the earth like a tree—grounded, safe, and secure.

fire agate

Sexuality | Creativity | Energy | Passion | Happiness

Fire agate has the following spiritual, physical, and emotional healing properties.

spiritual healing

- Provides an energetic shield of protection from negativity.
- Helps you ground yourself by reconnecting and putting your mind, body, and soul into alignment.
- Boosts creativity, success, inspiration, and expression.
- Enhances your spiritual awakening experience.

physical healing

- Helps overcome addictions.
- Boosts libido, energy, fertility, and vitality.
- Helps increase circulation flow.
- Can increase your metabolic rate and provide digestive relief.
- Helps treat disorders of the eyes, circulatory system, and nervous system.

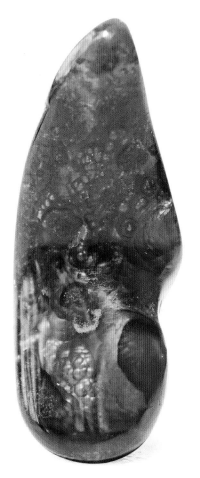

COLORS	brown, orange, yellow, green, blue, and mostly red
HARDNESS	6–7
CHAKRAS	root, sacral, and solar plexus
ZODIAC SIGNS	Gemini and Aries
ELEMENT	fire
CRYSTAL PAIRINGS	carnelian, sunstone, fire quartz, or orange calcite
PRECAUTIONS	Fire agate can be in the sunlight but not for too long, as the colors may begin to fade.
AFFIRMATION	I feel deeply rooted where I belong.

emotional healing

- Boosts confidence and courage.
- Helps you get out of a funk or rut and get back to your positive, energetic self again.
- Increases passion and zest for life.
- Helps increase your self-esteem and ability to make quicker decisions.
- Encourages you to become the best version of yourself.

Place a fire agate in your pocket or bra daily to give you an extra boost of energy and stamina throughout your day.

garnet

Strength | Love | Joy | Life Force | Power

Garnet has the following spiritual, physical, and emotional healing properties.

spiritual healing

- Works on releasing karmic contracts.
- Enhances and deepens your meditation.
- Increases Kundalini life force energy.
- Provides an energetic shield of protection from negativity.
- Increases feeling grounded into mother nature's healing energy.

physical healing

- Boosts fertility, passion, motivation, libido, and sensuality.
- Supports a healthy heart, lungs, and blood.
- Helps speed up the recovery process after surgery or an injury.
- Revitalizes, strengthens, and rejuvenates the physical body.

COLOR	deep red
HARDNESS	6.5–7.5
CHAKRA	root and heart
ZODIAC SIGNS	Aquarius, Capricorn, Aries, Leo, and Virgo
ELEMENT	earth and fire
CRYSTAL PAIRINGS	serpentine, vanadanite, pink tourmaline, ruby, red jasper, or green tourmaline
PRECAUTIONS	Garnet contains aluminum and can be toxic if ingested. Avoid putting it in direct sunlight, as its color will begin to fade.
AFFIRMATION	I am living my life with purpose, love, and passion.

emotional healing

- Can help you overcome anxiety, stress, worry, and fear.
- Helps relieve depression, chaos, and emotional trauma.
- Enhances understanding, trust, expression, and honesty with yourself and others.
- Encourages change, creativity, abundance, courage, and awareness.
- Can help with emotional stability and increasing one's ability to feel love.
- Brings feelings of warmth, love, nourishment, and romance.

If you are feeling numb to love and searching for answers on how to find it, go within. Meditate with a garnet over your heart chakra and imagine the last time you felt love. Really feel it and open your heart up to feeling that unconditional love again. Repeat this meditation daily until you feel back to your natural loving state of being.

orange calcite

Joy | Relationships | Creativity | Sexuality | Energy Flow

Orange calcite has the following spiritual, physical, and emotional healing properties.

spiritual healing

- Boosts creative flow and sparks new ideas.
- Helps you discover your soul purpose in this lifetime.
- Expands your life force and energy flow.
- Helps you embark on your new journey or endeavor.
- Increases your awareness of self.

physical healing

- Works to increase libido, vitality, sensuality, and physical energy.
- Helps bring your hormones back into a healthy and balanced state.
- Supports a healthy digestive, reproductive, and immune systems.
- Promotes stimulating the metabolism to increase healthy weight loss.
- Supports healthy skin and bones.

emotional healing

- Helps you attract positive relationships both romantically and in friendships.
- Helps you overcome old, negative patterns and habits.
- Encourages playfulness, lightheartedness, and passion.
- Helps you overcome depression and reduce fear-based thinking.
- Is a feel-good stone that boosts self-confidence, optimism, and joy.

If you need to bring that spark and passion back into your life, keep an orange calcite near your bedside. When you wake up in the morning, hold it in your hand and focus on its vibrant energy. Then affirm to yourself, "There are no limits to my possibilities." Allow the vibrations from the orange calcite to give you a boost of energy to spark your day with joy, gratitude, and passion.

COLORS	orange and white
HARDNESS	3
CHAKRAS	sacral
ZODIAC SIGNS	Cancer and Leo
ELEMENT	fire
CRYSTAL PAIRINGS	ocean jasper, bumblebee jasper, carnelian, citrine, sunstone, fire agate, honey calcite, sardonyx, or vanadinite
PRECAUTIONS	Orange calcite is a soft stone that shouldn't be placed in water or prolonged sun exposure.
AFFIRMATION	I am in charge of how I feel and today I am choosing happiness.

sunstone

Abundance | Joy | Creativity | Strength | Energy

Sunstone has the following spiritual, physical, and emotional healing properties.

spiritual healing

- Brings positive energy and abundance.
- Can aid in protection against negativity and evil spirits.
- Clears and energizes all seven chakras.
- Encourages you to be your most authentic self.
- Sparks new ideas, creativity, and visions.

physical healing

- Aids in improving overall health and well-being.
- Stimulates sexuality, passion, and libido.
- Assists in vitality, strength, energy, and longevity.
- Supports a healthy circulatory and nervous system.

emotional healing

- Can help relieve stress and conquer fears.
- Boosts feelings of optimism, euphoria, and self-care.
- Helps individuals battling depression find happiness and joy again.
- Encourages independence and originality.
- Boosts feelings of self-confidence, courage, and self-worth.
- Encourages healthy and positive relationships.

To attract more joy, happiness, and gratitude into your life, wear or carry sunstone on you. Rub or hold it anytime you start feeling down and repeat the affirmation "I am constantly in a state of joy!"

COLOR	orange
HARDNESS	6–6.5
CHAKRA	all, especially sacral
ZODIAC SIGNS	Leo and Libra
ELEMENT	fire
CRYSTAL PAIRINGS	fire agate, green opal, iolite, labradorite, mookaite jasper, ocean jasper, orange calcite, or vanadinite
PRECAUTIONS	Do not allow prolonged sun exposure.
AFFIRMATION	I am in charge of how I feel today, and today I choose joy.

carnelian

Creativity | Vitality | Energy | Confidence | Sensuality

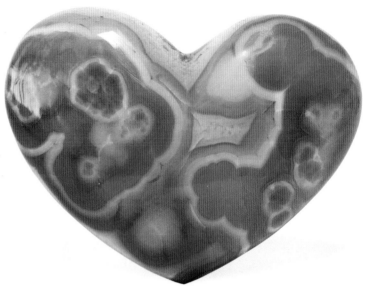

Carnelian has the following spiritual, physical, and emotional healing properties.

spiritual healing

- Boosts your ability to manifest your dreams and desires.
- Sparks creativity and imagination.
- Provides an energetic protection from negative and toxic energy.
- Boosts an abundance of love, positive energy, and light in your life.
- Can clear out negative energy from other crystals.

physical healing

- Boosts sex drive and fertility.
- Helps promote blood circulation and purification.
- Boosts energy, passion, stamina, motivation, and vitality.
- Provides peace during menstrual and menopausal symptoms.
- Supports a healthy immune system and reproductive system.

emotional healing

- Increases enthusiasm and optimism for enjoying everything life has to offer.
- Aids in the treatment of eating disorders and disordered thinking.
- Helps you set boundaries with others.
- Increases feelings of self-confidence and self-worth.
- Encourages healthy relationships with your partner, loved ones, and friendships.

To increase fertility, hold a carnelian heart or palm stone over your womb every night and imagine your child already in your womb.

COLORS	red, orange, yellow, and white
HARDNESS	7
CHAKRA	sacral
ZODIAC SIGNS	Virgo, Taurus, Cancer, and Leo
ELEMENT	fire
CRYSTAL PAIRINGS	orange calcite, citrine, rose quartz, red garnet, crazy lace agate, fire agate, flower agate, mookaite jasper, sardonyx, shiva lingam, or vanadinite
PRECAUTIONS	Carnelian is not safe in salt water.
AFFIRMATION	I have the energy and stamina to achieve anything I desire.

sardonyx

Loving Relationships | Security | Happiness |
Energy | Creativity

Sardonyx has the following spiritual, physical, and emotional healing properties.

spiritual healing

- Promotes energetic grounding and protection.
- Enhances your creativity, sparking new ideas and explorations.
- Urges you to strive for a fulfilling life.
- Is a stone of courage, good luck, and strength.

physical healing

- Boosts endurance, passion, vitality, and energy.
- Brings the metabolism back into balance.
- Helps maintain a healthy immune system.
- Supports healthy lungs and bones.

emotional healing

- Helps with lasting happiness and clear communication.
- Brings in feelings of positivity, optimism, and happiness.

- Can aid in eliminating hesitations.
- Aids in positive socializing, marriage, and relationships with others.
- Boosts feelings of joy and gratitude, helping one overcome depression.
- Enhances confidence and honesty within yourself.
- Promotes feelings of safety and security.

If you are struggling with any relationships in your life, wear or keep a sardonyx on you at all times to promote positive communication, joy, and compassion.

COLOR	orange, red, yellow, and black
HARDNESS	6
CHAKRA	sacral
ZODIAC SIGN	Virgo
ELEMENT	fire
CRYSTAL PAIRINGS	carnelian, orange calcite, or red jasper
PRECAUTIONS	none
AFFIRMATION	I attract happiness, security, and loving relationships.

vanadinite

Energy | Creativity | Adventurousness | Motivation | Focus

Vanadinite has the following spiritual, physical, and emotional healing properties.

spiritual healing

- Enhances and stimulates your creativity.
- Gives you that extra boost of motivation to pursue your goals and dreams.
- Provides a deep peace within the soul.
- Helps you see the beauty in all people, the earth, and all things.
- Can help resolve old karmic patterns.

physical healing

- Helps you sustain energy and remain focused through a full day of work.
- Can block off radiation that is caused by electronics.
- Helps women through PMS and both men and women through menopause.
- Helps bring your hormones back into a healthy and balanced state.
- Boosts libido and passion.

emotional healing

- Allows you to ignite your inner child, feeling free, adventurous, playful, and curious.
- Boosts feelings of confidence and self-worth.
- Helps you feel sexually desirable.
- Boosts your desire to take risks and let go of unwanted fears.
- Promotes feelings of optimism and joy.

If you are working toward a certain goal or dream, take out your journal and place your vanadinite next to or on it to amplify inspiration, creativity, new ideas, and guidance for manifesting how to achieve it.

COLORS	red, orange, and yellow
HARDNESS	3-4
CHAKRAS	root, sacral, solar plexus, and third eye
ZODIAC SIGN	Virgo
ELEMENT	fire
CRYSTAL PAIRINGS	garnet, orange calcite, sunstone, or carnelian
PRECAUTIONS	Do not put vanadinite in water. It is a very soft, brittle stone.
AFFIRMATION	I have an abundance of health, energy, and vitality.

bumblebee jasper

Joy | Energy | Confidence | Creativity | Abundance

Bumblebee jasper has the following spiritual, physical, and emotional healing properties.

spiritual healing

- Sparks creativity, adventure, new ideas, and explorations.
- Can free blocked energy from your spiritual body, especially the solar plexus chakra.
- Brings positive energy and abundance.
- Provides protection during spiritual enlightenment.
- Brings energetic support and grounding to bring you back into alignment.
- Provides spiritual guidance in helping you manifest your greatest desires and dreams.

physical healing

- Aids in the relief of an upset stomach.
- Helps one fight off infections and expel toxins from the body.
- Stimulates vitality, energy, and youthfulness.
- Works to regulate a healthy liver, kidneys, pancreas, and adrenal glands.

emotional healing

- Supports acceptance of change, new beginnings, and transformation.
- Works to increase feelings of self-worth, confidence, and courage.
- Promotes feelings of joy, hope, and gratitude.
- Aids in releasing fears and self-doubts.
- Helps stimulate mental clarity, focus, concentration, and assertiveness.

If you have an upset stomach, place a bumblebee jasper over the area until you feel relief.

COLOR	yellow, orange, black, and gray
HARDNESS	2.5–5
CHAKRA	root, sacral, and solar plexus
ZODIAC SIGN	Cancer and Leo
ELEMENT	earth and fire
CRYSTAL PAIRINGS	citrine, ocean jasper, orange calcite, carnelian, honey calcite, crazy lace agate, or septarian
PRECAUTIONS	Bumblebee jasper contains sulfur and can be toxic if ingested. Do not get it wet.
AFFIRMATION	I am proud of myself and all of my accomplishments.

citrine

Abundance | Joy | Digestive Balance | Wealth | Luck

Citrine has the following spiritual, physical, and emotional healing properties.

spiritual healing

- Radiates high vibrational energy, making it perfect when manifesting prosperity, success, and abundance.
- Guides us to find our soul purpose in this lifetime.
- Stimulates a deeper connection with your higher self and spirit guides.
- Promotes new perceptions, creativity, and ideas.
- Opens, activates, and balances the solar plexus chakra.

physical healing

- Helps bring balance and healing to the digestive system and metabolism.
- Is known to boost stamina, endurance, and physical energy.
- Works to regulate a healthy liver and kidneys.
- Helps support and balance the endocrine system and hormones.
- Supports healthy blood flow and circulation.

emotional healing

- Helps reduce fear, worry, and anxiety.
- Aids in stimulating mental focus, personal empowerment, productivity, and mental clarity.
- Can strengthen self-confidence, personal power, and self-esteem.
- Helps you develop a positive attitude toward anything that life swings at you.
- Provides support in releasing old limiting beliefs.

If you are feeling down, doubting yourself, or disapproving of yourself, try wearing a citrine bracelet or necklace daily to help boost your self-confidence.

COLORS	yellow
HARDNESS	7
CHAKRAS	solar plexus
ZODIAC SIGN	Cancer
ELEMENT	fire
CRYSTAL PAIRINGS	orange calcite, carnelian, pyrite, moldavite, Libyan desert glass, bumblebee jasper, golden healer, gold sheen obsidian, honey calcite, opal, or peridot
PRECAUTIONS	Citrine's color will fade in direct sunlight.
AFFIRMATION	I radiate joy and confidence in every cell of my being.

golden healer

Abundance | Golden Light |
Confidence | Happiness | Empathy

Golden healer has the following spiritual, physical, and emotional healing properties.

spiritual healing

- Harmonizes your yin and yang energies.
- Helps raise your vibrations.
- Connects and awakens you to the healing universal golden light.
- Works on clearing energetic blockages and restoring your body back into balance.
- Connects you to your higher self and personal power.

physical healing

- Enhances physical vitality and energy.
- Helps you make large life changes with little effort.
- Aids in cleansing and restoring all organs in the body.

- Boosts feelings of happiness and joy to bring health and abundance into the home.
- Supports a healthy digestive system.

emotional healing

- Brings feelings of joy, empathy, compassion, happiness, and love.
- Calms the mind, bringing a sense of peace and harmony.
- Boosts feelings of self-worth, self-confidence, and self-love.
- Helps heal old emotional wounds and release what no longer serves you.
- Encourages you to move forward after going through a negative experience.

If you struggle to be your authentic self in social settings, at work, or around your loved ones, carry or wear golden healer. Affirm to yourself before entering into your environment, "It's safe to be my authentic self. I am loved just as I am."

COLOR	yellow and white
HARDNESS	7
CHAKRA	solar plexus
ZODIAC SIGN	Leo
ELEMENT	water and air
CRYSTAL PAIRINGS	citrine, honey calcite, lemurian, Libyan desert glass, mookaite jasper, or ocean jasper
PRECAUTIONS	Do not keep golden healer in direct sunlight, as the color will begin to fade.
AFFIRMATION	I am constantly attracting positivity and abundance into my life.

libyan desert glass

Manifestation | Confidence | Joy |
Abundance | Highly Vibrational

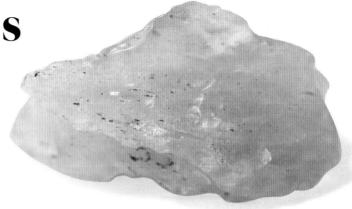

Libyan desert glass has the following
spiritual, physical, and emotional healing
properties.

spiritual healing

- Speeds up manifestations and
  self-transformation.
- Awakens the king or queen energy within you.
- Helps you find your soul purpose in life.
- Is highly vibrational and can even take you to
  other realms.
- Connects and awakens you to the healing
  universal golden light.
- Sparks and enhances your creativity and
  new ideas.

physical healing

- Can provide relief for any imbalances in the
  digestive tract.
- Helps support and balance the immune and
  endocrine systems.
- Brings balance to any physical symptoms that
  arise from stress.
- Provides a renewal of your physical vitality.

emotional healing

- Helps you set boundaries to form the ultimate
  love for yourself.
- Boosts inner feelings of joy, playfulness, and
  adequacy.
- Enables you to claim and strengthen your
  personal power.
- Boosts self-confidence to help you come out
  of your shell.
- Instills sympathy, filling your mind with kind,
  gentle, and understanding thoughts about
  others.

Write in your journal—with pictures—what exactly
you'd like to manifest and place Libyan desert
glass over the manifestation to amplify this abundant energy. As you do this, feel in your heart that
your manifestation has already come true.

COLOR	yellow
HARDNESS	6–7
CHAKRAS	all, especially solar plexus
ZODIAC SIGN	Virgo and Gemini
ELEMENTS	fire and storm
CRYSTAL PAIRINGS	moldavite, citrine, golden healer, gold sheen obsidian, honey calcite, herkimer diamond, prehnite, or serpentine
PRECAUTIONS	none
AFFIRMATION	I am divinely guided to manifest for my highest good.

crazy lace agate

Confidence | Energy | Flow | Balance | Creativity

Crazy lace agate has the following spiritual, physical, and emotional healing properties.

spiritual healing

- Provides a spiritual field of protection from negative energy.
- Helps you relax in order to trust and go with the flow of life.
- Harmonizes your yin and yang energies.
- Stimulates your creativity, imagination, and innovative thinking.
- Is grounding, reconnecting you to the earth's energy.

physical healing

- Helps increase physical energy, vitality, and stamina.
- Can improve concentration and overall mental function.
- Helps soothe and relieve any digestive issues.
- Works on cleansing out toxins in the pancreas and lymphatic system.
- Helps combat infections and blood vessel problems.

emotional healing

- Helps release negative attachments that no longer serve you.
- Aids in boosting self-confidence and self-esteem.
- Allows you to let go of control and go with the flow of life.
- Opens your eyes to the greatest joys of life.
- Encourages you to take action and diminish unwanted fears.

If you are an artist or have a job that uses lots of creativity, place a large crazy lace agate point on your desk to spark out-of-the box thinking.

COLORS	red, white, gray, orange, and yellow
HARDNESS	6.5–7
CHAKRAS	root, sacral, and solar plexus
ZODIAC SIGNS	Virgo, Pisces, Gemini, and Libra
ELEMENT	earth and fire
CRYSTAL PAIRINGS	carnelian, orange calcite, red jasper, smoky quartz, or bumblebee jasper
PRECAUTIONS	Keep crazy lace agate away from direct sunlight; the color will fade.
AFFIRMATION	I wake up every morning feeling happy and confident.

honey calcite

Joy | Confidence | Courage | Angels | Purpose

Honey calcite has the following spiritual, physical, and emotional healing properties.

spiritual healing

- Attunes you to higher angelic realms and consciousness.
- Cleanses and purifies your home's energy.
- Helps you strengthen your manifestations to achieve your higher purpose in life.
- Increases physical, mental, and spiritual energetic growth.
- Provides spiritual guidance in achieving your goals.

physical healing

- Promotes healthy blood sugar levels, endocrine function, and digestion.
- Encourages children's healthy development.
- Reduces inflammation.
- Helps detoxify the kidney, bladder, and bowels.

emotional healing

- Allows you to be more open-minded and embrace change with open arms.
- Brings feelings of joy, hope, and optimism.
- Allows you to let go of what no longer serves you.
- Works to increase your feelings of self-worth, inner strength, confidence, and courage.
- Can show you how to recognize and use your personal power.
- Helps you get back on your feet after being knocked down by a challenging situation.

To release what no longer serves you, hold two honey calcite spheres, one in each hand, focus on bringing up that negative emotion/feeling, and watch it wash away.

COLORS	yellow and orange
HARDNESS	3
CHAKRA	solar plexus
ZODIAC SIGNS	Cancer, Leo, Pisces, and Aries
ELEMENTS	fire and wind
CRYSTAL PAIRINGS	bumblebee jasper, golden healer, celestite, herkimer diamond, citrine, Libyan desert glass, orange calcite, or septarian
PRECAUTIONS	Do not put honey calcite in water, because it is a very soft, brittle stone. Do not put it in prolonged direct sunlight; it can become brittle and break.
AFFIRMATION	I am constantly beaming universal golden light that surrounds and protects me.

septarian

Grounding | Nurturing | Courage |
Confidence | Transformation

Septarian has the following spiritual, physical, and emotional healing properties.

spiritual healing

- Is a nurturing, protective, and grounding stone.
- Enhances your dreams and provides a vividness one has yet to experience.
- Harmonizes our inner and outer selves.
- Helps one dive into transformation by going deep within.
- Aids in restoring and regulating blocked energies in the solar plexus.

physical healing

- Can help calm an upset stomach or any imbalance in the digestive system.
- Aids in strengthening the bones, teeth, and muscles.
- Supports healthy blood and kidneys.
- Promotes overall good health and well-being.

COLORS	yellow and brown
HARDNESS	3.5–4
CHAKRAS	root, sacral, and solar plexus
ZODIAC SIGNS	Taurus, Leo, Virgo, Capricorn, and Scorpio
ELEMENTS	earth and fire
CRYSTAL PAIRINGS	mookaite jasper, honey calcite, bumblebee jasper, unakite jasper, or tiger's eye
PRECAUTIONS	Septarian is a soft stone; do not put it in water.
AFFIRMATION	I am grounded, safe, and protected at all times.

emotional healing

- Helps you keep your focus on one project at a time.
- Promotes courage, personal power, and bravery.
- Helps you get through extreme life changes by balancing and repairing your emotional body.
- Boosts feelings of joy, confidence, self-esteem, and gratitude.
- Helps you become more patient with others.
- Can help release emotional stress, anxiety, or depression.

If others are making you feel like you're not good enough, remember it is only a projection of themselves. To regain your self-confidence and self-worth, meditate with a septarian on your solar plexus chakra. During the meditation, feel the energy coming from the septarian and repeat the affirmation "I am amazing just as I am. I am enough."

amber

Joy | Purification | Radiance | Warmth | Healing

Amber has the following spiritual, physical, and emotional healing properties.

spiritual healing

- Helps one find their soul purpose in life.
- Aids in speeding up and amplifying your manifestations.
- Helps purify, protect, and expand your auric field.
- Can clear out all karmic debris and past-life traumas.
- Helps you connect to your higher consciousness and awareness.

physical healing

- Is said to absorb and remove pain from the body.
- Helps boost energy levels, longevity, and vitality.
- Connects us to the core of our overall well-being.
- Helps in maintaining a healthy immune system.
- Aids in reducing inflammation and swelling in the body.

emotional healing

- Boosts self-confidence and self-expression.
- Brings wisdom, balance, and patience.
- Boosts feelings of joy and gratitude, helping one overcome depression.
- Helps banish all fears so you can see life in an abundance of joy, radiance, and love.
- Promotes releasing and healing emotional traumas.

If you have any aches or pains, place an amber on the inflamed area until the pain has subsided. If you have pain all over or arthritis, try wearing an amber bracelet daily to bring relief.

COLORS	yellow, gold, and honey
HARDNESS	2–2.5
CHAKRA	solar plexus
ZODIAC SIGNS	Leo and Scorpio
ELEMENTS	earth
CRYSTAL PAIRINGS	lemurian or jet
PRECAUTIONS	Do not place amber in water; it is too soft.
AFFIRMATION	I have the willpower to set boundaries with love and grace, which allows me to be protected from negative energy.

mookaite jasper

Creativity | Change | Worthiness |
Relaxation | Joy

Mookaite jasper has the following spiritual,
physical, and emotional healing properties.

spiritual healing

- Sparks new ideas, creativity, and visions.
- Promotes grounding and connection to earth's
  healing and nourishing energies.
- Stimulates a deep desire for embarking on
  change and new ventures.
- Can bring you into greater connection with
  your ancestors and spirit guides.
- Frees you from your karmic cycle.

physical healing

- Aids in the rapid healing of wounds.
- Helps improve circulation and purification of
  the blood.

- Supports a healthy immune system and a
  healthy digestive system.
- Helps slow the aging process by increasing
  your vibrations.
- May reset the body's normal circadian rhythm
  for better sleep.
- Helps strengthen the hair and nails.

emotional healing

- Promotes a positive and peaceful mind-set.
- Boosts feelings of self-esteem, self-confidence,
  and self-worth.
- Aids in coping with loneliness, grief, and
  depression.
- Sparks creativity, motivation, and
  self-discovery.

If you are an artist or have a job that uses lots of
creativity, place a large mookaite jasper point on
your desk to spark new ideas and visions.

COLORS	red, orange, yellow, purple, gray, and brown
HARDNESS	6–7
CHAKRAS	root, sacral, and solar plexus
ZODIAC SIGNS	Virgo and Scorpio
ELEMENT	earth
CRYSTAL PAIRINGS	golden healer, red jasper, carnelian, sunstone, septarian, or tiger's eye
PRECAUTIONS	none
AFFIRMATION	I am worthy of love, happiness, and health.

unakite jasper

Compassion | Positive Thoughts | Grounding | Love | Release

Unakite jasper has the following spiritual, physical, and emotional healing properties.

spiritual healing

- Helps you visualize the things you most want in life.
- Promotes renewal, revitalization, and regeneration.
- Facilitates you in the rebirthing process.
- Brings your consciousness into the present moment, allowing you to be connected to both the physical earth and the spiritual world.
- Brings energetic support and grounding to bring you back into alignment.

physical healing

- Aids in healing the heart and lungs and after an injury.
- Helps relieve stress and tension in the body.
- Enables you to find the root cause of your physical disease.
- Works to clear any reproductive issues that have stemmed from past abuse.
- Helps calm and stabilize the nervous system.

emotional healing

- Releases negative energy and addictive thought patterns.
- Promotes healthy and loving relationships with others.
- Helps bring your emotions back into balance.
- Encourages feelings of gratitude, empathy, and compassion.
- Promotes a healthy balance of love you give to others, the world, and yourself.

Connect back to mother nature and ground into your infinite divine light being by keeping a unakite jasper in your pocket or bra daily.

COLORS	green and red
HARDNESS	6–7
CHAKRAS	root and heart
ZODIAC SIGNS	Taurus, Virgo, Capricorn, and Scorpio
ELEMENT	earth
CRYSTAL PAIRINGS	green aventurine, kambaba jasper, moss agate, petrified wood, or septarian
PRECAUTIONS	none
AFFIRMATION	I become healthier every day.

nephrite jade

Good Luck | Grounding | Protection | Health | Heart Healing

Nephrite jade has the following spiritual, physical, and emotional healing properties.

spiritual healing

- Brings good luck, protection, and fortune.
- Is an earth-healing stone that connects us with mother nature as one.
- Is known to change your negative energy into positive energy.
- Stimulates lucid and vivid dreaming.
- Brings balance to your feminine and masculine energies.
- Frees you from your karmic cycle.

physical healing

- Brings strength and health to the physical body.
- Helps heal all imbalances in the metabolism, skin, hair, kidneys, and adrenals.
- Aids in bringing the nervous system back into harmony.
- Helps strengthen the heart.
- Promotes a peaceful night's rest.

emotional healing

- Promotes happy and healthy relationships.
- Instills feelings of nostalgia, peace, harmony, and hope.
- Allows you to open your heart to love others at a deep level.
- Stimulates the release of limiting beliefs.

If you have been feeling under the weather or need to bring strength back into your physical body, meditate with a nephrite jade in your hand (or two, one in each hand), and repeat the affirmation "I feel strong, healthy, and harmonious."

COLOR	green
HARDNESS	6–6.5
CHAKRAS	root and heart
ZODIAC SIGNS	Virgo, Pisces, and Taurus
ELEMENT	earth
CRYSTAL PAIRINGS	epidote, green aventurine, kambaba jasper, pyrite, moss agate, serpentine, or shungite
PRECAUTIONS	Do not leave nephrite jade out in prolonged sunlight; its color may begin to fade.
AFFIRMATION	My body is constantly attracting what's best for me.

malachite

Emotional Release | Heart Healing | Highly Vibrational | Transformation | Love

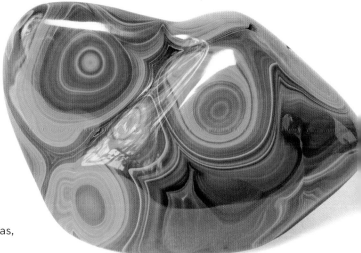

Malachite has the following spiritual, physical, and emotional healing properties.

spiritual healing

- Clears, activates, and balances all the chakras, especially the heart chakra.
- Increases positive light and vibrations for the auric field.
- Supports inner and creative visualizations.
- Is a stone of transformation, assisting you through big changes in your life.
- Helps you move beyond your ego to altruism.
- Enhances spirituality and psychic abilities.

physical healing

- Can align and cleanse cellular and DNA structures.
- Works to restore and increase physical strength and vitality.
- Can provide protection from all types of radiation.
- Supports a healthy immune system.
- Aids in the treatment of broken bones, swollen joints, asthma, and arthritis.

emotional healing

- Increases unconditional love for yourself and others.
- Helps heal old emotional abuse and wounds, especially from childhood trauma.
- Aids in releasing repressed emotions stored in the subconscious mind.
- Encourages healthy relationships based on love and compassion.

Malachite is a powerful heart chakra crystal, and I strongly suggest just using it on its own at first until you feel its energy. If you are working on healing old emotional abuse and wounds, especially childhood trauma, work with malachite during a therapy session or during a meditation in a more private setting to help you release old wounds and rekindle your loving heart.

COLOR	green
HARDNESS	3.5-4
CHAKRA	heart
ZODIAC SIGNS	Taurus, Virgo, Capricorn, and Scorpio
ELEMENTS	earth, water, and fire
CRYSTAL PAIRINGS	azurite, chrysocolla, tiger's eye, turquoise, or morganite
PRECAUTIONS	Do not place malachite in water; it contains copper and is a soft stone. Do not place it in direct sunlight, because the color will begin to fade.
AFFIRMATION	I let go of old emotional baggage that no longer serves me.

bloodstone

Flow | Release | Purification | Courage | Grounding

Bloodstone has the following spiritual, physical, and emotional healing properties.

spiritual healing

- Is grounding, reconnecting you to the earth's energy.
- Helps you live more present in the moment.
- Has been known and used for centuries to banish evil and dispel negativity.
- Expands and heightens your intuition.
- Opens and awakens communication with spiritual realms.

physical healing

- Can aid in your recovery from an illness, surgery, or injury.
- Helps bring your hormones back into a healthy and balanced state.
- Supports healthy blood flow and circulation.

- Helps detoxify and purify the physical body, especially the blood.
- Supports nutrient absorption.

emotional healing

- Calms the mind and increases your ability to make rational decisions.
- Aids in releasing emotional stress, temper, and aggression.
- Promotes calmness and emotional centering.
- Encourages selflessness, idealism, kindness, and generosity.
- Is a stone of courage, promoting strength to face your fears.

To encourage healthy circulation and blood flow, wear bloodstone as jewelry daily.

COLORS	green and red
HARDNESS	6
CHAKRAS	root, sacral, and heart
ZODIAC SIGNS	Aries, Pisces, and Libra
ELEMENT	earth
CRYSTAL PAIRINGS	black tourmaline, jet, black obsidian, or lemurian
PRECAUTIONS	Do not submerge bloodstone in water; it can rust.
AFFIRMATION	I am strong, courageous, and brave enough to conquer anything.

emerald

Heart Healing | Love | Compassion | Empathy | Kindness

Emerald has the following spiritual, physical, and emotional healing properties.

spiritual healing

- Helps you develop trust with the universe that everything happens in divine timing.
- Can enhance psychic abilities.
- Stimulates your ability to receive fortune and abundance.
- Bathes the auric field in an abundance of green healing light.
- Works to cleanse the energetic body of any karmic contracts.

physical healing

- Helps heal the heart from a heartbreak, physical imbalances of the heart, or heart diseases.
- Can lessen symptoms that stem from diabetes.
- Aids in relieving joint pain.
- Helps in recovering after an infection.
- Is known as a master physical healer, providing overall health and wellness.

emotional healing

- Helps attract or keep positive relationships with others.
- Opens the heart to feeling unconditional love for yourself and others.
- Stimulates empathy, sympathy, and kindness.
- Helps you overcome fears of abandonment, unworthiness, and loneliness.
- Is a nourishing stone, promoting forgiveness and compassion.

Whether you're grieving, feeling unloved, or feeling unworthiness, wear emerald as a necklace daily at heart level to stimulate and attract more love, nurturing, and gratitude into your life.

COLOR	green
HARDNESS	7.5–8
CHAKRA	heart
ZODIAC SIGNS	Taurus, Capricorn, and Virgo
ELEMENTS	earth and water
CRYSTAL PAIRINGS	rose quartz, kunzite, rhodochrosite, green aventurine, pink tourmaline, green tourmaline, morganite, prehnite, serpentine, or spirit quartz
PRECAUTIONS	Emerald contains aluminum and can be toxic if ingested. Direct sunlight should also be avoided; its color will fade.
AFFIRMATION	When I open my heart up to love, I am filled with an abundance of love and light.

green aventurine

Optimism | Luck | Abundance |
Emotional Well-Being | Vitality

Green aventurine has the following spiritual, physical, and emotional healing properties.

spiritual healing

- Magnifies your ability to manifest good luck and fortune.
- Encourages spiritual growth and development.
- Allows you to attract and receive abundance into your life.
- Releases negative attachments to other things, allowing you to reconnect with what matters.
- Energetically provides a shield of protection for your home and garden.

physical healing

- Boosts physical energy and vitality.
- Can help strengthen the muscles, lungs, and heart.
- Aids in improving overall health and well-being.
- Can reduce clumsiness by assisting with your center of gravity.
- Aids in detoxifying and cleansing the organs.

emotional healing

- Helps improve decision-making and leadership abilities.
- Aids in removing aggression, negative thoughts, and irritability.
- Promotes relaxation and emotional well-being.
- Helps you feel optimistic and motivated again.
- Encourages self-love and self-care.

Feeling unlucky lately? It's time you attract more luck back into your life! Wear a green aventurine necklace over your heart or a tumbled stone in your bra to attract more luck and abundance.

COLOR	green
HARDNESS	6.5–7
CHAKRA	heart
ZODIAC SIGNS	Taurus, Virgo, Capricorn, and Libra
ELEMENTS	earth and water
CRYSTAL PAIRINGS	rose quartz, emerald, unakite jasper, green opal, nephrite jade, prehnite, morganite, green tourmaline, or pyrite
PRECAUTIONS	Avoid putting green aventurine in direct sunlight; the color will begin to fade.
AFFIRMATION	I am a magnet for abundance.

garnierite

Emotional Stability | Unconditional Love | Well-Being | Kindness | Confidence

Garnierite has the following spiritual, physical, and emotional healing properties.

spiritual healing

- Works to balance your feminine energy.
- Helps you move beyond your ego to altruism.
- Helps you set boundaries.
- Works as a companion during your spiritual growth and development.
- Fills you up with unconditional love and light.

physical healing

- Provides an energy boost to get you through your day.
- Encourages a sense of overall health and well-being.
- Aids in strengthening the heart, lungs, and muscles.
- Helps if you struggle with being sensitive to sound.
- Increases strength, motivation, and perseverance.

emotional healing

- Guides you on how to fully love yourself and others unconditionally.
- Helps you conquer your fears in order to achieve and manifest your dreams.
- Helps bring your emotions into balance and stability.
- Increases feelings of self-confidence and self-worth.
- Brings mental clarity when seeking the truth.

If you feel emotionally unbalanced and want to bring release and more love into your life, go within and meditate while holding a garnierite on your heart chakra. Feel the release and refill your heart with unconditional love.

COLORS	green, blue, and gray
HARDNESS	4
CHAKRA	heart
ZODIAC SIGNS	Leo and Virgo
ELEMENT	water
CRYSTAL PAIRINGS	rainbow moonstone, rose quartz, morganite, kunzite, pink opal, or turquoise
PRECAUTIONS	Garnierite contains aluminum and can be toxic if ingested. It is a soft stone; do not put it in water. Avoid putting it in direct sunlight, as its color will begin to fade.
AFFIRMATION	I love my mind. I love my body. I love my spirit.

green tourmaline

Good Luck | Unconditional Love |
Healthy Heart | Vitality | Vibrancy

Green tourmaline has the following spiritual,
physical, and emotional healing properties.

spiritual healing

- Brings balance for both masculine and feminine energies.
- Attracts good luck, prosperity, and abundance.
- Helps transform negative energy into positive.
- Aids in assisting highly spiritual people enjoy the physical world.
- Teaches us to open our hearts to send healing love and light out into the world.

physical healing

- Works on maintaining healthy blood sugar levels and digestion.
- Can clear and purify any skin disorders or issues.

- Brings harmony, healing, strength, and flow to the physical heart.
- Can enhance physical vitality, stamina, and energy.
- Supports a healthy reproductive system.

emotional healing

- Helps you overcome jealousy or envy of others.
- Opens your heart to the sensation of unconditional love.
- Helps you conquer your fears and combat anxiety.
- Promotes a sense of belonging, compassion, and pure happiness.
- Helps bring emotional balance and stability.

If you feel like an outcast or judged by others,
wear green tourmaline as a necklace near your
heart or a small stone in your bra to open your
heart to the love you have for yourself and understanding that how others feel about you is just a
projection of themselves.

COLOR	green
HARDNESS	7–7.5
CHAKRA	heart
ZODIAC SIGNS	Libra, Capricorn, and Aries
ELEMENT	water
CRYSTAL PAIRINGS	green aventurine, ruby, pink tourmaline, aquamarine, emerald, garnet, or peridot
PRECAUTIONS	Green tourmaline contains aluminum and can be toxic if ingested. It is sensitive to sunlight and intense temperature changes.
AFFIRMATION	I value and love myself for exactly who I am.

kambaba jasper

Balance | Protection | Grounding | Peace | Courage

Kambaba jasper has the following spiritual, physical, and emotional healing properties.

spiritual healing

- Encourages positive change, renewal, and new beginnings.
- Promotes balanced energy from within.
- Is a great stone for empaths, providing energetic protection, peace, and nurture.
- Brings in wisdom and guidance from ancestral energies.
- Encourages grounding to mother nature healing energies, allowing you to be more present in every moment.
- Brings balance to the masculine and feminine energies.

physical healing

- Supports a healthy immune system.
- Can cleanse the body of all toxins.
- Can strengthen and improve your hair, skin, teeth, and nails.
- Helps balance and soothe any digestive imbalances.
- Supports the strengthening and regulation of a healthy heart.

emotional healing

- Opens the heart to receiving love.
- Promotes compassion, kindness, generosity, and patience.
- Boosts feelings of self-confidence, self-worth, inspiration, and courage.
- Assists in calming the mind and emotions by soothing the nerves.

If you feel tired or fatigued throughout your day, you may be feeling ungrounded. Wear kamababa jasper jewelry (skin contact) so you continue your day feeling grounded, centered, and energized.

COLORS	black and dark green
HARDNESS	6.5–7
CHAKRAS	root and heart
ZODIAC SIGNS	Aries and Scorpio
ELEMENT	earth
CRYSTAL PAIRINGS	unakite jasper, moss agate, nephrite jade, or petrified wood
PRECAUTIONS	none
AFFIRMATION	When I look within, I find peace, stillness, and tranquility.

moss agate

Earthiness | New Beginnings |
Abundance | Balance | Stability

Moss agate has the following spiritual, physical, and emotional healing properties.

spiritual healing

- Helps you go through change and new beginnings with ease and excitement.
- Helps one create and find their purpose in life.
- Facilitates connection to mother nature, helping you become more present and grounded in the physical world.
- Brings positive energy and abundance.
- Helps speed up the manifestation process.

physical healing

- Acts as an anti-inflammatory, helping treat skin and fungal infections.
- Brings the body back into alignment and balance.
- Stimulates the brain and memory functions.
- Helps heal the physical body.
- Supports a healthy immune system.

emotional healing

- Helps one release old, negative patterns and fears.
- Can relieve anxiety, stress, and worry.
- Brings in new friendships with like-minded energy and beliefs.
- Enhances mental stability, concentration, stamina, and completion.
- Helps balance the emotions, preventing irrational mood swings.

Open your heart to positive energy, transformation, and purpose by wearing a moss agate near your heart or in your bra. You will notice positive intuitive guidance from earth angels and your inner guidance.

COLORS	green and white
HARDNESS	6.5–7
CHAKRAS	root and heart
ZODIAC SIGNS	Capricorn, Virgo, and Taurus
ELEMENT	earth
CRYSTAL PAIRINGS	fluorite, epidote, kambaba jasper, green opal, petrified wood, unakite jasper, or nephrite jade
PRECAUTIONS	Never clean moss agate with household chemicals or leave it out in direct sunlight for hours because most moss agate contains quartz.
AFFIRMATION	I am nourished by mother nature and life itself.

moldavite

*Manifestation | Trauma Healing | Highly Vibrational |
Transformational | Raises Vibrations*

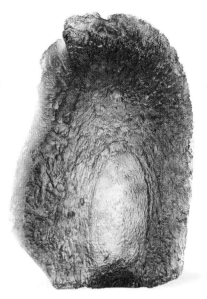

Moldavite has the following spiritual, physical, and emotional healing properties.

spiritual healing

- Awakens and balances your Kundalini energy.
- Connects you to higher spirit realms, your higher self, spirit guides, other dimensions, and extraterrestrials.
- Magnifies and speeds up the process of transformation and manifestations.
- Enhances your dream state; it is great for lucid dreaming and astral travel.
- Is extremely powerful and known to give you an energetic flush.
- Is an extremely high vibrational tektite, raising your vibrations to a whole new level quickly.
- Stimulates your intuition and psychic abilities.
- Assists in deepening your meditation and connecting to your higher consciousness.

physical healing

- Can provide relief for those who suffer from asthma, allergies, or rashes.
- Is only to be used if you are ready to bring up the root causes of your imbalances or illnesses, because it will create a "healing crisis."
- Awakens the presence of trapped emotions and spiritual wounds and brings them to the surface for them to be healed.

emotional healing

- Radiates love and opening of the heart.
- Helps remove irrational fears and doubts.
- Boosts feelings of personal power and will.
- Initiates creativity so you can make better decisions and solve problems with ease and clarity.

Moldavite is extremely powerful by itself and can be used daily to help you manifest your dreams. Just by wearing it you will raise your vibrations, thus increasing your attraction to more abundance in your life.

COLOR	green
HARDNESS	5.5–7
CHAKRAS	heart, third eye, and crown
ZODIAC SIGNS	All
ELEMENT	storm
CRYSTAL PAIRINGS	charoite, citrine, herkimer diamond, Libyan desert glass, black tourmaline, lemurian, or rainbow moonstone
PRECAUTIONS	Gradually adjust yourself to moldavite's high frequency. Start by wearing or using it for a minute at a time. It may take days or weeks until you're ready to use it for a full meditation or day.
AFFIRMATION	I welcome an abundant mindset.

peridot

Love | Prosperity | Health | Joy | Animal Communication

Peridot has the following spiritual, physical, and emotional healing properties.

spiritual healing

- Helps remove deep blockages located in the back of the chakras.
- Aids in animal communication and healing.
- Assists in protection from negative energy and evil spirits.
- Manifests spiritual abundance, success, and luck.
- Invites spiritual wisdom and connection.

physical healing

- Helps heal the heart, physically and emotionally.
- Aids in strengthening and promoting a healthy blood flow.
- Helps support and balance the endocrine system.
- Rejuvenates energy in the physical body.
- Promotes a healthy liver, gallbladder, spleen, intestines, heart, and lungs.

emotional healing

- Helps you manifest prosperity, health, and joy in abundance.
- Helps you recover from your addictions.
- Opens your heart to receiving love, grace, and gratitude.
- Builds your confidence and feelings of self-worth.
- Helps release built-up anger, tension, or jealousy.

To release any built-up anger, tension, or jealousy, hold a peridot to your heart and welcome the emotions that come up. This may feel weird at first because why would you want to feel this feeling even more? But once you have felt it, breathe into your heart, and let go of it. Keep releasing with your breath until you feel light and free.

COLORS	green
HARDNESS	6.5–7
CHAKRAS	solar plexus and heart
ZODIAC SIGNS	Leo, Virgo, and Taurus
ELEMENTS	earth and air
CRYSTAL PAIRINGS	herkimer diamond, morganite, prehnite, green tourmaline, watermelon tourmaline, ruby, or citrine
PRECAUTIONS	none
AFFIRMATION	I am a magnet for abundance.

serpentine

Kundalini Energy Awakening | Compassion | Love | Purification | Connection

Serpentine has the following spiritual, physical, and emotional healing properties.

spiritual healing

- Awakens and balances your Kundalini energy.
- Helps clear any blocked energies and then allows a natural healthy flow of energy to go through.
- Enhances animal, mother nature, and spiritual connections.
- Provides an energetic protection field in your aura so you don't have other toxic energies seep into yours.
- Is grounding, reconnecting you to the earth's healing energy.

physical healing

- Helps in cellular regeneration and in replenishing your energy.
- Supports a healthy digestive system.
- Promotes a healthy heart, kidneys, and skin.
- Helps improve circulation and purification of the blood.
- Helps rejuvenate the body's tissues.
- Aids in the treatment of diabetes or hypoglycemia symptoms.

emotional healing

- Allows you to release your fears of change and any fearful ideas of your future.
- Opens your heart to giving to others from the goodness of your heart.
- Promotes feelings of love, compassion, and forgiveness.
- Works to balance and stabilize emotions.

If your emotions have been feeling all over the place lately, work to rebalance and find stability by wearing a serpentine near your heart (skin contact) daily until you feel more emotionally balanced.

COLOR	green
HARDNESS	3–6
CHAKRAS	all, especially heart
ZODIAC SIGNS	Gemini, Scorpio, Taurus, Virgo, and Capricorn
ELEMENT	earth
CRYSTAL PAIRINGS	nephrite jade, Libyan desert glass, tiger's eye, emerald, or jet
PRECAUTIONS	Avoid cleansing serpentine in water; most serpentine is softer, so it can become brittle and crack with water.
AFFIRMATION	Today I will be mindful, happy, and live in the moment.

prehnite

Love | Surrender | Healing | Detoxification | Acceptance

Prehnite has the following spiritual, physical, and emotional healing properties.

spiritual healing

- Enhances angelic and spirit guide communication.
- Stimulates intuition and psychic abilities.
- Opens your heart to surrender to what is.
- Enhances more vivid dreams and recalling dreams.

physical healing

- Helps balance and heal the circulatory, diges-tive, urinary, and lymphatic systems.
- Can cleanse the body of all toxins.
- Helps alleviate nightmares, night terrors, and deep-rooted fears.
- Assists you in uncovering and healing the deep traumas that have developed into disease through the years.
- Aids in boosting the metabolism.

COLORS	green
HARDNESS	6-6.5
CHAKRAS	solar plexus and heart
ZODIAC SIGNS	Libra and Capricorn
ELEMENTS	earth and water
CRYSTAL PAIRINGS	green aventurine, peridot, Libyan desert glass, lepidolite, scolecite, emerald, or pink tourmaline
PRECAUTIONS	Prehnite contains aluminum and can be toxic if ingested.
AFFIRMATION	I forgive all that has come before me and all that is yet to come.

emotional healing

- Brings union of the heart and the will.
- Helps release ego identification with past wounds.
- Is a stone of unconditional love, bringing peace and protection to the heart.
- Helps you accept yourself and others for exactly who you and they are.
- Helps you declutter your mind and motivates you to declutter your space.
- Opens your heart up to forgiving yourself and others.

Keep a prehnite under your pillow or on your nightstand to help alleviate nightmares and night terrors. Before you close your eyes at night, think of the things you are grateful for that happened that day.

green opal

Joy | Love | Peace | Earthiness | Balance

Green opal has the following spiritual, physical, and emotional healing properties.

spiritual healing

- Sparks creativity, new ideas, and perspectives.
- Harmonizes your yin and yang energies.
- Aids in spiritual awareness, hypnosis, and divination.
- Helps ground you to earth's healing energy.
- Allows you to open your heart to accepting change and healing that needs to be done for you to become your most healthy and authentic self.

physical healing

- Promotes cleansing and purification in the body.
- Helps strengthen the immune system.
- Aids in bringing the adrenal glands and digestive system back into balance.
- Promotes a deeper sleep and helps reduce insomnia and nightmares.
- Aids in the treatment of colds, flus, and sinus infections.

emotional healing

- Encourages and strengthens positive and loving relationships.
- Boosts feelings of joy, love, and gratitude.
- Helps release and heal emotional trauma.
- Helps you focus on your breath to feel calm down when you are feeling irritated or impatient.
- Brings out the butterfly and giddy feelings regarding your significant other.

Opening your heart back up to love can be challenging and hard to accept. Go within, lie down, and meditate with a green opal on your heart chakra. Affirm to yourself, "I open my heart to love again."

COLORS	green and brown
HARDNESS	5
CHAKRA	heart
ZODIAC SIGNS	Scorpio, Sagittarius, and Aries
ELEMENTS	earth and water
CRYSTAL PAIRINGS	green aventurine, moss agate, epidote, pink opal, sunstone, or amazonite
PRECAUTIONS	Do not get green opal wet or put it in direct sunlight because it can break. It is not recommended for elixirs.
AFFIRMATION	With every breath I take, I breathe in inner peace and loving light.

epidote

Heart Opener | Positivity | Balance |
Confidence | Emotional Stability

Epidote has the following spiritual, physical, and
emotional healing properties.

spiritual healing

- Brings in a balanced and stabilized energetic
  flow.
- Works to raise your vibrations.
- Encourages a sense of connection to mother
  nature, allowing you to be more present.
- Works to amplify and speed up your
  manifestations.
- Provides an energetic shield of protection
  from negative energy.

physical healing

- Works on finding healing and hope for those
  who struggle with an unknown physical
  disease.
- Helps those suffering from brain disorders
  such as Parkinson's, Alzheimer's, or dementia.

- May aid in the healing and balance of the
  digestive system.
- Helps calm and stabilize the nervous system.
- Supports a healthy thyroid, gallbladder, adrenal glands, and liver.

emotional healing

- Helps one get through emotional
  breakthroughs.
- Opens your mind and heart to understanding
  others' perspectives
- Allows emotional blocks to be released by
  opening your heart.
- Boosts personal power and self-confidence.
- Brings mental clarity, insightfulness, patience,
  and focus.

Keep a small epidote tumble on you daily to help
you stay focused, grounded, and centered. Our
outer world can become chaotic sometimes, and
when it does, hold on to your epidote to bring you
back into your inner peace.

COLORS	green and white
HARDNESS	6-7
CHAKRA	heart
ZODIAC SIGNS	Gemini and Libra
ELEMENTS	earth and water
CRYSTAL PAIRINGS	herkimer diamond, nephrite jade, moss agate, or green opal
PRECAUTIONS	Epidote contains aluminum and can be toxic if ingested.
AFFIRMATION	I open my heart to receive unconditional love.

ocean jasper

Happiness | Relaxation | Optimism |
Self Awareness | Safety

Ocean jasper has the following spiritual, physical, and emotional healing properties.

spiritual healing

- Surrenders you to accepting love and light in the midst of darkness.
- Releases negative energy and replaces it with positivity.
- Helps you feel protected, secure, and safe.
- Helps you move forward and feel whole again by healing emotional and spiritual traumas.
- Promotes deep relaxation by reconnecting your spirit to earth and its healing vibrations.

physical healing

- Calms and soothes the nervous system.
- Works to strengthen and heal the physical heart.
- Helps bring the body back into its natural state and energetic rhythm.
- Assists in replenishing and restoring the adrenal glands when they've been on overdrive.
- Promotes cellular regeneration.

emotional healing

- Brings feelings of happiness and joy.
- Can assist individuals who are feeling depressed in regaining their enthusiasm for life.
- Enhances your self-discovery and inner power.
- Can relieve stress and tension in the emotional body.
- Encourages you to be kind, empathetic, and understanding.

Ocean jasper is a great pick-me-up stone to carry in your pocket or bra to bring positive energy, joy, and gratitude to your mind, body, and spirit throughout your day. Anytime you feel yourself spiraling into a negative mind-set, rub or hold your ocean jasper and repeat the affirmation "I am the creator of my own life and I choose to be happy."

COLORS	all
HARDNESS	6.5–7
CHAKRAS	all
ZODIAC SIGNS	Capricorn, Virgo, Libra, and Scorpio
ELEMENTS	earth and water
CRYSTAL PAIRINGS	fire quartz, bumblebee jasper, agate, sunstone, orange calcite, golden healer, or opal
PRECAUTIONS	Never clean ocean jasper with household chemicals or leave it out in direct sunlight for hours because most ocean jasper contains quartz.
AFFIRMATION	I am a magnet for all things that bring me joy, positivity, and miracles.

agate

Grounding | Awakening | Harmony |
Connection | Release

Agate has the following spiritual, physical, and
emotional healing properties.

spiritual healing

- Brings good luck, protection, and fortune.
- Cleanses and expands your auric field.
- Increases spiritual awakening and growth.
- Brings balance and harmony to your mind,
  body, and spirit.
- Allows you to become more present in the
  moment by grounding and connecting to
  mother nature.

physical healing

- Promotes overall health and well-being.
- Helps you overcome any negative habits or
  addictions.

- Can aid in the relief of back pain caused by
  the avoidance of unpleasant feelings.
- Brings comfort and healing for the skin.
- Promotes peaceful sleep.

emotional healing

- Aids in the release of anger and tension in
  the body.
- Enhances mental clarity, focus, and attention
  to detail.
- Helps you feel safe and emotionally stable.
- Opens your heart up again to accept uncondi-
  tional love.
- Promotes positivity, joy, and peace.

Keep an agate in any area of your home or sacred
space to bring feelings of joy, positivity, and bliss.

COLORS	all
HARDNESS	7-7.5
CHAKRAS	all
ZODIAC SIGN	Gemini
ELEMENT	earth
CRYSTAL PAIRINGS	smoky quartz, red jasper, ocean jasper, clear quartz, jet, or hematite
PRECAUTIONS	Never clean with household chemicals or leave out in the direct sunlight for hours because most agates contain quartz.
AFFIRMATION	I am grounded, protected, and balanced.

blue lace agate

Serenity | Peace | Trust | Empathy | Relief

Blue lace agate has the following spiritual, physical, and emotional healing properties.

spiritual healing

- Promotes positive acceptance of everything that unfolds in your life.
- Can link your thoughts to calm a spiritual vibration, bringing you overall serenity.
- Connects us more closely to our spiritual guides, who can assist us in finding answers.
- Opens your heart up to trust yourself and others.
- Can help you connect to higher spiritual realms and consciousness.

physical healing

- Assists in the relief of sore throats, aching, congestion, and swollen glands.
- Can improve and promote healthy skin, providing relief for skin conditions.

- Known to balance the thyroid and thymus glands.
- Promotes a good night's rest.
- Supports a healthy respiratory system.

emotional healing

- Promotes calming the mind, peace, and lightheartedness.
- Can help alleviate any anxiety, stress, or tension in the body.
- Helps you stay focused on the present moment, especially when you are stressed.
- Increases feelings of self-confidence and self-esteem.
- Helps maintain a level head, allowing for reasonable thinking.

If you have built-up tension in your body from stress or worry, hold a blue lace agate in both of your hands during your meditation and imagine the blue lace dissolving any tension in the body.

COLOR	baby blue
HARDNESS	6.5–7
CHAKRA	throat
ZODIAC SIGNS	Gemini and Pisces
ELEMENTS	air and water
CRYSTAL PAIRINGS	blue calcite, aquamarine, blue chalcedony, howlite, lepidolite, or larimar
PRECAUTIONS	none
AFFIRMATION	I experience a sense of peace and tranquility with every breath I take.

larimar

Tranquility | Communication | Soothing | Goddess Energy | Authenticity

Larimar has the following spiritual, physical, and emotional healing properties.

spiritual healing

- Connects one to the energy of a goddess.
- Helps you discover and align with who you truly are.
- Brings the soul into energetic harmony and inner peace.
- Opens your throat chakra so you can surrender to what is and let go of what was.
- Brings energetic healing to your inner child.

physical healing

- Can be healing for the hair, lungs, circulatory system, and feet.
- Supports a healthy thyroid and thymus gland.
- Helps support a healthy and strong physical heart.

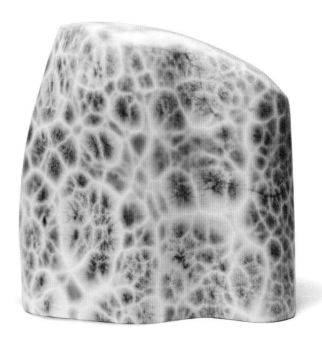

- Can reduce PTSD symptoms, panic attacks, anxiety, and stress in the body.
- Aids in the treatment of urinary tract infections.

emotional healing

- Calms and brings nurturing.
- Helps you heal any guilt, fear, grief, abandonment, rejection, and aggression.
- Can aid in the release from being addicted to the materialistic world.
- Works to break down emotional walls and release emotional blockages in the heart.
- Encourages positive communication on an energetic level.

Our outer world can feel chaotic, stressful, and out of balance at times. If you are currently experiencing this, keep larimar in your pocket or bra and hold or rub it to bring inner peace and serenity.

COLOR	blue, white, and gray
HARDNESS	4.5–5
CHAKRAS	heart and throat
ZODIAC SIGNS	Cancer and Leo
ELEMENT	water
CRYSTAL PAIRINGS	blue chalcedony, chrysocolla, howlite, blue lace agate, aquamarine, turquoise, or lemurian
PRECAUTIONS	Do not leave larimar in water or the sun for a prolonged time.
AFFIRMATION	I am at peace with exactly who I am.

turquoise

Communication | Peace | Mindfulness | Kindness | Authenticity

Turquoise has the following spiritual, physical, and emotional healing properties.

spiritual healing

- Helps you be mindful and live in the present moment.
- Allows the soul to open and express itself from a place of peace and love.
- Helps you remain on an enlightened path that is for your highest good.
- Encourages us to adapt to change.
- Is known to bring good luck, protection, and fortune.

physical healing

- Helps oxygenate the blood and increase the amount of life force in the physical body.
- Aids in combating PTSD, depression, chronic fatigue, and anxiety.
- Helps you maintain a healthy immune system.
- Works to decrease inflammation and tension in the body.
- Can alleviate pain, including menstrual cramps.

emotional healing

- Brings you back to the present moment, especially when you are stressed.
- Helps you articulate and bring forth your deepest authentic self.
- Helps you forgive others, accept yourself for who you are, and release regrets.
- Enlightens you so you can see love, light, compassion, kindness, and generosity within yourself and others.
- Promotes speaking your truth with integrity.

Become more mindful and present in your daily life by wearing turquoise as jewelry. Anytime you feel your mind become chaotic, stressed, worried, or living in the past, rub or hold your turquoise and bring your attention inward.

COLORS	blue and green
HARDNESS	5-6
CHAKRA S	heart and throat
ZODIAC SIGNS	Sagittarius, Aquarius, Pisces, and Scorpio
ELEMENTS	air and water
CRYSTAL PAIRINGS	amazonite, aquamarine, garnierite, larimar, or malachite
PRECAUTIONS	Turquoise contains aluminum and copper and can be toxic if ingested.
AFFIRMATION	I speak my truth with clarity and wisdom.

angelite

Angelic Connection | Communication | Emotional Balance | Peace | Positivity

Angelite has the following spiritual, physical, and emotional healing properties.

spiritual healing

- Awakens your spiritual connection to higher realms.
- Connects you to love, support, and protection from your angels.
- Enhances your meditation, positive affirmations, and intentions.
- Activates a greater sense of belonging in this world.
- Facilitates and induces the rebirthing process, the journey of spiritual awakening.

physical healing

- Promotes a peaceful night's rest provided by angels.
- Works to regulate and bring balance to the thyroid, the thymus, and throat infections.
- Supports healthy and strong bones.
- Can help maintain a healthy digestive system.
- Supports healthy water balance and fluid levels in the body.

emotional healing

- Encourages positive communication with others and yourself.
- Enhances confidence and honesty within yourself.
- Helps calm the mind, bringing feelings of peace and serenity.
- Aids in releasing negative self-talk, fears, and phobias.
- Helps bring a sense of peace and relief during times of grief.

Hold an angelite palm stone or sphere during your meditation to connect you to your angels and spirit guides.

COLOR	blue
HARDNESS	3.5
CHAKRAS	throat, third eye, and crown
ZODIAC SIGNS	Aquarius
ELEMENT	wind
CRYSTAL PAIRINGS	celestite, herkimer diamond, amethyst, aquamarine, or orca agate
PRECAUTIONS	Do not put angelite in water; it may dissolve.
AFFIRMATION	I am surrounded by pure love, support, protection, and light from my angels.

aquamarine

Calming | Tranquility | Soothing | Communication | Cooling

Aquamarine has the following spiritual, physical, and emotional healing properties.

spiritual healing

- Provides a deeper connection to your spirit guides and higher self.
- Promotes deep spiritual development and awareness.
- Clears stagnant energy in both the heart and throat chakras.
- Provides an energetic shield around the aura and subtle bodies.
- Assists in activating the memory to help you remember past-life experiences.

physical healing

- Works to minimize inflammation and swelling in the body.

- Assists in the healing of your nose, eyes, ears, and throat.
- Can reduce fevers by cooling the body.
- Promotes healthy skin and youthfulness.

emotional healing

- Brings feelings of inner peace and tranquility within.
- Enables you to be compassionate toward yourself and others.
- Helps you feel empowered and courageous.
- Helps you overcome grief and emotional traumas.
- Helps you release old negative thoughts and emotional patterns.
- Helps you speak your truth with clear communication.

If you are feeling overwhelmed, stressed, or worried, carry or wear aquamarine to bring in feelings of inner peace and serenity.

COLORS	green and blue
HARDNESS	7.5–8
CHAKRAS	throat and heart
ZODIAC SIGNS	Pisces and Aquarius
ELEMENT	water
CRYSTAL PAIRINGS	larimar, kunzite, morganite, emerald, chrysocolla, turquoise, celestite, green tourmaline, or spirit quartz
PRECAUTIONS	Aquamarine contains aluminum and can be toxic if ingested. It is sensitive to sunlight and intense temperature changes.
AFFIRMATION	I am flowing through life with ease, kindness, and inner peace.

blue calcite

Calming | Peace | Soothing | Communication | Optimism

Blue calcite has the following spiritual, physical, and emotional healing properties.

spiritual healing

- Provides a calm, expanded light to the auric field.
- Dispels negative energy and replaces it with positive energy.
- Can aid in the development of sensitivity and empathy.
- Increases telepathy, intuition, and psychic connection.
- Boosts ability to recall dreams.

physical healing

- Can lower blood pressure.
- Supports a healthy endocrine system.
- Helps cool the body, making it good for healing sore throats and any respiratory illness.

- Works to minimize inflammation and pain in the body, especially headaches or migraines.
- Promotes healthy bones, teeth, and skin.

emotional healing

- Helps release any negative feelings or thoughts about yourself.
- Helps you find your voice to express your truth with confidence.
- Aids in the relief of nervousness, tension, stress, and anxiety.
- Promotes feelings of peace, rest, and relaxation.
- Enhances creativity and communication and is amazing for writers struggling with writer's block.

If you feel nervous about an upcoming event, keep a blue calcite in your pocket to rub and focus your attention on to ease your nerves.

COLOR	baby blue
HARDNESS	3
CHAKRA	throat
ZODIAC SIGNS	Cancer and Pisces
ELEMENTS	fire and air
CRYSTAL PAIRINGS	blue lace agate, aquamarine, blue chalcedony, howlite, or orca agate
PRECAUTIONS	Blue calcite is too soft to be put in water.
AFFIRMATION	Every breath I take fills me up with inner peace and mental clarity.

celestite

Peace | Angels | Serenity | Communication | Relaxation

Celestite has the following spiritual, physical, and emotional healing properties.

spiritual healing

- Helps you communicate with your higher self, angels, and spirit guides.
- Magnifies your spiritual awakening and experience.
- Attracts good luck and fortune.
- Stimulates clairvoyant communication.
- Helps you acknowledge and accept your spiritual gifts from the Divine.
- Works on releasing stuck energies in the aura, subtle bodies, and chakras.
- Harmonizes your yin and yang energies.

physical healing

- Brings peace, stillness, and harmony to the body.
- Aids in the treatment of the ears, mouth, head, nose, and throat.
- Aids in minimizing inflammation and pain in the body.
- Helps soothe and relieve any digestive issues.
- Promotes a peaceful night's rest.

emotional healing

- Helps combat any fears of flying, agoraphobia, speaking in public, or large crowds.
- Can relieve stress and anxiety.
- Helps maintain emotional balance and stability.
- Instills feelings of inner peace, serenity, hope, and tranquility.

To bring a sense of peace and tranquility to your mind, whether you are at work, at home, or with others, carry a celestite with you daily. Keep a larger piece next to your bedside to promote a peaceful night's rest.

COLOR	baby blue
HARDNESS	3–3.5
CHAKRAS	throat, third eye, and crown
ZODIAC SIGNS	Gemini and Cancer
ELEMENT	wind
CRYSTAL PAIRINGS	angelite, amethyst, clear quartz, aquamarine, blue chalcedony, or honey calcite
PRECAUTIONS	Do not keep celestite in direct sunlight, as the color will fade. Avoid using it in water, as the stone is very soft and may break into pieces.
AFFIRMATION	I release all doubts and welcome inner peace.

chrysocolla

Gentleness | Joy | Emotional Stability |
Peace | Communication

Chrysocolla has the following spiritual,
physical, and emotional healing properties.

spiritual healing

- Instills world and inner peace.
- Stimulates intuition and psychic abilities.
- Works to balance and connect to your divine femininity.
- Allows you to accept what is and go with the flow of life.
- Helps you become attuned to the earth's energetic healing vibrations.

physical healing

- Is beneficial during PMS symptoms, reducing menstrual cramps.
- Aids in releasing stress, anxiety, worry, and tension in the body.
- Supports a healthy thyroid, thymus, and respiratory system.
- Assists in replenishing and restoring the adrenal glands.
- Helps assist in the regulation of insulin and balancing blood sugar levels.

COLORS	blue and green
HARDNESS	2–4
CHAKRAS	heart and throat
ZODIAC SIGNS	Sagittarius, Gemini, Virgo, and Taurus
ELEMENT	water
CRYSTAL PAIRINGS	aquamarine, azurite, larimar, or malachite
PRECAUTIONS	Chrysocolla contains copper and can be toxic if ingested. It is a soft stone that shouldn't be placed in water.
AFFIRMATION	I am able to express myself from a place of love and honesty.

emotional healing

- Increases feelings of empathy toward others.
- Assists you in recovering emotionally from a partner's abuse.
- Increases your capability to receive and give love.
- Helps banish guilt, which allows room for more joy and happiness.
- Encourages you to speak your truth by communicating from the heart.

Keep a chrysocolla in your bra or pocket throughout your day to accept what is and go with the flow of life.

amazonite

Tranquility | Communication | Comfort | Truth | Health

Amazonite has the following spiritual, physical, and emotional healing properties.

spiritual healing

- Soothes and rejuvenates all seven chakras.
- Illuminates and refills your aura.
- Helps you set boundaries with others.
- Boosts creativity and imagination.
- Enhances communication to help you speak and honor your truth.

physical healing

- Assists in the recovery process following a traumatic surgery or injury.
- Encourages a happy and healthy lifestyle.
- Helps bring the adrenal and thyroid glands back into balance after they are overworked because of anxiety or too much stress.
- Supports a healthy immune system.
- Works on strengthening the bones and joints.

emotional healing

- Opens the heart up again to receive love from others.
- Helps release and heal emotional trauma.
- Aids in calming a troubled mind.
- Promotes feelings of peace, joy, and serenity.
- Allows you to accept and understand your feelings with ease.

If you are struggling to speak your truth or have a speech to make in front of others, keep an amazonite tumbled stone in your pocket throughout the day. Before you speak, you can also meditate with an amazonite and repeat the affirmation "I allow my voice to speak from the heart with love and kindness."

COLORS	green and blue
HARDNESS	6–6.5
CHAKRAS	throat and heart
ZODIAC SIGNS	Virgo, Aquarius, and Pisces
ELEMENTS	air and water
CRYSTAL PAIRINGS	aquamarine, larimar, chrysocolla, turquoise, or green opal
PRECAUTIONS	Do not use amazonite in an elixir because it contains copper.
AFFIRMATION	I am at peace with who I am today.

blue chalcedony

Tranquility | Harmony | Transformation | Communication | Balance

Blue chalcedony has the following spiritual, physical, and emotional healing properties.

spiritual healing

- Supports balance of the mind, body, emotions, and spirit.
- Helps you communicate clearly through divine guidance.
- Aids in strengthening and repairing any energetic leaks in the aura.
- Facilitates a deeper meditation and inner channeling.
- Stimulates telepathic visions and psychic abilities.

physical healing

- Can help treat conditions of the female reproductive system.
- Works to cool the body to provide relief from throat inflammation and infections.
- Is a great stone for singers because it can strengthen your vocal cords.
- Promotes a deep and peaceful sleep.
- Can help treat conditions of the eyes, ears, nose, and respiratory system.

emotional healing

- Brings feelings of peace and tranquility while combating stress, nervousness, and anxiety.
- Helps you express your truth with love, comfort, and ease.
- Helps cool the body to release anger, tension, and fear that is emotionally stuck in the body.
- Boosts feelings of joy, optimism, and self-confidence.
- Allows you to release what no longer serves you so you can feel most at peace internally.

Keep a blue chalcedony under your pillow or meditate with it before you go to bed at night to quiet your mind and promote a good night's rest.

COLOR	blue
HARDNESS	6-7
CHAKRAS	throat and third eye
ZODIAC SIGNS	Aquarius, Pisces, and Libra
ELEMENT	water
CRYSTAL PAIRINGS	blue lace agate, aquamarine, blue calcite, howlite, lapis lazuli, larimar, or celestite
PRECAUTIONS	none
AFFIRMATION	I let go of anything I cannot control and find inner peace within what I can control.

amethyst

Protection | Divinity | Intuition | Peace | Balance

Amethyst has the following spiritual, physical, and emotional healing properties.

spiritual healing

- Is known as the "healer of people, animals, and plants."
- Provides protection from negative energy and psychic attacks.
- Boosts psychic gifts and intuition.
- Enhances meditation and connection to higher realms.
- Helps release any negative or stuck energies in the spiritual, physical, or emotional body.
- Works to stabilize and expand the aura.

physical healing

- Can be used to treat migraines and headaches.
- Supports overall health and well-being.
- Promotes a peaceful night's rest.
- Due to the high iron content, can help improve oxygen levels in the body.
- Helps calm the nervous system and bring it back into balance.

emotional healing

- Brings feelings of peace and harmony while combating stress and anxiety.
- Shifts negative thought patterns into positivity and optimism.
- Helps you recognize the root cause of your negative thoughts and behaviors.
- Helps you overcome any recurring negative bad habits, thought patterns, or addictions.

Wear amethyst as any form of jewelry daily to provide a shield of protection from negative energy or psychic attacks.

COLOR	purple
HARDNESS	7
CHAKRAS	third eye and crown
ZODIAC SIGNS	Aquarius, Virgo, Capricorn, and Pisces
ELEMENTS	air, water, and ether (spirit)
CRYSTAL PAIRINGS	All varieties of quartz, such as clear quartz, citrine, rose quartz, or smoky quartz. If you are using amethyst for protection, it pairs well with black tourmaline, jet, or black obsidian. If you are using it for recovering from addictions or negative thought patterns, kyanite is the perfect pairing.
PRECAUTIONS	Do not leave amethyst out in direct sunlight; the color will fade.
AFFIRMATION	I am connected and protected by divine light.

sugilite

Spiritual Wisdom | Confidence | Nurture | Spiritual Protection | Deep Connection

Sugilite has the following spiritual, physical, and emotional healing properties.

spiritual healing

- Enables you to open your mind to all of life's endless possibilities.
- Is great for empaths and highly sensitive people, providing a sense of grounding and protection.
- Represents spiritual love, deep connection, and wisdom.
- Encourages you to live in the present moment.
- Helps clear out negative energy trapped in the aura, chakras, and meridians.

physical healing

- Can reduce migraines and headaches.
- Is known to boost endurance, vitality, and energy.
- Helps with all sleeping disorders, including nightmares or night terrors.
- Due to the high iron content, can help improve oxygen levels and iron deficiencies in your body.
- Supports a healthy immune system and a healthy nervous system.

emotional healing

- Is a stone for mental balance, creativity, courage, and self-confidence.
- Aids in your ability to express yourself with ease, confidence, and flow.
- Can help with hostility, anger, jealousy, and forgiveness.
- Brings feelings of love, nurture, and care into your romantic relationships.
- Aids in releasing emotional blockages caused by trauma.

If you are prone to getting headaches or migraines, wear sugilite jewelry (skin contact) daily to keep your third-eye and crown chakras balanced to prevent pain from arising. You can also keep a pocket stone on you and pull it out to gently rub in circles on your third-eye chakra.

COLOR	purple
HARDNESS	6
CHAKRAS	third eye and crown
ZODIAC SIGN	Virgo and Capricorn
ELEMENT	wind
CRYSTAL PAIRINGS	super 7, charoite, iolite, jet, lapis lazuli, or rutilated quartz
PRECAUTIONS	Sugilite contains aluminum and can be toxic if ingested. Putting it in direct sunlight should also be avoided because the color will fade.
AFFIRMATION	I deserve to be happy and successful.

super 7

Chakra Balancing | Intuition | Letting Go | Mental Clarity | Spirituality

Super 7 is a naturally occurring mixture of seven crystals: amethyst, quartz, smoky quartz, cacoxenite, rutile, goethite, and lepidocrocite. It has the following spiritual, physical, and emotional healing properties.

spiritual healing

- Is spiritually cleansing and purifying.
- Is perfect for healing, balancing, and energizing all seven chakras.
- Stimulates and awakens your spiritual intuition, psychic abilities, and wisdom.
- Helps you align with your true authentic self.
- Provides an energetic shield of protection from negative energy.
- Deepens meditation and stimulates your awareness and connection to higher consciousness.
- Sparks imagination and self-discovery.

physical healing

- Stimulates regeneration and renewal of the physical body.
- Helps you heal stomach, digestive, adrenal, and thyroid imbalances.
- Promotes healthy blood flow.
- Helps with all sleeping disorders, including nightmares or night terrors.

emotional healing

- Enables you to let go of all your fears, stressors, and anxieties.
- Increases compassion, connection, and passion in your relationships.
- Promotes a deep feeling of harmony, peace, and contentment.
- Provides mental clarity to speak rationally and truthfully.

As you journal at night, keep a super 7 on your journal or near you to stimulate intuitive guidance, self-discovery, and imagination.

COLORS	purple, black, red, and white
HARDNESS	7
CHAKRAS	all
ZODIAC SIGNS	all
ELEMENTS	earth and storm
CRYSTAL PAIRINGS	iolite, spirit quartz, sugilite, or clear quartz
PRECAUTIONS	Super 7 contains aluminum and can be toxic if ingested. Putting it in direct sunlight should also be avoided, as the color will fade.
AFFIRMATION	My chakras are aligned and balanced at all times.

spirit quartz

Spiritual Connection | Intuition |
Master Healer | Divine Love | Protection

Spirit quartz has the following spiritual, physical, and emotional healing properties.

spiritual healing

- Balances yin and yang energies, helping you feel more balanced.
- Provides protection from negative energy.
- Activates and balances the meridians, aura, chakras, and Kundalini energy.
- Enhances your spiritual connection and awareness.
- Promotes a deeper sense of awareness and clarity.
- Opens the heart to feeling and connecting with divine love.

physical healing

- Is known to detoxify the physical body.
- Considered to be the "master healer" that provides healing for all the physical body.
- Helps provide relief for skin disorders such as eczema, psoriasis, and rosacea.
- Supports a healthy brain and nervous system.

emotional healing

- Helps one through the process of grieving when losing a loved one.
- Brings feelings of peace and harmony and a decrease in stress.
- Promotes forgiveness and unconditional love for others.
- Boosts feelings of compassion, sympathy, kindness, and generosity.
- Helps release bottled-up emotions, fear, and emotional pain.

COLORS	purple and white
HARDNESS	7
CHAKRAS	third eye and crown
ZODIAC SIGNS	Libra, Virgo, Aquarius, Pisces, and Capricorn
ELEMENTS	ether (spirit) and fire
CRYSTAL PAIRINGS	aquamarine, emerald, morganite, herkimer diamond, super 7, kunzite, or kyanite
PRECAUTIONS	Do not leave spirit quartz out in direct sunlight; the color will fade.
AFFIRMATION	I am the whole, unique spirit of light and love that shines from deep within.

If you are working on healing your physical body, meditate lying down with a spirit quartz at your crown chakra and tap into the energy of abundance, healing, and freedom. Let that energy fill your mind, body, and spirit with infinite healing light.

fluorite

Focus | Clarity | Divinity | Intuition | Protection

Fluorite has the following spiritual, physical, and emotional healing properties.

spiritual healing

- Provides an energetic shield to protect you from negative energy.
- Cleanses and restores all seven chakras.
- Protects, repairs, and seals the energy in the aura.
- Increases intuition, telepathy, and psychic abilities.
- Enhances and deepens your meditation.

physical healing

- Aids in the treatment of colds, flu, staph infections, or strep infections.
- Helps you feel more balanced, especially when experiencing vertigo.
- Aids in the mobility of joints.
- Aids in stimulating the mind, increasing concentration, focus, learning, and memory.
- Initiates cleansing and purification of the body's organs.

emotional healing

- Instills happy, healthy, and positive relationships with others.
- Works to balance the emotions and keep them stabilized.
- Calms the mind, reducing stress in the body.
- Encourages you to search within for answers instead of listening to outside influences.
- Awakens the mind to be open to endless opportunities.

If you struggle to focus at work or even during meditation, use a fluorite worry stone or palm stone to help you concentrate and bring mental clarity. If you struggle with brain fog, you can even wear it all day long as jewelry to help stimulate, balance, and refocus the mind.

COLORS	green, purple, white, blue, pink, red, brown, and black
HARDNESS	4
CHAKRAS	heart, throat, third eye, and crown
ZODIAC SIGNS	Capricorn and Pisces
ELEMENT	wind
CRYSTAL PAIRINGS	amethyst, black tourmaline, labradorite, rose quartz, clear quartz, moss agate, or orca agate
PRECAUTIONS	Do not put fluorite in direct sunlight; the color will begin to fade. Do not put it in water, as it can be toxic and dissolve.
AFFIRMATION	I am focused and concentrated on achieving my goals.

lepidolite

Peace | Balance | Harmony | Healing | Tranquility

Lepidolite has the following spiritual, physical, and emotional healing properties.

spiritual healing

- Aids in astral travel and rebirth.
- Helps you live in the present moment.
- Helps you move beyond your ego to altruism.
- Releases spiritual "baggage" and limiting beliefs.
- Provides assistance during big transitions in your life.
- Can be used to locate energy blockages within your body.

physical healing

- Helps you fall and stay asleep at night.
- Supports a healthy digestive system and metabolism.
- Helps balance the nervous system by soothing the nerves.
- Helps people with ADD and ADHD become more present and focused.
- Can increase flexibility in the joints.

emotional healing

- Aids in relieving anxiety, stress, depression, worry, and distrust.
- Opens your heart to love, forgiveness, and acceptance.
- Helps release trapped emotional anger, tension, and trauma.
- Works on balancing the emotions.

If you are prone to feeling anxious, keep a lepidolite on you at all times in your purse, pocket, or bra, or even as jewelry. This will bring your emotional state and mind-set back to a place of peace, safety, and joy. Taking it out to rub throughout your day activates your senses to bring you back into your body and calm down your nerves.

COLOR	Purple
HARDNESS	2.5–3
CHAKRAS	heart and third eye
ZODIAC SIGNS	Libra, Virgo, Cancer, and Gemini
ELEMENTS	earth and air
CRYSTAL PAIRINGS	blue lace agate, blue chalcedony, aquamarine, smoky quartz, hematite, amethyst, prehnite, or scolecite
PRECAUTIONS	Avoid placing lepidolite in water or in direct sunlight.
AFFIRMATION	I am in control of my thoughts and happiness.

charoite

Intuition | Protection | Positivity |
Spirituality | Boundaries

Charoite has the following spiritual, physical, and
emotional healing properties.

spiritual healing

- Releases lack of harmony and negative energy
  in the body.
- Stimulates intuition and psychic abilities.
- Brings high spiritual energy into union with
  unconditional love, which allows you to fully
  release and connect to your higher power.
- Allows you to deepen your meditation.
- Provides an energetic protection from toxic
  people, psychic attacks, and negative energies.

physical healing

- Works to build up your physical strength
  and mobility.
- Helps regulate a healthy blood pressure and
  heart rate.

- Aids in healing the liver, kidneys, digestive
  tract, spleen, and pancreas.
- Helps alleviate aches and pains in the body.
- When taken as an elixir, can help cleanse and
  purify the body.

emotional healing

- Helps you set healthy boundaries with others.
- Promotes compassion and empathy.
- Promotes inner reflection and encourages a
  positive outlook on any situation.
- Aids in opening the heart to forgiving yourself
  and others.
- Helps ground and stabilize the emotional body.

To strengthen your intuition and spiritual messages, place a charoite on your third-eye chakra
while lying down during your meditation.

COLORS	purple and black
HARDNESS	5-6
CHAKRAS	root, solar plexus, heart, third eye, and crown
ZODIAC SIGNS	Sagittarius, Pisces, and Scorpio
ELEMENT	wind
CRYSTAL PAIRINGS	sugilite, amethyst, moldavite, kunzite, jet, black tourmaline, shungite, or tiger's eye
PRECAUTIONS	none
AFFIRMATION	I am grounded, I am safe, and I am fully protected everywhere I go.

rose quartz

Unconditional Love | Forgiveness |
Compassion | Self-Love | Joy

Rose quartz has the following spiritual, physical,
and emotional healing properties.

spiritual healing

- Immerses the mind, body, and soul with the
  highest vibration, love.
- Deepens your connection with angels and
  angelic realms.
- Enhances affirmations that are repeated
  during meditation.
- Helps cleanse the emotional body of the aura.

physical healing

- Helps bring physical healing and strength to
  all areas of the heart.
- Helps men and women get through their mid-
  life crises.

- Aids in the treatment of any chest, lungs, or
  thymus imbalances.
- Can increase fertility, passion, and romance
  with your partner.
- Supports healthy circulation, reproductive
  organs, and skin.

emotional healing

- Is known to boost feelings of unconditional
  love for yourself and others.
- Promotes feelings of kindness, compassion,
  empathy, and generosity.
- Aids in recovery from abuse and heartbreak.
- Is known to increase feelings of overall happiness and joy.
- Helps bring a sense of peace and relief during
  times of grief.
- Opens the heart to allow you to forgive others
  and release the emotional trauma that's block-
  ing the heart from wanting or receiving love.

If you are feeling a lack of love, meditate lying
down and place a rose quartz heart over your
heart chakra. Focus on the loving energy coming
from the rose quartz and bring it into your heart
to feel unconditional love for yourself.

COLOR	pink
HARDNESS	7
CHAKRA	heart
ZODIAC SIGNS	Gemini and Taurus
ELEMENT	water
CRYSTAL PAIRINGS	morganite, emerald, pink tourmaline, rhodochrosite, rhodonite, pink opal, amethyst, carnelian, flower agate, fluorite, garnierite, green aventurine, kunzite, or thulite
PRECAUTIONS	Rose quartz will fade in direct sunlight.
AFFIRMATION	I love myself unconditionally.

rhodonite

*Love | Positive Relationships | Emotional
Balance | Trauma Healing | Self-Esteem*

Rhodonite has the following spiritual, physical,
and emotional healing properties.

spiritual healing

- Can provide healing for emotional and past-life trauma.
- Aids you in living your life to the fullest and with self-actualization.
- Harmonizes feminine and masculine energies.
- Helps you understand your purpose in life and your spiritual life path.
- Encourages spiritual growth and transformation.

physical healing

- Can treat infertility and PMS symptoms.
- Helps one lose weight and detoxify the body.

- Can help men and women through menopause.
- Supports a healthy immune system.
- Aids in reducing inflammation in the body.

emotional healing

- Aids in the relief of anxiety, stress, mental unrest, and confusion.
- Promotes healthy relationships and helps bond families closer together.
- Promotes feelings of unconditional love, self-esteem, and self-love.
- Helps clear energetic blockages that stem from past emotional wounds and scars.
- Promotes emotional balance and stability.

If you will be seeing family, friends, or loved ones who may be harder to connect and bond with, keep a large rhodonite in the center of the space where you will gather to bring in feelings of unconditional love, compassion, and kindness.

COLORS	pink and white
HARDNESS	5.5–6
CHAKRA	heart
ZODIAC SIGNS	Scorpio and Taurus
ELEMENT	fire and earth
CRYSTAL PAIRINGS	rose quartz, rhodochrosite, morganite, pink amethyst, pink opal, or scolecite
PRECAUTIONS	Do not keep rhodonite in direct sunlight; the color will fade. Avoid using it in water, as the stone is softer and may crack or break.
AFFIRMATION	I use my gifts to fulfill my soul's purpose.

rhodochrosite

Unconditional Self-Love | Deep Healing | Kindness | Forgiveness | Empathy

Rhodochrosite has the following spiritual, physical, and emotional healing properties.

spiritual healing

- Energizes and brings balance to the heart chakra.
- Assists in the healing of childhood trauma and past lives.
- Enhances your creativity, sparking new ideas and explorations.
- Renews passion and excitement for life.
- Emits the strongest vibration in the universe, love. It shows us the true meaning of unconditional love.

physical healing

- Can increase libido, physical energy, and sensuality.
- Aids in healthy development for babies.
- Brings the nervous system back into balance.
- Helps stimulate the mind and boosts memory.
- Supports a healthy spleen, heart, kidney, and circulation.

emotional healing

- Boosts feelings of unconditional love for yourself and others.
- Promotes feelings of courage, love, forgiveness, confidence, kindness, and compassion.
- May bring repressed feelings and trauma to the surface to be healed.
- Enables you to express yourself from the heart.
- Provides emotional stability and balance.

COLORS	pink and white
HARDNESS	3.5–4
CHAKRA	heart
ZODIAC SIGNS	Scorpio, Taurus, Cancer, and Pisces
ELEMENTS	fire and water
CRYSTAL PAIRINGS	rose quartz, emerald, eudialyte, morganite, pink amethyst, pink tourmaline, rhodonite, or thulite
PRECAUTIONS	Do not keep rhodochrosite in direct sunlight; the color will fade. Avoid using it in water, as the stone is very soft and may break into pieces.
AFFIRMATION	My needs and feelings are valid.

The only approval you ever need is from yourself. If you are being hard on yourself, wear rhodochrosite near your heart all day (skin contact) to promote an unconditional love and approval of self. Reaffirm, while you feel it in your heart, "I love and approve of myself."

pink tourmaline

Deep Healing | Empathy | Love | Happiness | Purpose

Pink tourmaline has the following spiritual, physical, and emotional healing properties.

spiritual healing

- Attracts love in the spiritual realms.
- Helps you connect to your soul purpose in this lifetime.
- Can help you release negative attachments and energy.
- Helps repair leakages and blockages in your aura.
- Nurtures and balances the feminine energies.

physical healing

- Supports a healthy menstrual cycle and reproductive system.
- Assists in creating a stronger bond with your newborn.
- Supports a healthy heart, lungs, and skin.
- Can provide protection against harmful radiation.
- Helps balance your mental state and the biochemistry in your brain.

emotional healing

- Helps you open your heart up and feel more empathetic toward others.
- Can alleviate stress, worry, and emotional pain.
- Promotes feelings of joy, love, and happiness.
- Bathes you in unconditional love of yourself and others.
- Helps you recognize the love and care you need to give yourself that you so willingly give to others.

If you are searching for love outside of yourself, go within and meditate with pink tourmaline on your heart chakra. Grasp onto a time when you truly felt love for yourself, feel it in your heart, and allow that loving energy to fill up your entire being.

COLOR	pink
HARDNESS	7–7.5
CHAKRA	heart
ZODIAC SIGN	Libra
ELEMENT	water
CRYSTAL PAIRINGS	green tourmaline, kunzite, garnet, eudialyte, morganite, pink amethyst, watermelon tourmaline, rhodochrosite, rose quartz, ruby, prehnite, or thulite
PRECAUTIONS	Pink tourmaline contains aluminum and can be toxic if ingested. It is sensitive to sunlight and intense temperature changes.
AFFIRMATION	I am constantly choosing to fill my cup up first.

morganite

Love | Compassion | Emotional Balance |
Angelic Guidance | Surrender

Morganite has the following spiritual, physical,
and emotional healing properties.

spiritual healing

- Allows you to open your heart to angelic guidance and love.
- Surrenders you to accepting love and light in
  the midst of darkness.
- Allows you to trust your spirit guides and feel
  their support.
- Helps you reach self-actualization and alignment with your higher self in this lifetime.

physical healing

- Helps strengthen the physical heart and provide support during a heartbreak.

- Boosts inner and physical strength.
- Aids in the treatment of asthma, emphysema,
  and tuberculosis.

emotional healing

- Helps you be receptive to love from others
  and less protective of your heart.
- Helps you recognize and heal old emotional
  patterns of judgment, fear, self-hatred, and
  manipulation.
- Brings feelings of peace, support, and love
  during times of grief.
- Provides emotional protection and balance.
- Boosts feelings of joy, patience, confidence,
  and compassion.
- Encourages positive and loving relationships,
  both romantically and in friendships.

If you have just lost a loved one, carry a morganite
near your heart at all times of the day to bring
feelings of peace, support, and love during the
grieving process.

COLOR	pink
HARDNESS	7.5–8
CHAKRA	heart
ZODIAC SIGNS	Taurus and Cancer
ELEMENTS	earth and water
CRYSTAL PAIRINGS	aquamarine, garnierite, green aventurine, kunzite, malachite, rose quartz, pink tourmaline, rhodochrosite, ruby, watermelon tourmaline, emerald, peridot, pink amethyst, pink opal, rhodonite, spirit quartz, or thulite
PRECAUTIONS	Morganite contains aluminum and can be toxic if ingested. It is sensitive to sunlight and intense temperature changes.
AFFIRMATION	Divine love enters through the light of my heart.

pink opal

Unconditional Love | Care | Trust | Letting Go | Emotional Balance

Pink opal has the following spiritual, physical, and emotional healing properties.

spiritual healing

- Encourages you to communicate with your angels.
- Helps heal past-life and ancestral wounds.
- Brings love and gentle healing to the aura.
- Brings gentle resolution and healing to painful traumatic memories.
- Enhances your spiritual awakening experience.

physical healing

- Promotes a good night's rest.
- Supports a healthy heart, spleen, and lungs.
- Aids in the treatment of diabetes and hypoglycemia.

- Helps support a healthy recovery after an injury.
- Can provide relief and soothing to the skin.

emotional healing

- Opens the heart to love, trust, kindness, and sympathy.
- Helps you achieve and maintain a positive mind-set.
- Brings emotional healing and balance.
- Helps you express yourself openly and let go of any irrational fears.
- Calms the mind, allowing stress and anxiety to be released.

If your mind tends to wander off into negativity, refocus by rubbing or holding a pink opal tumble and repeating the affirmation "I am the creator of my life, and I choose to be positive about everything in my life!"

COLOR	pink
HARDNESS	6–7
CHAKRA	heart
ZODIAC SIGNS	Libra, Scorpio, Cancer, and Pisces
ELEMENT	water
CRYSTAL PAIRINGS	pink amethyst, garnierite, green opal, rhodonite, rose quartz, or morganite
PRECAUTIONS	Pink opal is not recommended for use in direct sunlight or for gem elixirs.
AFFIRMATION	Taking care of myself is my top priority.

eudialyte

Self-Love | Forgiveness | Uplifting |
Healing | Spiritual Discovery

Eudialyte has the following spiritual, physical, and emotional healing properties.

spiritual healing

- Assists you in discovering your life's path.
- Purifies and protects you from negative energies.
- Helps you connect deeper to find answers from your spirit guides.
- Keeps you grounded and aligned with goals.
- Sparks creativity and new ideas.

physical healing

- Helps you become more present and loving in your physical body.
- Helps calm and stabilize the nervous system.
- Works with the body to help it self-heal.
- Aids in treating problems in the pancreas, thyroid, and eyes.
- Helps stabilize, balance, and heal the heart.

COLOR	pink, red, white, and black
HARDNESS	5-6
CHAKRAS	root and heart
ZODIAC SIGNS	Taurus, Aries, and Virgo
ELEMENTS	earth and water
CRYSTAL PAIRINGS	rhodochrosite, ruby, pink tourmaline, or black tourmaline
PRECAUTIONS	Eudialyte is a soft stone and slightly radioactive. Do not put it in water.
AFFIRMATION	I fully open my heart to love myself and others.

emotional healing

- Helps you overcome fears, self-doubt, and self-criticism.
- Opens the heart to forgiving others and loving yourself unconditionally.
- Provides a blanket of love when you are going through the grieving process.
- Helps uplift your mood on days when you feel down.
- Promotes healing from childhood abuse and trauma.

Holding on to guilt, shame, or regret only builds up more walls surrounding your heart. It's time to release the walls and open your heart back up to feeling that unconditional love you have within you. Take the time to meditate lying down with eudialyte on your heart chakra.

flower agate

Blossoming | Love | Positivity | Passion | Joy

Flower agate has the following spiritual, physical, and emotional healing properties.

spiritual healing

- Represents you blossoming and realizing your full potential, as shown by the seeds and flowers on the crystal structure.
- Helps you manifest, transform, and achieve your dreams.
- Sparks creativity and artistic expression.
- Infuses you with unconditional love and support from the Divine.
- Supports your overall well-being, mind, body, and spirit.

physical healing

- Boosts libido, physical stamina, vitality, and zest for life.
- Provides stability and release to put the body back into harmony.
- Helps with nutrient absorption and supports a healthy digestive system.
- Helps you have a peaceful night's rest.
- Supports a healthy urinary tract and reproductive system.

emotional healing

- Encourages self-growth, self-expression, and personal development.
- Increases enthusiasm and drive, which is ideal for entrepreneurs who want to pursue their business ventures.
- Aids in releasing fearful thinking, old emotional patterns, and self-doubts.
- Eases the feeling of restlessness.
- Instills deeper connection and greater love for your beauty and body.

If you are working toward blossoming into your most beautiful abundant self, use flower agate at all times of the day. Keep one in your pocket, a larger piece in your office space, and even one on your nightstand. This will help you reach your goals, encourage self-development, and help you reach your full potential.

COLORS	pink, white, and gray
HARDNESS	6.5–7
CHAKRA	all
ZODIAC SIGNS	Gemini and Virgo
ELEMENT	earth
CRYSTAL PAIRINGS	pyrite, rose quartz, carnelian, or rainbow moonstone
PRECAUTIONS	none
AFFIRMATION	My life is blossoming into its most beautiful version.

kunzite

*Unconditional Love | Compassion |
Expression | Flow | Emotional Healing*

Kunzite has the following spiritual, physical, and emotional healing properties.

spiritual healing

- Removes negative energy and acts as a protective shield around your auric field.
- Is highly vibrational, exuding divine love and light.
- Helps you release energy blockages in the heart, allowing you to become more open to love again.
- Induces a deep meditative state.
- Provides a blanket of love, helping you feel safe and secure.

physical healing

- Helps relieve heartache and heartbreak.
- Helps calm the nervous system.

- Keeps the body in flow, healing the circulatory system and blood pressure.
- Enhances femininity and female sexuality.
- Helps strengthen and regulate a healthy heart.

emotional healing

- Brings in feelings of unconditional love, self-love, expression, and flow.
- Promotes calmness, self-esteem, and control.
- Can relieve depression, anxiety, and stress.
- Helps release fears to let you experience life with joy and love.
- Helps you open your heart up to love again.

When we feel unconditional love from within, we reciprocate that love tenfold to others. Wear kunzite daily to radiate unconditional love for yourself and others.

COLORS	pink and purple
HARDNESS	6.5–7
CHAKRA	heart
ZODIAC SIGNS	Taurus, Leo, and Scorpio
ELEMENT	water
CRYSTAL PAIRINGS	aquamarine, charoite, emerald, garnierite, morganite, rose quartz, pink tourmaline, or spirit quartz
PRECAUTIONS	Kunzite contains aluminum and can be toxic if ingested. It is sensitive to sunlight and intense temperature changes.
AFFIRMATION	I release outer influences and am filled with divine love.

pink amethyst

*Love | Forgiveness | Compassion |
Protection | Peace*

Pink amethyst has the following spiritual,
physical, and emotional healing properties.

spiritual healing

- Promotes lucid and vivid dreaming.
- Frees you from your karmic cycle.
- Provides a protective energetic shield from
  negative energy.
- Is a great stone for meditation, bringing you
  into a deeper state of consciousness.
- Cleanses the aura of any stagnant or blocked
  energy preventing you from receiving and
  giving unconditional love.

physical healing

- Brings harmony, healing, strength, and flow
  to the physical heart.
- Aids in recovery from addiction and other
  bad habits.
- Supports and balances healthy hormones.
- Can release physical and emotional pain.
- Promotes a peaceful night's rest.

emotional healing

- Promotes unconditional love of yourself
  and others.
- Helps release doubts in a romantic
  relationship.
- Brings gentle feelings of kindness, empathy,
  and forgiveness.
- Aids in releasing overwhelming sensations of
  fear, anxiety, worry, or stress.
- Transforms negative thought patterns into
  optimism and enthusiasm.

Meditate with a pink amethyst at your heart
chakra. Feel and grab onto a moment you felt
truly loved. Sink into that sensation in your heart
and imagine the loving energy traveling throughout your entire body.

COLOR	pink
HARDNESS	7
CHAKRA	heart
ZODIAC SIGN	Pisces
ELEMENT	wind
CRYSTAL PAIRINGS	amethyst, pink opal, rhodonite, morganite, rhodochrosite, or pink tourmaline
PRECAUTIONS	Do not leave pink amethyst out in direct sunlight; the color will fade.
AFFIRMATION	I love myself exactly as I am.

ruby

Passion | Love | Vitality | Sexuality | Courage

Ruby has the following spiritual, physical, and emotional healing properties.

spiritual healing

- Helps you ground to the physical world.
- Activates the meridians and Kundalini energy.
- Strengthens your life force (prana) and chi throughout the body.
- Opens your heart to feeling and connecting with divine love.
- Provides an energetic loving shield of protection over the heart chakra.

physical healing

- Aids in bringing circulation and energy flow to the feet and legs.
- Helps stimulate vitality, energy, and burning passion for life.

- Boosts libido and sexual energy and can help you overcome infertility.
- Helps you become more focused, attentive, and aligned.
- Aids in recovering from any addictions, abuse, or childhood trauma.

emotional healing

- Helps you express love toward yourself.
- Brings enthusiasm and openheartedness for life.
- Is a stone of courage, helping you become comfortable with the unknown.
- Boosts emotional strength, stability, balance, and stamina.
- Increases passion and lust for your romantic partner.

If you are feeling scared of the unknown, meditate with a ruby in your hand and surrender and release to the universe. You are always guided to receive answers and may notice the unknown is actually the most known.

COLORS	red and magenta
HARDNESS	9
CHAKRAS	root and heart
ZODIAC SIGNS	Aries and Leo
ELEMENTS	earth and fire
CRYSTAL PAIRINGS	sapphire, eudialyte, green tourmaline, watermelon tourmaline, pink tourmaline, garnet, morganite, peridot, or thulite
PRECAUTIONS	Ruby contains aluminum and can be toxic if ingested. It is sensitive to sunlight and intense temperature changes.
AFFIRMATION	I am grounded and present.

thulite

Love | Pleasure | Generosity |
Deep Healing | Compassion

Thulite has the following spiritual, physical, and emotional healing properties.

spiritual healing

- Stimulates healing and regeneration within one's life force.
- Aids in speeding up and amplifying your manifestations.
- Opens the heart chakra for deep healing to be activated.
- Enlightens you on your true soul purpose in this lifetime.

physical healing

- Has a strong healing ability to regenerate and heal the body.
- Stimulates sexual energy and libido.
- Works to clear any reproductive issues that have stemmed from past abuse.
- Brings vitality, energy, and restoration for your health and is especially beneficial for those struggling with chronic fatigue.
- Helps increase physical balance and coordination.

emotional healing

- Encourages happiness, pleasure, passion, affection, and enthusiasm.
- Helps maintain good relationships, find new compatible friends, and initiate a romantic relationship.
- Helps us rest the pains of our past and move forward with compassion for ourselves and others.
- Opens the heart to unconditional love for yourself and others.
- Aids you in overcoming detrimental addictions that make you feel unworthy of a wonderful life.

If you are holding onto the past, anger, or resentment, meditate with thulite over your heart chakra to help you bring in the energy of forgiveness, love, and compassion. You can also wear thulite as jewelry to further this release and reconnection back to love..

COLORS	pink and red
HARDNESS	6–6.5
CHAKRAS	sacral, solar plexus, heart, and throat
ZODIAC SIGNS	Gemini and Taurus
ELEMENTS	wind and water
CRYSTAL PAIRINGS	pink tourmaline, rhodochrosite, ruby, morganite, or rose quartz
PRECAUTIONS	Thulite contains aluminum and can be toxic if ingested.
AFFIRMATION	I am constantly in the vibration of love.

watermelon tourmaline

Joy | Love | Inner Peace | Higher-Self Activator | Serenity

Watermelon tourmaline has the following spiritual, physical, and emotional healing properties.

spiritual healing

- Awakens and balances the higher heart (in between the heart and throat chakras).
- Balances yin and yang energies.
- Stimulates, balances, and energizes your connection with your higher self.
- Helps you express your affirmations and intentions with love and clarity.
- Promotes awareness of the world around you without your soaking in any negative energies.

physical healing

- Can release stress, nervousness, and tension from the physical body.

- Helps strengthen the heart and lungs.
- Helps minimize ADD and ADHD, helping one become more present and attentive.
- Supports healthy hormones, menstrual cycle, and reproductive system.

emotional healing

- Teaches us the true meanings of joy, happiness, and love.
- Promotes calmness and inner peace.
- Helps resolve issues in relationships, filling them with joy and love.
- Works to alleviate depression and old pain.
- Increases feelings of compassion, empathy, and sympathy.
- Strengthens our ability to love ourselves and others unconditionally.

Strengthen your ability to open your heart and love yourself unconditionally by keeping a watermelon tourmaline on your heart center.

COLORS	green, pink, blue, and yellow
HARDNESS	7-7.5
CHAKRA	heart
ZODIAC SIGNS	Virgo and Gemini
ELEMENT	water
CRYSTAL PAIRINGS	morganite, peridot, pink tourmaline, or ruby
PRECAUTIONS	Watermelon tourmaline contains aluminum and can be toxic if ingested. It is sensitive to sunlight and intense temperature changes.
AFFIRMATION	My heart is open to giving and receiving love.

black tourmaline

Grounding | Protection | Purification | Positivity | Connection

Black tourmaline has the following spiritual, physical, and emotional healing properties.

spiritual healing

- Repels, deflects, and protects you from negative energy.
- Works to release stagnant energy in your aura, chakras, or subtle bodies.
- Cleanses and removes toxic energy and replenishes it with energy from the earth.
- Increases spiritual growth and abundance.
- Facilitates speeding up your manifestations.
- Connects you deeply to mother nature, allowing you to feel more grounded and centered.

physical healing

- Can reduce pain and numbness.
- Protects you from harmful radiation from EMFs (electromagnetic fields).
- Aids in the detoxification of the body of all poisons and chemicals.
- Supports a healthy immune system and adrenal glands.
- Works to increase physical vitality and energy.

emotional healing

- Encourages cooperation and optimism.
- Helps reduce stress, anxiety, and worried thoughts.
- Supports a healthy emotional state and stability.
- Can reduce or eliminate suicidal thoughts and excessive fear.

If you struggle with any side effects of harmful radiation from EMFs, such as brain fog, sleep disturbances, or headaches, keep a large black tourmaline near or on your electronic devices.

COLOR	black
HARDNESS	7–7.5
CHAKRA	root
ZODIAC SIGNS	Libra, Scorpio, and Capricorn
ELEMENT	earth
CRYSTAL PAIRINGS	jet, smoky quartz, selenite, hematite, amethyst, black obsidian, eudialyte, larvikite, moldavite, black onyx, shungite, or charoite
PRECAUTIONS	Black tourmaline may contain aluminum and can be toxic if ingested.
AFFIRMATION	My mind, body, and spirit are protected and filled with infinite light.

black obsidian

Protection | Grounding | Purification | Acceptance | Positivity

Black obsidian has the following spiritual, physical, and emotional healing properties.

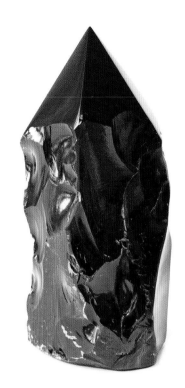

spiritual healing

- Provides an energetic shield, protecting you from negative energy.
- Helps you connect to the spiritual world and heal any past-life issues.
- Works to remove any negative attachments stuck in the energy field.
- Encourages you to find your soul purpose.
- Grounds you into your body and mother nature.
- Sparks creativity and imagination.

physical healing

- Can alleviate pain and tension in the body.

COLOR	black
HARDNESS	5-6
CHAKRA	root
ZODIAC SIGNS	Scorpio and Capricorn
ELEMENT	earth
CRYSTAL PAIRINGS	black tourmaline, howlite, jet, smoky quartz, black onyx, petrified wood, or rutilated quartz
PRECAUTIONS	none
AFFIRMATION	I am divinely protected from all negative energy and shielded by beaming white light.

- Aids in regulating a healthy digestive system and metabolism.
- Works to heal any reproductive issues that have stemmed from past abuse.
- Supports a healthy flow of blood in the body.

emotional healing

- Helps you conquer issues relating to past misuse of personal power.
- Works to release your limiting and negative beliefs about yourself.
- Helps you feel empowered enough to take control and responsibility for your own healing.
- Enhances your capacity to exercise self-control and resist temptation to achieve your goals.
- Helps you overcome any recurring negative bad habits, thought patterns, or addictions.

If you want to release trapped emotions or stuck negative energy, lie down and place a black obsidian at the bottom of your feet during your meditation. Imagine the black obsidian pulling out all the negative energy trapped in your body.

black moonstone

New Beginnings | Femininity | Focus |
Purpose | Connection

Black moonstone has the following spiritual,
physical, and emotional healing properties.

spiritual healing

- Strengthens intuition and psychic abilities.
- Encourages positive change, renewal, and new beginnings.
- Works to balance feminine energy.
- Provides an energetic shield to protect you from negative energy.
- Supports deep introspection and self-discovery.
- Connects you to mother nature, allowing you to feel more grounded and centered.

physical healing

- Helps bring your hormones back into a healthy and balanced state.
- Can treat infertility and PMS symptoms.
- Helpful for stroke recovery and brain function.
- Promotes healthy skin and youthfulness.

emotional healing

- Helps you focus and concentrate on a specific task or project.
- Works on releasing any worries or fears.
- Can remove feelings of jealousy, possessiveness, or desire to control others.
- Helps you find your direction and purpose in life.
- Calms the mind so you can maintain focus and have clarity for decision-making.

To guide you through large transformations in your life, carry or wear black moonstone during your day.

COLORS	brown and black
HARDNESS	6–6.5
CHAKRAS	root, sacral, third eye, and crown
ZODIAC SIGN	Cancer
ELEMENT	water
CRYSTAL PAIRINGS	rainbow moonstone, black tourmaline, amethyst, carnelian, labradorite, or petrified wood
PRECAUTIONS	Black moonstone may contain aluminum and can be toxic if ingested.
AFFIRMATION	I embrace change with open arms.

shungite

EMF Protection | Grounding | Vitality |
Purification | Balance

Shungite has the following spiritual, physical,
and emotional healing properties.

spiritual healing

- Provides protection against negative energy in
  the body or home.
- Promotes grounding and connection to earth's
  healing and nourishing energies.
- Purifies and balances the body, yin and yang
  energies, and chakras.
- Provides direction to help you fulfill your soul
  purpose in this lifetime.
- Acts as a catalyst for spiritual growth and
  transformation.

physical healing

- Provides protection against any harmful envi-
  ronmental energies that affect your physical
  body.

- Works to increase physical energy and
  stamina, relieving fatigue and insomnia.
- Purifies your water (when using elite shungite,
  a specific type of shungite).
- Is known to absorb and eliminate any health
  hazards in your life.
- Protects you from harmful radiation from
  EMFs (electromagnetic fields).
- Supports a healthy digestive system, skin, and
  immune system.

COLOR	black
HARDNESS	3.5–4
CHAKRA	root
ZODIAC SIGNS	Scorpio, Capricorn, and Cancer
ELEMENTS	fire, wind, and storm
CRYSTAL PAIRINGS	smoky quartz, black tourmaline, hematite, black onyx, copper, charoite, or nephrite jade
PRECAUTIONS	Shungite is a soft stone but is safe in water.
AFFIRMATION	I live my life fearlessly.

emotional healing

- Helps calm an overactive mind, releasing
  panic, worry, fear, stress, stuck emotions,
  and anxiety.
- Helps calm the mind to achieve ultimate peace
  and harmony.
- Aids in releasing aggressive energy and fills
  your energy with love.

If you struggle with any side effects of harmful
radiation from EMFs, such a brain fog, sleep
disturbances, or headaches, keep a large shungite
near or on your electronic devices.

black onyx

Intention | Protection | Grounding |
Strength | Personal Power

Black onyx has the following spiritual, physical, and emotional healing properties.

spiritual healing

- Enhances protection from negative energy.
- Helps one ground themselves to mother nature.
- Enhances spiritual vision and dream experiences.
- Amplifies your intentions and allows you to think clearly.
- Harmonizes masculine and feminine energies.

physical healing

- Boosts the retention of memory and encourages attention to detail.
- Can increase physical strength, vitality, and stamina.

- Helps you release any unwanted excess energy.
- Can calm and soothe the nervous system.
- Aids in the treatment of disorders related to the feet, bone marrow, and tissues.

emotional healing

- Assists in boosting personal power, inner strength, and willpower.
- Brings forth a calm state of mind in heated situations.
- Helps you create a more structured, controlled, and disciplined life.
- Helps release any anger or anxiety stuck in your emotional body.
- Encourages positivity and happiness.

To bring your masculine and feminine energies back into balance, hold a black onyx in each hand during meditation or before bed. To add to the union of the energies, you can add the chant *laam* (which is a sound that corresponds to the root chakra).

COLOR	black
HARDNESS	7
CHAKRAS	root, solar plexus, and third eye
ZODIAC SIGNS	Taurus and Scorpio
ELEMENT	earth
CRYSTAL PAIRINGS	black tourmaline, black obsidian, gold sheen obsidian, rainbow moonstone, rainbow obsidian, or shungite
PRECAUTIONS	Do not put black onyx out in the sun for a prolonged period.
AFFIRMATION	I release all negativity from my mind, body, and soul.

jet

Rejuvenation | Protection | Purification | Stress Relief | Positivity

Jet has the following spiritual, physical, and emotional healing properties.

spiritual healing

- Provides protection against negative energy in the body or home.
- Clears the energy field of negative attachments and addictive patterns.
- Assists in awakening one's psychic awareness and gifts.
- Can stimulate financial abundance and business success.
- Deepens your meditation and raises your Kundalini energy.

physical healing

- Energetically cleanses and rejuvenates the liver and kidneys.
- Helps ease pain from migraines, upset stomach, and the flu.
- Is beneficial during PMS symptoms, reducing menstrual cramps.
- Aids in the treatment of epilepsy, colds, and lymphatic swelling.

emotional healing

- Lets you see the lessons in negative experiences and helps you integrate those lessons.
- Helps bring emotional balance and stability.
- Helps you step into your personal power and full potential.
- Helps alleviate depression, bringing that spark back into your life, filling it with joy and love.
- Can reduce stress and worried thinking.
- Aids in reducing depression, anxiety, and unwanted fears.

If you are surrounded with negative people at work, keep a large jet on your desk and in your pocket for when you speak to them to provide a protective shield of energy.

COLOR	black
HARDNESS	2.5–4
CHAKRA	root
ZODIAC SIGNS	Gemini, Aries, and Taurus
ELEMENT	earth
CRYSTAL PAIRINGS	black obsidian, black tourmaline, amber, amethyst, bloodstone, charoite, hematite, lepidolite, sugilite, rutilated quartz, or serpentine
PRECAUTIONS	Do not put jet in water; it is a very soft, brittle stone.
AFFIRMATION	My mind, body, and spirit are grounded, centered, and purified.

herkimer diamond

High Vibrational | Amplifier | Protector | Dreamer | Mental Clarity

Herkimer diamond has the following spiritual, physical, and emotional healing properties.

spiritual healing

- Infuses more energetic light into the body to help you feel full of it at all times.
- Is a stone of dreams and vision work.
- Assists in removing energetic cords or negative patterns.
- Amplifies all energies, crystals, and intentions.
- Assists highly spiritual people in enjoying the physical world.
- Promotes lucid dreaming and astral traveling.
- Can be utilized to attune yourself with another person, place, or activity.
- Enhances your intuition and psychic abilities.

physical healing

- Aids in purifying and cleansing the physical body.
- Helps boost the immune system.
- Provides a layer of protection from physical burnout.
- Boosts one's overall physical energy and stamina.

emotional healing

- Aids in clearing the mind of unconscious fears and repressions.
- Assists you in achieving self-actualization, where your life's full potential is reached.
- Facilitates healing and overall emotional well-being.

Use a herkimer diamond alongside any crystal to amplify its healing properties. If you are currently working on reaching self-realization or your full potential, keep a herkimer diamond near or on your journal as you write.

COLOR	clear and white
HARDNESS	7
CHAKRAS	third eye and crown
ZODIAC SIGNS	Libra, Scorpio, and Sagittarius
ELEMENT	air
CRYSTAL PAIRINGS	all, especially moldavite
PRECAUTIONS	Herkimer diamond's color will fade, and it can cause a fire when in direct sunlight.
AFFIRMATION	I am constantly radiating love and light.

clear quartz

Master Healer | Divinity | Spirituality | Manifestor | Amplification

Clear quartz has the following spiritual, physical, and emotional healing properties.

spiritual healing

- Is used to amplify crystals, the physical body, energy, thoughts, and intentions.
- Provides an energetic shield of protection against negative energy.
- Facilitates the manifestation process.
- Repairs leakages and expands your auric field.
- Known as the "master healer" because of its ability to be programmed to work on any physical, mental, emotional, or spiritual ailment.
- Facilitates communicating and connecting with your higher consciousness and spirit guides.
- Increases clarity in understanding your intuition or psychic messages better.
- Helps clear and activate all energy centers of the body.

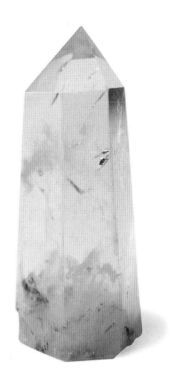

physical healing

- Has the ability to work with any health condition in the body to help bring it back into balance.
- Brings vitality, energy, and restoration for your health.
- Aids in pain relief.
- Supports a healthy nervous system and immune system.

emotional healing

- Helps stimulate the mind and boost your memory.
- Works with emotional energy to stimulate positive and joyful feelings.
- Helps treat any mental or emotional disorders.
- Aids in releasing negative emotional attachments to others.

Clear quartz will magnify any other crystal's energy. To use it on its own, place it at your crown chakra during meditation to raise your vibrations, strengthen your aura, and connect with your higher consciousness.

COLOR	clear
HARDNESS	7
CHAKRA	crown
ZODIAC SIGNS	all
ELEMENT	air, water, and fire
CRYSTAL PAIRINGS	all
PRECAUTIONS	Clear quartz is sensitive to light and can cause a fire when in prolonged direct sunlight.
AFFIRMATION	I honor and accept the Divine within me.

lemurian

Healing | Divinity | Highly Vibrational |
Manifestation | Expansion

Lemurian has the following spiritual, physical,
and emotional healing properties.

spiritual healing

- Expands your inner light.
- Helps speed up the manifestation process.
- Helps improve your quality of life.
- Is perfect for using during Reiki healing
  sessions or any energy work.
- Connects you to your spirit guides, angels,
  and higher self.
- Promotes karmic healing and removal of
  negative attachments.

physical healing

- Supports a healthy heart, brain, immune
  system, and nervous system.
- Can minimize inflammation and pain in
  the body.
- Aids in a speedy recovery after a surgery,
  bruise, injury, or physical trauma.

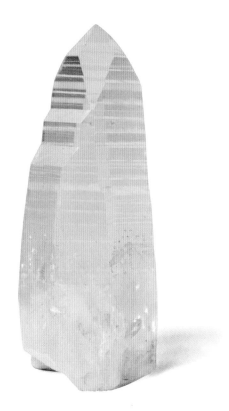

- Has the ability to work with any health condition in the body to help bring it back into
  balance.

emotional healing

- Brings greater connection so you can see
  and love your authentic self.
- Calms the mind, bringing peace and
  tranquility.
- Can provide healing from emotional trauma.
- Provokes feelings of love, nurture, and
  connection.
- Helps you feel emotionally connected
  and understand that you aren't ever alone in
  this world.

If you were just in an accident, injured yourself,
or have a small bruise, use a lemurian wand in the
area in need of healing. If possible, keep it on that
spot as you sleep to aid in a quicker recovery. Do
this daily until the area has healed.

COLORS	white and clear
HARDNESS	7
CHAKRA	crown
ZODIAC SIGN	Gemini
ELEMENT	wind and storm
CRYSTAL PAIRINGS	all
PRECAUTIONS	Lemurian is sensitive to light and can cause a fire when in direct sunlight.
AFFIRMATION	I am a beacon of healing love and light.

howlite

Calm | Peace | Awareness |
Restful Sleep | Bone Strength

Howlite has the following spiritual, physical, and emotional healing properties.

spiritual healing

- Allows you to deepen your meditation.
- Provides a deep insight into your past lives.
- Helps you find your authentic self.
- Facilitates connecting to your higher consciousness, realms, and awareness.
- Absorbs negative energy.

physical healing

- Can provide pain relief.
- Is great for keeping in your nightstand or under your pillow at night for a peaceful sleep.
- Helps stimulate the mind and improve memory.
- Is great for strengthening the bones, teeth, and soft tissues, due to high calcium absorption.

emotional healing

- Helps stabilize your emotions.
- Assists in motivation and ambition for reaching your goals.
- Can help quiet and calm the mind, increasing relaxation.
- Aids in reducing frustration, anxiety, tension, worries, stress, and anger.
- Removes the possibility of becoming conceited or self-centered.
- Encourages emotional expression.

If you struggle to quiet your mind or keep a positive mind-set before falling asleep, hold a howlite in your hand (or one in each hand), close your eyes, focus on each of your body parts in turn—head, eyes, nose, mouth, jaw, all the way to your toes—and ask it to relax. Take a deep breath in and out with each relaxation.

COLORS	white and gray
HARDNESS	3.5
CHAKRA	crown
ZODIAC SIGNS	Virgo, Gemini, and Cancer
ELEMENT	air
CRYSTAL PAIRINGS	lepidolite, black obsidian, blue calcite, larimar, or scolecite
PRECAUTIONS	Howlite contains boron and can be toxic if ingested. It is a soft stone, so do not submerge it in water.
AFFIRMATION	I am at peace and harmony with everyone and everything.

rainbow moonstone

New Beginnings | Insight | Femininity |
Balance | Divine Connection

Rainbow moonstone has the following spiritual,
physical, and emotional healing properties.

spiritual healing

- Stimulates intuition, insight, and creativity.
- Provides spiritual guidance to help you find
  your soul purpose in life.
- Provides protection when working with lucid
  dreaming of visionary quests.
- Helps you go through change and new beginnings with ease and excitement.
- Provides protection and repairs any leakages
  in the auric field.
- Can offer protection and provide good fortune
  when you are traveling.

COLORS	white and black with flashes of blue
HARDNESS	6–6.5
CHAKRAS	sacral and crown
ZODIAC SIGNS	Gemini, Cancer, Scorpio, and Libra
ELEMENTS	water and ether (spirit)
CRYSTAL PAIRINGS	labradorite, garnierite, flower agate, black moonstone, azurite, herkimer diamond, moldavite, black onyx, opal, and rainbow obsidian
PRECAUTIONS	Do not keep rainbow moonstone exposed to prolonged sunlight.
AFFIRMATION	I embrace the positive changes to come with open arms.

physical healing

- Helps heal any imbalances in the
  digestive tract.
- Eases menopause and premenstrual
  symptoms.
- Helps women with fertility, childbirth, hormonal imbalances, and sexuality issues.
- Supports healthy ears, skin, hair, eyes,
  and organs.
- Provides connection between the physical,
  emotional, and spiritual bodies.

emotional healing

- Boosts feelings of self-confidence, optimism,
  joy, and hope.
- Aids in releasing anger, frustration, and
  irritability.
- Brings peace, calmness, and composure to
  the mind.
- Helps you understand your emotions from
  a place of love and promotes emotional
  well-being.
- Encourages feelings of love, compassion,
  and understanding.

Keep a rainbow moonstone in your pocket or
bra to provide you with an infinite white light of
protection surrounding you during your travels.

selenite

Spiritual Guidance | Physical Healing |
Protection | Harmony | Authenticity

Selenite has the following spiritual, physical,
and emotional healing properties.

spiritual healing

- Provides access to understanding and connecting to your past and future lives.
- Provides a bright, energetic white light shielding your auric field and your home.
- Enhances telepathy, intuition, and clairvoyant
  sensations.
- Connects you to angelic guidance and
  communication.
- Cleanses and charges all other crystals.
- Enhances meditation and connection to
  higher realms.

physical healing

- Can alleviate pain, inflammation, and tension in
  the body.
- May clear blockages that initiate physical
  healing.
- Promotes a healthy balanced nervous system.
- On a cellular level, can counteract the effects
  of "free radicals" to heal and restore.
- Supports a healthy spine and alignment.

emotional healing

- Helps you recognize your best and most
  authentic self.
- Helps you stay mentally focused, alert, and
  concentrated, reducing mental fog.
- Helps calm the mind to promote inner peace
  and a sense of tranquility.
- Aids in emotional balance and stability.

Charge your crystals overnight in a selenite bowl.
This is an easy way to make sure your crystals are
loved, recharged, and taken care of daily.

COLORS	white and clear
HARDNESS	2
CHAKRA	crown
ZODIAC SIGNS	Cancer, Scorpio, Pisces, and Taurus
ELEMENTS	air and water
CRYSTAL PAIRINGS	all
PRECAUTIONS	Do not put selenite in prolonged sunlight. It is a very soft stone; do not put it in water.
AFFIRMATION	I release any negative energy that no longer serves my highest good.

scolecite

Soothing | Inner Peace | Awareness | Harmony | Spiritual Connection

Scolecite has the following spiritual, physical, and emotional healing properties.

spiritual healing

- Brings a sense of tranquility, inner peace, and serenity that can gently lift one to higher planes of awareness.
- Enhances your dream state; is great for lucid dreaming.
- Awakens the heart when connecting to your spirit.
- Helps one receive spiritual inspiration and insight.
- Connects you to higher spirit realms, your higher self, spirit guides, other dimensions, and extraterrestrials.
- Provides spiritual guidance to help you find your soul purpose in this lifetime.

physical healing

- Helps support proper serotonin levels, to keep one happy and joyful throughout the day.
- Promotes a deep and restful sleep.
- Helps empaths and introverts recharge their energy after being drained by others.
- Supports a healthy digestive system, spine, lungs, eyes, and circulatory system.

emotional healing

- Clears mental "debris" so your true inner light can shine.
- Helps one stay balanced and calm when faced with difficult situations.
- Brings feelings of peace and harmony while combating stress and anxiety.
- Boosts feelings of self-love and self-confidence.
- Promotes compassion and empathy.

If you struggle to quiet your mind or keep a positive mind-set before falling asleep, hold a scolecite in your hand (or one in each hand), close your eyes, and focus on your breath. With each exhale, let go of any tension you may be holding on to from the day.

COLOR	white
HARDNESS	5–5.5
CHAKRAS	third eye and crown
ZODIAC SIGN	Capricorn
ELEMENTS	wind and ether (spirit)
CRYSTAL PAIRINGS	orca agate, prehnite, rhodonite, howlite, azurite, lepidolite, selenite, or sodalite
PRECAUTIONS	Scolecite is a soft stone; do not put it in water. Prolonged sun exposure may damage the crystal.
AFFIRMATION	I am always at a state of peace and harmony.

pyrite

Fool's Gold | Good Luck | Confidence | Abundance | Manifestation

Pyrite has the following spiritual, physical, and emotional healing properties.

spiritual healing

- Provides an energetic shield to protect you from negative energy.
- Gives you a sense of safety, security, stability, and grounding.
- Helps increase your vibration and speed up the manifestation process.
- Magnifies your attraction to prosperity, good luck, and abundance.

physical healing

- Supports a healthy endocrine system.
- Helps stimulate the mind and enhances memory recall.
- Helps heal the digestive system and boost metabolism.
- Works to purify the body of infection, toxins, and diseases.
- Supports a healthy male reproductive system, especially in regard to impotence and infertility.

emotional healing

- Helps you overcome deep, profound fears.
- Can help you become more motivated and ambitious.
- Strengthens your personal power and assertiveness.
- Boosts feelings of self-confidence, courage, and self-worth.
- Encourages healthy and positive relationships.

To attract more wealth into your life, keep a raw pyrite in your wallet daily.

COLOR	gold
HARDNESS	6-6.5
CHAKRA	solar plexus
ZODIAC SIGNS	Leo and Gemini
ELEMENT	earth
CRYSTAL PAIRINGS	citrine, flower agate, gold sheen obsidian, lapis lazuli, green aventurine, or nephrite jade
PRECAUTIONS	Do not put pyrite in water; it can fade in color or rust.
AFFIRMATION	Money comes to me easily and effortlessly.

gold sheen obsidian

Abundance | Protection | Manifestation |
Personal Power | Guidance

Gold sheen obsidian has the following spiritual, physical, and emotional healing properties.

spiritual healing

- Provides grounding and protection from negative energy.
- Helps you discover hidden talents and unique skills.
- Works on cleansing and purifying your aura.
- Is powerful for manifesting and attracting abundance.
- Assists in connecting you with your spirit guides.
- Provides guidance in helping you find your life purpose.

physical healing

- Supports a healthy digestive system.
- Can reverse damage that has been done to the cells, which accelerates recovery from wounds, injury, or bruising.
- Assists in providing a direct path that is needed to heal.
- Can help alleviate pain in the body.

emotional healing

- Helps you find or realign with your personal power.
- Assists you in diving deep into conquering your deepest, darkest fears.
- Helps turn down the ego, so you are able to think from your most authentic self.
- Provides guidance and insight in the direction you need to be.

To help you realign with your personal power, keep a gold sheen obsidian in your pocket or bra daily. Anytime you feel your personal power being taken away from you, hold it or rub it and reaffirm your personal power.

COLORS	gold and black
HARDNESS	5-6
CHAKRAS	root, solar plexus, and third eye
ZODIAC SIGN	Sagittarius
ELEMENT	earth
CRYSTAL PAIRINGS	black obsidian, citrine, rainbow obsidian, pyrite, Libyan desert glass, black onyx, or rainbow moonstone
PRECAUTIONS	none
AFFIRMATION	I am protected and filled with positive energy everywhere I go.

rutilated quartz

Manifestation | Spiritual Inspiration |
Energy | Purpose | Higher Consciousness

Rutilated quartz has the following spiritual,
physical, and emotional healing properties.

spiritual healing

- Speeds up and magnifies the energy of intentions, manifestations, and affirmations.
- Helps you connect to the spiritual world and heal any past-life issues.
- Helps you receive spiritual inspiration.
- Enhances intuition and psychic abilities.
- Aids in psychic channeling, astral travel, and spiritual connection.
- Expands your consciousness to the greater spiritual realms.

physical healing

- Can boost your overall energy levels and combat lethargy.
- Works with the body to detoxify mercury poisoning in the blood.
- Helps support and balance the endocrine system.
- Aids in decreasing unhealthy food cravings and addictions.
- Helps restore and regenerate the body back into balance.

emotional healing

- Helps you feel less overwhelmed and more at ease with life's responsibilities and stressors.
- Can promote self-expression and enhance communication.
- Encourages the healing of emotional, spiritual, and physical wounds.

To expand your consciousness during meditation,
lie down and place a rutilated quartz point facing
inward toward your head at the crown chakra to
raise your vibrations and expand your consciousness into greater spiritual realms.

COLOR	clear with silver, gold, red, green, and black
HARDNESS	7
CHAKRA	all
ZODIAC SIGNS	Leo, Taurus, and Gemini
ELEMENT	storm
CRYSTAL PAIRINGS	moldavite, sugilite, black obsidian, jet, lemurian, smoky quartz, or herkimer diamond
PRECAUTIONS	Do not put rutilated quartz outside in prolonged sunlight.
AFFIRMATION	Life supports me in every way possible.

hematite

Protection | Grounding | Connection |
Positivity | Balance

Hematite has the following spiritual, physical, and emotional healing properties.

spiritual healing

- Harmonizes your yin and yang energies.
- Balances the mind, body, and spirit.
- Provides an energetic shield protecting you from negative energy.
- Is one of the most powerful stones for grounding into mother nature's healing energies, allowing you to become more present in the moment.
- Helps you identify your inner strengths and limitations so that you may use them to improve, conquer, and succeed on all levels.

physical healing

- Aids in detoxifying the liver and organs.
- Accelerates the body's natural healing process.
- Provides protection against harmful EMFs (electromagnetic fields).

- Assists in the absorption of iron and formation of red blood cells.
- Promotes healthy blood flow and circulatory system.

emotional healing

- Instills strength, ambition, love, and courage.
- Helps release judgment of yourself and others.
- Helps you remember your thought patterns, ideas, and memories.
- Assists in releasing negative habits and addictive thought patterns.
- Facilitates the attainment of inner peace and happiness.

If you are feeling spacy or have brain fog, take a hematite outside with you into mother nature. As you hold it in your hand, allow the energy to flow from it through your hands, through your body, to your legs, and out your feet, connecting to the ground below you.

COLOR	black
HARDNESS	5.5–6.5
CHAKRA	root
ZODIAC SIGN	Aquarius
ELEMENT	earth
CRYSTAL PAIRINGS	agate, black tourmaline, black obsidian, shungite, or jet
PRECAUTIONS	Do not submerge hematite in water; it can rust.
AFFIRMATION	I am grounded, centered, and balanced.

smoky quartz

Protection | Grounding | Peace |
Restoration of Energy | Balance

Smoky quartz has the following spiritual, physical, and emotional healing properties.

spiritual healing

- Helps cleanse the aura and chakras of any blockages.
- Provides a shield of protection from negative energies.
- Harmonizes your yin and yang energies.
- Is grounding, reconnecting you to the earth's healing energy.
- Deepens your meditation, allowing for clear thoughts and the ability to be more present in the moment.

physical healing

- Helps align the body back into equilibrium.
- Can relieve chronic pain, including migraines and cramps.

- After an illness, can restore your vitality and physical energy.
- Protects you from harmful radiation from EMFs (electromagnetic fields).
- Promotes a restful night's sleep.

emotional healing

- Works to reduce anxiety, stressful thoughts, panic attacks, and self-harm thoughts.
- Calms the mind, so it is perfect for use during meditation.
- Can release negative thoughts associated with fear, jealousy, or anger.
- Supports mental clarity and emotional balance.
- Is known to increase cooperation and unification with others so you can reach the same goal or desire.

If you tend to go through your day with your mind feeling chaotic or swirly, you may need to ground and find your connection to your body and mother nature. Keep a smoky quartz on you to wear or pull out when you need to find your center again.

COLORS	black, brown, and white
HARDNESS	7
CHAKRA	root
ZODIAC SIGNS	Capricorn, Scorpio, Taurus, and Virgo
ELEMENT	earth
CRYSTAL PAIRINGS	agate, crazy lace agate, black obsidian, amethyst, black tourmaline, lepidolite, red jasper, or rutilated quartz
PRECAUTIONS	The color of a smoky quartz will fade or change due to prolonged sun exposure.
AFFIRMATION	I am grounded and present in the moment at all times.

petrified wood

Transformation | Earthiness | Security |
Balance | Energy

Petrified wood has the following spiritual,
physical, and emotional healing properties.

spiritual healing

- Is grounding, reconnecting you to the
  earth's energy.
- Helps you become aligned with your ultimate
  purpose in this lifetime.
- Helps release any stuck or scattered energies.
- Provides a foundation for new goals, transformation, or changing of your life path.
- Provides access to and understanding of your
  past lives.

physical healing

- Can help improve your overall physical health
  and well-being.
- Works to strengthen the bones and joints.
- Boosts physical vitality and energy in the body.

- Works on healing the organs in the sacral
  chakra.

emotional healing

- Teaches patience and understanding of how
  to go with the flow of life.
- Helps release feelings of stress and worry.
- Increases passion and joy for life.
- Helps bring balance to your emotional
  well-being.
- Promotes feelings of safety and security.

Connect to mother nature and ground into your
infinite being by keeping petrified wood in your
pocket or bra daily.

COLORS	brown, red, white, black, purple, and orange
HARDNESS	7–8
CHAKRAS	root and sacral
ZODIAC SIGNS	Leo, Virgo, Capricorn, Taurus, and Scorpio
ELEMENT	earth
CRYSTAL PAIRINGS	kambaba jasper, moss agate, unakite jasper, black obsidian, black moonstone, or red jasper
PRECAUTIONS	none
AFFIRMATION	I embrace transformation.

tiger's eye

Courage | Open-Mindedness | Strength | Good Luck | Grounding

Tiger's eye has the following spiritual, physical, and emotional healing properties.

spiritual healing

- Is great for boosting intuition, psychic processes, spiritual awakening, and intuitive impressions.
- Brings good luck and prosperity.
- Provides protection against negative energy.
- Is grounding, providing a deeper connection to mother earth.
- Harmonizes yin and yang energy.

physical healing

- Helps healing from an injury or broken bone.
- Helps with all sleeping disorders, including nightmares or night terrors.
- Can reduce unhealthy and addictive cravings.
- Works to increase physical energy, strength, and vitality.

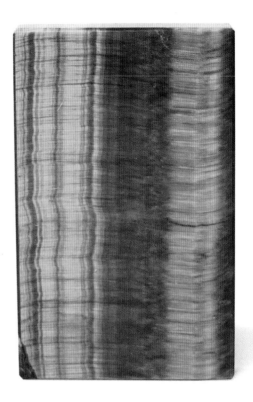

- Supports healthy adrenal glands, reproductive system, and vision.

emotional healing

- Can promote open-mindedness.
- Brings a sense of balance, harmony, and inner peace.
- Helps combat fear, worry, and depression.
- Gives you courage, especially when you're starting anything new.
- Can strengthen your personal power, self-discipline, and confidence.

Keep a tiger's eye under your pillow or on your nightstand to help alleviate nightmares and night terrors. Before you close your eyes at night, think of the things you are grateful for that happened that day.

COLORS	brown and yellow
HARDNESS	7
CHAKRAS	root and solar plexus
ZODIAC SIGNS	Aries and Capricorn
ELEMENTS	fire and earth
CRYSTAL PAIRINGS	malachite, septarian, serpentine, mookaite jasper, or charoite
PRECAUTIONS	Do not submerge tiger's eye in water. It is toxic if ingested.
AFFIRMATION	I am filled with warmth, courage, and strength.

shiva lingam

Balance | Fertility | Kundalini Energy
Awakening | Enlightenment | New Beginnings

Shiva lingam has the following spiritual, physical, and emotional healing properties.

spiritual healing

- Awakens Kundalini energy, starting at the base of the spine and spiraling upward.
- Balances feminine and masculine energies.
- Awakens the auric field, igniting the "fire" within.
- Symbolizes primeval energy of the creator, god, or higher power.
- Opens and balances all seven chakras.
- Awakens and deepens your connection to higher consciousness.

physical healing

- Can treat infertility and imbalances in the reproductive system.
- Is known to boost libido in both sexes.
- Aids in increasing physical strength and vitality.
- Helps improve overall health and well-being.

emotional healing

- Helps remove unwelcome sexual tension.
- Assists in overcoming fearful and negative thinking.
- Is a great stone for welcoming new beginnings and encouraging fresh ideas and solutions.
- Can help release negative thoughts and judgments of others.
- Can aid in opening your heart to compassion and empathy for others.

Boost your libido by keeping a shiva lingam near your bedside. You can also place it on your sacral chakra for a couple of hours when you find time in your day to relax.

COLOR	brown
HARDNESS	7
CHAKRAS	all
ZODIAC SIGNS	Scorpio, Aries, and Cancer
ELEMENTS	earth, wind, water, fire, and storm
CRYSTAL PAIRINGS	carnelian or clear quartz
PRECAUTIONS	none
AFFIRMATION	I bring balance and serenity to every aspect of my life.

copper

Optimism | Energy | Purification | Healing | Amplifier

Copper has the following spiritual, physical, and emotional healing properties.

spiritual healing

- Connects you between heaven and earth, making it perfect for amplifying your manifestations.
- Can clear out all negative energy and rebalance all seven chakras.
- Conducts and magnifies the energies surrounding it.
- Provides an energy protection shield.
- When used with other crystals, is known to amplify and purify their healing properties.
- Brings good luck and prosperity.

physical healing

- Can boost your libido, energy, stamina, and vitality.
- Aids in relieving pain from broken bones, rheumatism, and arthritis.
- Helps boost the immune system and fight off infectious diseases.

- Works to keep your body in flow, which can improve your circulation and oxygen levels.
- Can stabilize and balance blood flow in the body.
- Helps maintain overall health and wellness.

emotional healing

- Helps combat non-acceptance of yourself by bringing self-love and optimism to the surface.
- Can strengthen personal power and self-esteem.
- Helps us align with our soul purpose and true inner potential.

Copper is a great cleanser! If you are feeling under the weather, wear copper on you all day to cleanse out the negative energy and bring your body back into a healthy balance and flow.

COLOR	copper
HARDNESS	2.5–3
CHAKRA	all
ZODIAC SIGNS	Taurus and Sagittarius
ELEMENT	earth and water
CRYSTAL PAIRINGS	all
PRECAUTIONS	Do not put copper in water. It is toxic if ingested.
AFFIRMATION	I am spiritually connected to manifest anything I desire.

blue apatite

Restoration | Communication | Longevity | Psychic Awareness | Vitality

Blue apatite has the following spiritual, physical, and emotional healing properties.

spiritual healing

- Enhances psychic abilities and intuition.
- Helps clear out karma and negativity from your past and present.
- Awakens the third-eye chakra to help you dive deep into understanding your past life, Akashic records, and soul purpose.
- Stimulates lucid dreaming and astral travel.
- Deepens your meditation and raises your Kundalini energy.
- Harmonizes your yin and yang energies.

physical healing

- Helps with vertigo and dizziness by restoring the body's natural state of balance.
- Stimulates vitality, energy, and youthfulness.

- Can suppress your appetite and curb your cravings to help you lose weight.
- Supports a healthfully functioning heart.
- Supports healing of the organs and glands energetically.

emotional healing

- Promotes inner clarity, mental clarity, and self-insight.
- Works to improve overall feelings of self-worth and self-confidence.
- Helps you speak your truth with confidence in a social setting.
- Promotes a positive mind-set, especially when it comes to thoughts about your body.

If you're feeling imbalanced or experiencing vertigo, sit or lie down, close your eyes, and meditate with two blue apatite stones, one in each hand. Focus on your center of balance.

COLOR	blue
HARDNESS	5
CHAKRAS	throat and third eye
ZODIAC SIGN	Gemini
ELEMENT	wind
CRYSTAL PAIRINGS	amethyst, carnelian, lapis lazuli, citrine, or orca agate
PRECAUTIONS	Do not submerge blue apatite in water or keep it in direct sunlight for long periods of time; the color will fade.
AFFIRMATION	My body deserves love, support, and respect.

iolite

Intuition | Expansion | Insight | Meditation | Life Path

Iolite has the following spiritual, physical, and emotional healing properties.

spiritual healing

- Awakens the third-eye chakra and psychic gifts.
- Recharges and expands the auric field.
- Facilitates intuitive insight and visualization.
- Helps strengthen the energetic bond between the heart and brain, to find deep feelings of peace and joy.
- Supports deep meditation, dreaming, and visualization.

physical healing

- May help ease the pain of headaches, migraines, and eye strain.
- Stimulates the memory to prevent memory loss.
- Helps you fall asleep and stay asleep at night.
- Helps detoxify and regenerate the liver, especially damage due to alcoholism.
- Supports healthy eyes, nervous system, and respiratory system.

emotional healing

- Can calm an overactive mind to help you reach a state of meditation.
- Helps one gain emotional distance and find a clearer perspective on any life situation.
- Helps you uncover the lost part of yourself and offers you the chance to take your inner path to your deep self.
- Aids in diminishing fears of the unknown.
- Eases the need to be perfect and have control over every little thing.

If you want more intuitive guidance, meditate with iolite on your third-eye chakra. During your meditation, focus on your third-eye chakra and ask your question. You may not receive the answer right then, but this will activate your intuition to direct or guide you toward the answer.

COLOR	indigo blue
HARDNESS	7-7.5
CHAKRA	third eye
ZODIAC SIGNS	Sagittarius, Pisces, and Cancer
ELEMENTS	air and water
CRYSTAL PAIRINGS	amethyst, azurite, sodalite, super 7, sugilite, spirit quartz, sunstone, lapis lazuli, or sapphire
PRECAUTIONS	Iolite contains aluminum and can be toxic if ingested. Avoid putting it in prolonged direct sunlight, as the color may begin to fade.
AFFIRMATION	I trust in my own actions and intuition.

sodalite

Communication | Intuition | Concentration | Self-Expression | Harmony

Sodalite has the following spiritual, physical, and emotional healing properties.

spiritual healing

- Stimulates lucid dreaming.
- Provides deep spiritual insight and direction into understanding your most authentic self.
- Helps you move beyond your ego to a state of altruism.
- Enhances intuition and psychic abilities.
- Increases spiritual development and awareness.

physical healing

- Can balance blood pressure and flow.
- Aids in memory stimulation and the reduction of mental fog.
- Aids in treating any digestive disorders.
- Supports a healthy lymphatic system, immune system, and vocal cords.
- Promotes a deeper sleep and helps reduce insomnia.

emotional healing

- Works to calm the mind and balance emotions.
- Helps you release anger and trapped emotions.
- Provides mental clarity so you can speak rationally and truthfully.
- Can promote self-expression, speaking your truth, and enhanced communication.
- Increases self-esteem and self-trust.

If you are working on moving beyond your ego and into a state of altruism, meditate lying down with a sodalite on your third-eye chakra to activate higher consciousness and be guided to a greater state of love, compassion, and understanding that we are all one.

COLORS	blue and white
HARDNESS	5.5–6
CHAKRAS	throat and third eye
ZODIAC SIGNS	Virgo and Libra
ELEMENTS	earth and water
CRYSTAL PAIRINGS	iolite, lapis lazuli, blue sapphire, or scolecite
PRECAUTIONS	Avoid putting sodalite in prolonged sunlight; the color will fade.
AFFIRMATION	I am staying true to myself despite judgment from others.

lapis lazuli

Wisdom | Awareness | Deep Connection | Intuition | Goddess

Lapis lazuli has the following spiritual, physical, and emotional healing properties.

spiritual healing

- Boosts psychic abilities and intuition.
- Brings you to a higher awareness of yourself.
- Enhances visualization and deep connection during meditation.
- Helps provide you with deeper insight and answers about your past life.
- Assists in spiritual expansion, awakening, awareness, and realization of consciousness.
- Helps you learn from and understand your spiritual experiences.

physical healing

- Helps relieve insomnia, vertigo, and dizziness.
- Enhances higher cognitive thinking.
- Can reduce pain and inflammation in the body.
- Supports healthy endocrine, nervous, and immune systems.

emotional healing

- Can help you overcome depression.
- Brings inner peace, mental balance, and tranquility.
- Aids in relaxation and healthy relationships.
- Encourages mental endurance, wisdom, self-acceptance, and creativity.
- Supports emotional and mental clarity.

If you are going through a spiritual awakening, it can be an exciting experience, but you may have fears as to what your life will be like next. Go within and meditate with a lapis lazuli stone on your third eye and surrender to the universe. You will be guided in the most loving ways.

COLORS	blue, gold, and gray
HARDNESS	5–5.5
CHAKRAS	throat and third eye
ZODIAC SIGNS	Libra and Sagittarius
ELEMENT	wind
CRYSTAL PAIRINGS	blue apatite, iolite, blue chalcedony, pyrite, sugilite, larvikite, blue sapphire, or sodalite
PRECAUTIONS	Do not put lapis lazuli in water; it contains aluminum and is toxic to ingest.
AFFIRMATION	I am divinely guided and protected at all times.

kyanite

Positive Thoughts | Balance | Communication | Spiritual Guidance | Tranquility

Kyanite has the following spiritual, physical, and emotional healing properties.

spiritual healing

- Facilitates a deep meditative state.
- Harmonizes the masculine and feminine energies.
- Is highly vibrational, bringing you into greater connection with your spirit guides.
- Strengthens intuition and understanding of that "gut feeling."
- Helps bring the chakras and layers of the aura into balance.

physical healing

- Can help support the throat, muscles, and brain.
- Aids in treating conditions of the sensory organs.
- Helps you remember things more clearly by improving your memory.
- Helps one recover from a stroke, improving speech, coordination, and mobility.
- Provides overall balance for the nervous system.

emotional healing

- Is known for bringing calmness and tranquility.
- Helps release feelings of remorse and regret.
- Encourages mental stamina and positive communication.
- Helps you overcome any negative bad habits, recurring thought patterns, or addictions.
- Helps release anger, frustration, and tension in the emotional body.

If you are currently struggling with any addictions or recovering from one, keep a kyanite on you (skin contact) all day to help you overcome any recurring negative bad habits, thought patterns, or addictions. If you notice any addictive feelings or thoughts come up throughout your day, hold or rub your kyanite, focus on its healing energy, and repeat, "I am in charge of my own happiness."

COLORS	blue
HARDNESS	4.5–7
CHAKRAS	throat and third eye
ZODIAC SIGNS	Taurus, Sagittarius, Pisces, and Cancer
ELEMENTS	storm, water, and air
CRYSTAL PAIRINGS	amethyst, clear quartz, labradorite, selenite, or spirit quartz
PRECAUTIONS	Do not put kyanite in water. It contains aluminum and is a very brittle stone.
AFFIRMATION	Today, I replace old, negative habits with positive ones.

azurite

Intuition | Visionary | Clarity |
Divinity | Personal Discovery

Azurite has the following spiritual, physical, and emotional healing properties.

spiritual healing

- Stimulates your psychic ability and intuition.
- Helps you find a greater connection with your higher self.
- Works to strengthen the astral and etheric bodies, providing you protection from the negative energies of others.
- Strengthens your auric field.
- Provides a way to deepen and awaken your meditation with ease.
- Helps ignite diving deep into your past lives to promote spiritual healing.
- Is known as the "stone of heaven" and provides deep guidance to the heavenly self.

physical healing

- Helps heal all issues in the brain and head, such as headaches, vertigo, and tinnitus.
- Supports a healthy liver, thyroid, and nervous system.
- Helps clear toxins from the body.

emotional healing

- Helps you dive deep into the root cause of your greatest fears and how to seek love over fear.
- Helps you understand others' true motives instead of assuming the worst.
- Provides a gateway for deep discovery of yourself.
- Aids in breaking free of being judgmental toward others.
- Stimulates the release of limiting beliefs.

If you need spiritual guidance, meditate with azurite on your third-eye chakra to awaken your intuition, bring you clarity, and call in insightful answers.

COLOR	dark blue
HARDNESS	3.5–4
CHAKRAS	third eye and crown
ZODIAC SIGNS	Pisces, Aquarius, and Gemini
ELEMENT	wind
CRYSTAL PAIRINGS	malachite, chrysocolla, fluorite, amethyst, rainbow moonstone, scolecite, iolite, or sapphire
PRECAUTIONS	Azurite contains copper and can be toxic if ingested. Do not place it in direct sunlight; the color will begin to fade.
AFFIRMATION	I fully trust my inner guidance.

labradorite

Transformation | Intuition | Expansion | Protection | Revelation

Labradorite has the following spiritual, physical, and emotional healing properties.

spiritual healing

- Stimulates your imagination, intuition, and psychic abilities.
- Provides a protective energetic shield from negative or evil energies around you.
- Is a stone of transformation, helping you overcome obstacles to reach your destiny.
- Encourages spiritual development and awareness.
- Helps you recognize and see your inner light.

physical healing

- Can reduce high blood pressure.
- Aids in the treatment of disorders of the eyes and brain.

- Can alleviate stress and anxiety in the body.
- Can help you discover the root cause of why you may have developed a physical disease or illness.
- Helps release pain or inflammation from the body.
- Supports healthy digestion, regulation, and metabolism.

emotional healing

- Helps reduce social anxiety and impulsive behavior.
- Can help one remove and overcome fear-based thinking.
- Boosts self-confidence, imagination, harmony, and mental clarity.
- Helps you release negative thoughts about yourself that are stored in your subconscious mind.

To dispel negative or evil energies, wear labradorite jewelry (skin contact) on you daily. This will provide a protective energetic shield around you.

COLORS	gray with flashes of blue, pink, purple, green, yellow, and orange
HARDNESS	6–6.5
CHAKRAS	throat, third eye, and crown
ZODIAC SIGNS	Leo, Scorpio, and Sagittarius
ELEMENTS	water and air
CRYSTAL PAIRINGS	rainbow moonstone, black moonstone, fluorite, kyanite, clear quartz, sunstone, or larvikite
PRECAUTIONS	Labradorite contains aluminum and can be toxic if ingested.
AFFIRMATION	I welcome change and transformation into my life with open arms.

larvikite

Inner Strength | Positivity |
Greater Connection | Intuition | Peace

Larvikite has the following spiritual, physical, and emotional healing properties.

spiritual healing

- Can repel negative energy.
- Stimulates intuition and psychic abilities.
- Can refract the energies surrounding you that usually make you feel off or imbalanced.
- Connects you to your higher self.
- Helps ground and connect you to earth's healing energy.
- Increases your sense of security and inner strength.

physical healing

- Encourages youthfulness and vitality.
- Helps balance hormones.
- Helps one recover from a stroke, improving speech, brain function, and mobility.
- Assists in calming the nervous system.

- Helps initiate the cleansing and purification of the body's tissues.

emotional healing

- Can clear your mind of cluttered and unwanted thoughts.
- Works on giving you the inner strength to overcome emotional battles.
- Reduces stress or worried thinking.
- Stimulates attention to detail and focus.

A lot of times when we grow up in an unsafe environment, we look externally for safety from others. If you are currently searching for safety, look within. Meditate with a larvikite in your hand, cuddle up in a fetal position, and repeat the affirmation "It is safe to be within my body. I am safe. I am secure."

COLORS	deep blue, black, and silver
HARDNESS	6–6.5
CHAKRAS	root, throat, and third eye
ZODIAC SIGN	Aquarius
ELEMENT	earth
CRYSTAL PAIRINGS	lapis lazuli, black tourmaline, amethyst, or labradorite
PRECAUTIONS	Larvikite contains aluminum and can be toxic if ingested.
AFFIRMATION	My inner strength moves mountains.

orca agate

Inner Peace | Communication | Emotional Release | Mental Clarity | Spiritual Growth

Orca agate has the following spiritual, physical, and emotional healing properties.

spiritual healing

- Provides guidance for divine channeling work.
- Increases spiritual growth and awakening.
- Cleanses and repairs any leaks in the aura or energetic fields.
- Works to transform negative energy into positive energy.
- Helps you connect to the spiritual world and heal any past-life issues.
- Stimulates telepathic and different dimensional communication.

physical healing

- Stimulates healthy flow of the lymph nodes.
- Helps stimulate the mind and boost memory.
- Works to regulate and bring balance to the thyroid, thymus, and throat infections.
- Is a great stone for singers because it can strengthen your vocal cords.

emotional healing

- Promotes stillness, inner peace, and tranquility.
- Opens your throat chakra to let you communicate with others from a place of love.
- Helps heal inner rage and stress and provides a sense of safety.
- Can improve mental function, clarity, concentration, and perception.
- Aids in releasing self-doubt and self-loathing.

If you need help stimulating your mind and focusing your energy on a project, keep a large orca agate on your desk.

COLORS	blue and white
HARDNESS	6.5–7
CHAKRA	throat
ZODIAC SIGN	Gemini
ELEMENT	water
CRYSTAL PAIRINGS	blue apatite, blue calcite, sapphire, fluorite, or scolecite
PRECAUTIONS	none
AFFIRMATION	I speak and articulate my thoughts from the heart.

blue sapphire

Awareness | Intuition | Self-Discovery | Communication | Focus

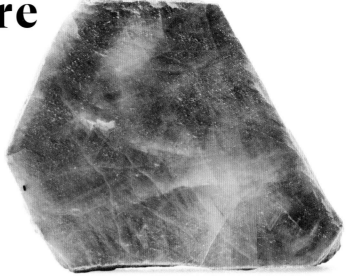

Blue sapphire has the following spiritual, physical, and emotional healing properties.

spiritual healing

- Is a great stone for meditation, bringing you into a deeper state of consciousness and awareness.
- Stimulates the lucid dream state.
- Boosts psychic abilities and intuition.
- Helps you find a greater connection with your higher self.
- Helps release negative attachments with your ego to achieve altruism.

physical healing

- Helps heal headaches, eye problems, inner ear imbalances, and vertigo.
- Can strengthen the mind, increase learning, and increase focus.
- Balances the thyroid and thymus glands.
- Helps calm the nervous system.
- Helps detoxify and purify the body, making it great for supporting weight loss.

emotional healing

- Helps you find your own voice, if you are easily persuaded.
- Activates determination, discipline, and motivation.
- Can strengthen your love life and help you let go of any insecurities you have with your significant other.
- Provides a gateway for deep discovery of yourself.
- Helps improve mental clarity, strength, and focus.

To stimulate your intuition or psychic abilities, meditate with a blue sapphire on your third-eye chakra. During your meditation, focus on your third-eye chakra and ask any questions you may have. You may not receive the answer right then, but this will activate your intuition and psychic abilities to direct or guide you toward the answer.

COLORS	blue
HARDNESS	9
CHAKRAS	throat and third eye
ZODIAC SIGN	Capricorn, Aquarius, and Virgo
ELEMENT	wind and earth
CRYSTAL PAIRINGS	orca agate, ruby, lapis lazuli, iolite, azurite, or sodalite
PRECAUTIONS	Blue sapphire contains aluminum and can be toxic if ingested. It is sensitive to sunlight and intense temperature changes.
AFFIRMATION	I am constantly speaking my truth.

opal

Beauty | Imagination | Emotional Release | Angels | Good Luck

Opal has the following spiritual, physical, and emotional healing properties.

spiritual healing

- Instills the aura with a frequency of joy.
- Enhances imagination and creativity.
- Balances and aligns all seven chakras.
- Expands your life force and angelic connection.
- Is known to bring good luck and fortune.
- Helps you embrace change with open arms.

physical healing

- Helps provide relief from skin disorders such as eczema, psoriasis, and rosacea.
- Can bring the kidneys back into healthy alignment.
- Aids in strengthening your hair, nails, and skin.
- Supports a healthy female reproductive system.

emotional healing

- Promotes beauty, inside and out.
- Helps you release your anger, fears, self-doubt, wounds, and negativity.
- Helps you become more positive and loving.
- Allows you to release what no longer serves you, so you can begin your emotional healing.
- Helps restore emotional balance and stability.

To expand your aura and fill it with the frequencies of love, use your opal to trace your entire aura. Then wear your opal, preferably as jewelry for skin contact, to keep your aura abundant and full.

COLOR	rainbow
HARDNESS	5.5–6.5
CHAKRA	all
ZODIAC SIGNS	Virgo, Scorpio, and Libra
ELEMENTS	water and air
CRYSTAL PAIRINGS	herkimer diamond, citrine, opal, rainbow moonstone, or lemurian
PRECAUTIONS	Most opals have a high water content, so exposure to bright light for extended periods can cause breakage or cracks. Most opals need to be submerged in water so they don't crack.
AFFIRMATION	I allow my emotional healing to begin.

rainbow obsidian

From Darkness to Light | Protection | Happiness | Enjoyment | Release

Rainbow obsidian has the following spiritual, physical, and emotional healing properties.

spiritual healing

- Allows one to see the light in a dark tunnel.
- Can turn around bad fortune.
- Is great for empaths, shielding you from negative energy and releasing energy that's not yours.
- Cleanses and balances all seven chakras.
- Surrenders you to accepting light in the midst of darkness.
- Stimulates intuition and psychic abilities.

physical healing

- Can provide pain relief.
- Aids in rejuvenating the bones and tissue in the body.
- Can help one discover the root cause of a physical disease or illness.
- Aids in strengthening and supporting a healthy heart.
- Can improve circulation and healthy blood flow.

emotional healing

- Helps those suffering from depression and paralyzing fears.
- Brings love, happiness, joy, hope, optimism, and light into one's life.
- Works to clear the emotional body of any blockages from past trauma.
- Creates a burning desire to enjoy life to the fullest.

If you need to find guidance in a dark place (depression, emotional trauma, grief, etc.), meditate lying down with rainbow obsidian touching your crown chakra. Release your need to know the answer and be present in the moment; your spirit guides will guide you to the light.

COLORS	black, shining rainbow
HARDNESS	5-6
CHAKRAS	root and solar plexus
ZODIAC SIGNS	Libra and Cancer
ELEMENT	earth
CRYSTAL PAIRINGS	gold sheen obsidian, black onyx, or rainbow moonstone
PRECAUTIONS	none
AFFIRMATION	Energy freely flows through my energy centers.

8 | pairing crystals using intentions

IF YOU'RE ANYTHING LIKE I was when first starting out with crystals, you have a whole list of physical, mental, emotional, and spiritual imbalances that you are ready to change. I remember thinking, "Well if I wear lepidolite for my anxiety, moldavite for transformation, sunstone for my depression, kunzite to calm my nervous system, rose quartz to love myself unconditionally, citrine for my stomach issues, and carnelian for a midday pick-me-up, I will feel awesome!" I understand, we want to change everything at once because we are so tired of feeling sick and know it's not who we are anymore. It's important to take one step at a time and enjoy the process along the way. Instead of overwhelming your energy with so many things you want to change, choose one intention at a time. For instance, if you want to work on increasing your overall energy and vitality, you'll want to use the right intentions along with the right crystal pairings. Such as: carnelian and shungite. When you use your crystals in proper pairs, you enhance, amplify, and speed up your body's response to intentional change. Each suggested crystal pairing in this chapter has worked for me, my loved ones, and thousands of my clients. However, what works for most people may not work for you. All our energies are different. As you learn more and practice connecting with your crystals intuitively, you may find that unexpected crystal pairs work for you, and that's completely fine! Please listen to what's best for your body—these pairings are a guide, not an ultimatum.

intention: **ANXIETY RELIEF**
Pairing: Lepidolite (to calm the nervous system) and hematite (to help you feel safe, present, and grounded)

intention: **PAIN RELIEF**
Pairing: Black tourmaline (for pulling out stuck energy) and amber (for pain relief)

intention: **WEIGHT LOSS**
Pairing: Blue apatite (to curb cravings) and carnelian (to boost motivation and energy)

intention: **ACCELERATING HEALING AFTER AN INJURY**
Pairing: Lemurian (to accelerate the body's natural healing process) and celestite (to ease pain and minimize inflammation in the body)

intention: **STRESS RELIEF**
Pairing: Blue lace agate (for calming and instilling peaceful thoughts) and smoky quartz (for removing excess negative energy)

intention: **FERTILITY**
Pairing: Carnelian (to boost fertility) and shiva lingam (to help remove sexual tension or stuck energy in the sacral chakra)

intention: **PREGNANCY BOND WITH BABY**
Pairing: Rose quartz (to increase feelings of unconditional love, support, gratitude, and connection with the baby) and rhodochrosite (to help release your childhood traumas and fears about childbirth)

intention: **BOOSTING LIBIDO**
Pairing: Carnelian (to boosts libido, passion, vitality, and motivation) and ruby (to bring joy in your sexual relationship)

intention: **SLEEP**
Pairing: Lepidolite (to bring peace and harmony to the parasympathetic nervous system) and

angelite (to calm the mind due to anxiousness or overthinking)
Pairing: Rose quartz (to soothe the body and re-establish the circadian rhythm, allowing you to fall asleep again at night) and kyanite (to release any negative thoughts)

intention: **LESSENING THE SYMPTOMS OF PREMENSTRUAL SYNDROME (PMS)**
Pairing: Rainbow moonstone (to calm the ovaries and any PMS symptoms) and hematite (to release any negative energy tied to the sacral chakra or idea of menstruation)

intention: **IMMUNE SYSTEM BALANCE**
Pairing: Mookaite jasper (to support a healthy immune system) and orange calcite (to strengthen the immune system)

intention: **HORMONAL BALANCE**
Pairing: Orange calcite (to help bring your hormones back into balance) and chrysocolla (to promote inner peace)
Pairing: Pink amethyst (to assist in the production of healthy hormones) and amazonite (to help boost hair follicles and nail growth lost during hormonal changes)

intention: **ENERGY AND VITALITY**
Pairing: Carnelian (for boosting energy, vitality, and endurance) and shungite (for releasing any stuck energy that is making you feel lethargic)

intention: **MIGRAINE RELIEF**
Pairing: Amethyst (to release any stuck energy causing the pain) and celestite (to relax the body and relieve discomfort)

intention: **DECREASE STOMACH INFLAMMATION**
Pairing: Citrine (to balance the digestive system) and celestite (to minimize inflammation in the body)

for mental and emotional healing

intention: **UNCONDITIONAL LOVE**
Pairing: Rose quartz (to promote feelings of unconditional love toward yourself and others) and garnet (to help with emotional stability and increasing one's ability to feel love)

intention: **SELF-LOVE**
Pairing: Rose quartz (to bathe you in unconditional love toward yourself) and morganite (to help you recognize and heal old emotional patterns of judgment, fear, self-hatred, and manipulation)

intention: **PEACE AND HARMONY**
Pairing: Blue lace agate (to bathe you in feelings of peace) and hematite (to keep you grounded)

intention: **OVERCOMING OVERWHELMING EMOTIONS**
Pairing: Blue calcite (for bringing in the vibrations of peace, serenity, and tranquility) and black tourmaline (for releasing excess overwhelming energy to bring you back into balance and the present moment)

intention: **COPING WITH GRIEF AND LOSS**
Pairing: Eudialyte (to provide a blanket of love and acceptance) and black obsidian (to release the idea of what could've been)
Pairing: Morganite (to bring feelings of peace, support, and love) and rose quartz (to help you overcome the heartache and pain)

intention: **JOY AND HAPPINESS**
Pairing: Eudialyte (to lift your mood) and sunstone (to provide support for you to achieve happiness or joy)
Pairing: Black obsidian (for acceptance of what is) and ocean jasper (to bring in feelings of pure joy, happiness, and gratitude)

intention: **BOOSTING SELF-CONFIDENCE**
Pairing: Citrine (to boost self-confidence) and rose quartz (to bathe you in unconditional love and acceptance for exactly who you are)

intention: **POSITIVE RELATIONSHIPS**
Pairing: Amazonite (to help you speak your truth and understand the other person's feelings) and pink opal (to open the heart to love, trust, and compassion in a relationship)

intention: **OVERCOMING ADDICTION**
Pairing: Amethyst (to help you overcome your addiction) and kyanite (to help you get through the recovery from addictions and negative thought patterns)
Pairing: Rhodochrosite (to help release any trauma that sparked your addiction) and rose quartz (to increase the unconditional love, kindness, and compassion toward yourself throughout the recovery process)

intention: **REDUCING ANGER**
Pairing: Lepidolite (to replace anger with peaceful thoughts) and smoky quartz (to release trapped energy that has been built up over time)

intention: **COMPASSION**
Pairing: Emerald (for stimulating feelings of empathy, sympathy, and kindness) and epidote (for opening your mind and heart to listening to others from a place of unconditional love)

intention: **FORGIVING OTHERS**
Pairing: Rhodochrosite (for allowing you to forgive others by opening your heart) and sugilite (for igniting deep healing that needs to be done in order to forgive others)

intention: **FOCUS AND CONCENTRATION**
Pairing: Fluorite (to boost concentration, learning, and memory) and blue sapphire (to strengthen the mind and focus)

intention: **POSITIVE THOUGHTS**
Pairing: Unakite jasper (to release negative energy and thoughts) and blue apatite (to promote a positive mind-set)
Pairing: Kyanite (to help release negative thought patterns) and charoite (to encourage a positive outlook on any situation)

intention: **SPEAKING YOUR TRUTH**
Pairing: Aquamarine (for helping you feel empowered and courageous enough to speak your truth) and chrysocolla (for allowing you to communicate from the heart)

intention: **FEELING WORTHY**
Pairing: Garnierite (for expanding the love you have for yourself) and citrine (for appreciation and respect for your own value)

intention: **RELEASING FEARS**
Pairing: Gold sheen obsidian (to assist you in diving deep into releasing and conquering your deepest, darkest fears) and kunzite (to open your heart back up to experiencing life with a new perspective of joy and love)

intention: **SETTING BOUNDARIES**
Pairing: Libyan desert glass (for helping you set boundaries with others to form the ultimate love for yourself) and sunstone (for enhancing support, guidance, and awareness to help you set boundaries with others)

crystal pairings

for spiritual healing and growth

intention: **BOOSTING INTUITION**
Pairing: Amethyst (to boost psychic abilities and intuition) and iolite (to facilitate intuitive insight and visualization)

intention: **EMPATH PROTECTION AND REFILL**
Pairing: Black obsidian (to provide an energetic shield of protection and release any negative energy you may have taken on from others) and scolecite (to recharge your energy after it has been drained by others)

intention: **ANGELIC GUIDANCE**
Pairing: Angelite (to help you connect with and receive answers from your angels) and kunzite (to open your heart to divine love and light)

intention: **AURA CLEARING AND REFILLING**
Pairing: Smoky quartz (to cleanse the aura of any blockages) and azurite (to strengthen and refill your aura)

intention: **ATTRACTING ABUNDANCE**
Pairing: Citrine (to strengthen your ability to manifest and attract abundance into your life) and emerald (to stimulate your ability to receive abundance from the universe)
Pairing: Gold sheen obsidian (to release any limiting beliefs you may have around whether you can have abundance) and green tourmaline (to attract abundance into your life)

intention: **BOOSTING CREATIVITY AND IMAGINATION**

Pairing: Carnelian (to stimulate new perceptions, creativity, and ideas) and labradorite (to promote psychic imagination and connection)

intention: **SPIRITUAL PROTECTION**

Pairing: Black onyx (for protection from negative energy) and serpentine (for an energetic protection field in your aura so toxic energies don't seep into it)

intention: **GROUNDING**

Pairing: Hematite (for grounding you in the physical world) and fire agate (for helping put your mind, body, and soul back into alignment)

intention: **SPIRITUAL AWAKENING**

Pairing: Sugilite (to open your third-eye and crown chakras to greater awareness and consciousness) and clear quartz (to enhance your spiritual connection)

intention: **SPEEDING UP YOUR MANIFESTATIONS**

Pairing: Moldavite (to speed up manifestations and raise your vibrations quickly) and herkimer diamond (to amplify all energies, crystals, and intentions)

intention: **DEEPENING MEDITATION**

Pairing: Howlite (to deepen meditation) and iolite (to calm an overactive mind to reach a state of meditation)

other
crystal pairings

intention: **ATTRACTING MORE WEALTH**

Pairing: Pyrite (to increase wealth, luck, and abundance) and gold sheen obsidian (to release any limiting beliefs around whether you can have wealth in abundance)

Pairing: Herkimer diamond (for amplifying all energies, crystals, and intentions) and citrine (for powerfully manifesting wealth and abundance)

intention: **TRAVEL PROTECTION**

Pairing: Aquamarine (to calm the mind and bring protection when traveling) and rainbow moonstone (to offer protection when traveling)

intention: **FINDING A BETTER JOB**

Pairing: Moldavite (to boost the speed of finding a job) and kyanite (for strengthening your intuition to guide you to the best job)

9 | crystal healing for animals

I **AM PARTICULARLY** passionate about crystal healing for animals because I have three dogs of my own who mean the entire world to me. Pets cannot verbally tell us what is going on, but crystal healing can give us a greater insight as to what it is.

One of my dogs, Ruger, is a German shorthaired pointer who suffers from extreme anxiety. We tried every pill in the book and nothing worked for him. Every veterinarian told us it was the worst case of anxiety they had ever seen, and that there was nothing else they could do. So I began to explore using crystals on Ruger. I made sure to cleanse, charge, and set my intentions before initiating the crystal healing process. I placed two lepidolite palm stones on his temples and held them there. I wasn't exactly sure what I was doing at the time, but it was worth a try. Within a couple of minutes, Ruger stopped trembling and fell into a peaceful sleep.

Animals are a great reminder of how connected we are to energy and how crystal healing can help put our energy centers back into alignment.

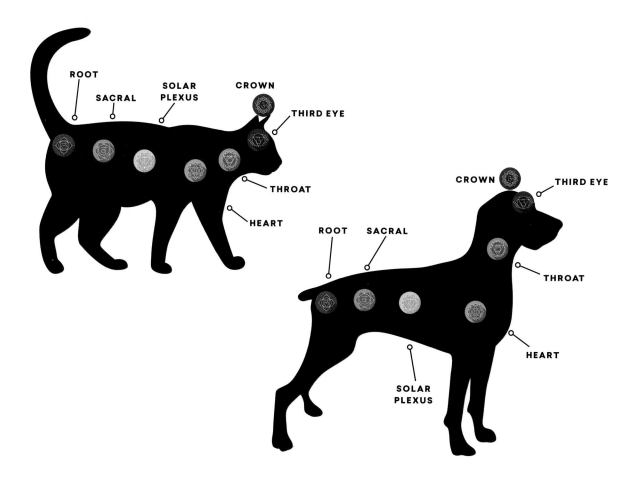

animals chakras

Just like humans, animals have seven chakras. Chakras are the seven major energy centers that spiral up the spine. Each chakra consists of the physical piece of the anatomy as well as emotional and spiritual well-being.

Animals have different body shapes than us, so their chakras are in slightly different areas. Their chakras start at the tip of their tail and go up to the tip of their nose.

Animal chakra locations:

- **Root chakra**: where the tail meets the body
- **Sacral chakra**: waist and pubic area
- **Solar plexus chakra**: at the midpoint of body, stomach, and back
- **Heart chakra**: the heart and in between the shoulder blades
- **Throat chakra**: center of the neck in the front and back body
- **Third-eye chakra**: center of the forehead, in between the eyebrows
- **Crown chakra**: top of the head

When animal chakras are in a healthy alignment, they are 3 to 4 inches (7.5 to 10 cm) in diameter, starting from the physical body and extending into the auric field (the energy field that surrounds your physical body).

understanding which chakras are

overactive, underactive, or balanced

Physical symptoms and illnesses can begin to arise when one or more chakras are out of alignment for a time. Fortunately, one of the most common ways to get your pet's chakras back into balance is to use crystal healing. We can start by checking the energy of each chakra by using a crystal pendulum or scanning the energy with your hands.

crystal pendulum method

1. Cleanse and charge the crystal in your pendulum. (See page 197 for more on pendulums.) Place a journal next to you so you can write down notes.

2. Hold the pendulum chain between your thumb and pointer finger.

3. Start at your animal's root chakra and ask the pendulum to show you whether the chakra is overactive, underactive, blocked, or balanced. Take note of the pendulum's movements for the answer.
   Overactive: chaotic motion
   Underactive: counterclockwise or side to side motion
   Blocked: no motion
   Balanced: clockwise or front to back motion

4. Repeat for each chakra, moving from the root chakra up to the crown chakra. Write down your observations from the pendulum's answers.

The pendulum method is the best method for getting the most accurate and direct answers.

energy scan method

1. Place a journal next to you so you can write down notes. Begin by firmly rubbing your palms together for 30 seconds to a minute, or until you feel a sense of heat rising.

2. Gently pull your hands apart and place them either hovering around or touching your animal's crown chakra.

3. Ask for verbal or energetic feedback on whether the chakra is overactive, underactive, blocked, or balanced. Take note of the energy senses for the answer.
   Overactive: extreme heat or chaotic energy
   Underactive: cold or empty energy
   Blocked: heavy, dense, or sticky energy
   Balanced: smooth and peaceful energy

4. Repeat for each chakra, moving from the crown chakra down to the root chakra. Write down your observations from the channeled guidance.

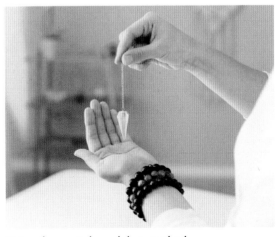

Using the crystal pendulum method

how to perform
a healing session

1. Before you begin any crystal healing session on your fur baby, cleanse and charge your crystals, your space, and yourself.

2. Make sure your animal is in a place where they feel safe and comfortable. Consider turning on meditation music to relax them before your session.

3. You can ask your animal to choose the crystals, choose the crystals that you feel intuitively called to for them, or choose from the crystal remedy recommendations below.

4. Set your intentions with the crystal(s).

5. Gently place the crystals in the direct area of the desired healing. You can put your hands on top of the crystals to keep them in place and let your animal know that what you're doing is safe.

6. Animals are more sensitive to crystal healing than we are. Therefore, they don't need the same amount of time with crystal healing as we do. I would recommend 10 to 15 minutes maximum.

7. Once your animal signals that they are done, gently take off each crystal, one by one.

8. Signs the crystal healing session is done: The crystal consistently falls off your animal. The energy flow seems to have stopped. The animal starts moving and getting uncomfortable.

Important: Watch your animal throughout the entire session because some may think a crystal is a toy and try to lick, bite, play with, or even ingest it. Crystals shouldn't be ingested like food and can be very toxic for your animal if they are.

Place amethyst in your home to promote peace, comfort, and protection for your pets

remedies

pain relief

Crystals:
- 1 amber (to decrease pain)
- 1 lepidolite (to promote peace)
- 2 clear quartz points (to simultaneously release and restore any stuck energy)

Place the amber directly on the area in pain, the lepidolite on your animal's third-eye chakra, one clear quartz point directed toward the area of pain, and the other point directly opposite from the first, pointing outward from the body.

weight loss

Crystals:
- 2 carnelian (to boost energy, stamina, motivation, and vitality)
- 1 blue apatite (to help your animal feel full and aid in healthy weight loss)

Place the carnelian on the front and back side of your animal's body on the sacral chakra and the blue apatite in between their eyebrows on their third-eye chakra.

arthritis

Crystals:
- 1 rhodochrosite (for joint health)
- 1 amber, possibly more depending on the severity of your animal's arthritis (for pain relief)
- 1 smoky quartz (to release any stuck energy)

Place the amber on the area where your pet appears to be in arthritic pain. For instance, if the pain is in their knees, then you will want to place an amber on each knee. Place the rhodochrosite in the center of their heart chakra and the smoky

quartz where the tail meets the body on the root chakra.

anxiety and stress relief

Crystals:
- 1 lepidolite (to decrease anxiousness and restore the body back into balance)
- 1 black tourmaline (to give your animal a sense of safety and security)
- 1 blue lace agate (to bring in peaceful thoughts)

Place the lepidolite on your animal's third-eye chakra, black tourmaline where the tail meets the body on the root chakra, and blue lace agate on the throat chakra on the back side of their body.

aura clearing

Crystal:
- 1 selenite wand (to cleanse the aura of any stuck, negative, or stagnant energies)

Hold the selenite wand parallel to and a few inches above your animal's body. Start at the crown chakra and move down to the root chakra. Take note of any changes that the selenite wand makes or feels; this will indicate areas where the energy was cleared.

stomach relief

Crystals:
- 1 citrine (to help heal the digestive tract)
- 1 aquamarine (to calm an upset stomach)
- 1 blue apatite (to regulate the appetite)

Place the citrine on your animal's belly, the aquamarine on their throat chakra on the front side of their body, and the blue apatite on their third-eye chakra.

boosting energy and vitality

Crystals:
- 2 carnelian (to boost energy, motivation, stamina, and vitality)
- 1 green aventurine (to rejuvenate the body)

Place the carnelian on your animal's front and back body on the sacral chakra and the green aventurine on their heart.

dental problems

Crystals:
- 1 blue calcite (to strengthen the teeth)
- 1 orange calcite (to promote healthy gums)
- 1 howlite (to strengthen the teeth)

Place the orange calcite on the back side of your animal's body in line with the sacral chakra, the blue calcite on their throat chakra on the front side of their body, and the howlite on their crown chakra on top of their head.

releasing anger

Crystals:
- 1 rose quartz (to encourage cooperation)
- 1 blue lace agate (to calm the mind)
- 1 black onyx (to release anger)

Place the black onyx on your animal's root chakra, the blue lace agate on their throat chakra on the front of their body, and the rose quartz on their heart.

bone strength

Crystals:
- 1 rainbow obsidian (to rejuvenate the bones and tissues)
- 1 septarian (to strengthen the bones)
- 2 angelite (to support strong bones)

Place the rainbow obsidian on your animal's root chakra, the septarian on their heart, and the angelite on the front and back of their throat chakra.

chakra balance

Crystals:
- 1 red jasper (for root chakra balance)
- 1 orange calcite (for sacral chakra balance)
- 1 citrine (for solar plexus chakra balance)
- 1 rose quartz (for heart chakra balance)
- 1 angelite (for throat chakra balance)
- 1 lepidolite (for third-eye chakra balance)
- 1 howlite (for crown chakra balance)

Place each crystal on your animal's corresponding chakra.

unconditional love

Crystals:
- 6 rose quartz (boosts feelings of unconditional love)

Place all six rose quartz around your animal's aura, 1 to 2 inches (2.5 to 5 cm) away from their body: one at the top of their head, one at their tail, and two spaced evenly on each side of their body.

crystal grids
for animal healing

Crystal grids are a great option for crystal healing work, especially if your animal is squirmy, highly energetic, or has a hard time sitting still. You can also use crystal grids to activate long-distance healing on an animal who may be struggling and lives with your family, friends, or loved ones.

Here's how to set up and activate a crystal grid:

1. Start with an intention.

2. Pick a grid or crystal base that best suits what your intentions are. (See page 36.)

3. Place a picture of your animal or some form of representation of your animal in the center of your grid.

4. Choose a central stone that aligns with your overall purpose and place it on top of the representation you chose for your animal.

5. Pick and place all your supporting stones to further support your intentions.

6. If you like, add any other elements that may enhance your intentions, such as copper, a pyramid, photos, affirmations, or flowers.

7. Activate the crystal grid.

You can keep this grid activated for as long as you desire, but I recommend a minimum of 24 hours. See chapter 4 for more guidance on intentions, grid setting, or numerology for your crystal grid.

10 | using crystals with intention & intuition

what works for you may not work for others

EVERYTHING THAT **I** have taught you about crystals is a guide, but your greatest guide is the one within. When you learn to tune into that guide, *intuition*, you will know exactly which crystals will put your body back into alignment without ever looking up their meanings. Think about it like this: Have you ever been in a crystal shop and found yourself drawn to a particular stone? You may look up the properties and think, "Wow, that is exactly what I needed!" This is your intuition guiding you.

In this chapter, I want you to get to know your intuition on a deeper level. By awakening it, you will be able to understand when and where your energy is off, which crystals you need, and where you should place them.

intuitive are you?

There are several different ways your intuition may speak to you. Think about your experiences as you read the following descriptions. Do any of them resonate with you?

clairvoyant
someone who has clear seeing

You notice people's aura or energy field, visualize dreams and goals easily, are a vivid dreamer, prefer to see things than discuss or read about them, and are imaginative and creative.

claircognizant
someone who has clear knowing

You get external confirmation of intuitively knowing the answer, experience déjà vu, have answers come easily to you without having context, feel spontaneous, pick up skills easily, and are full of endless ideas and possibilities.

clairaudient
someone who has clear hearing

You can hear things no one else can, prefer to listen than discuss or read about things, hear buzzing or ringing in your ears, love music, can communicate with animals, provide comfort to others, and converse with yourself.

clairalient
someone who has clear smelling

You smell spirits when someone passes away, smell things that no one else does, enjoy fragrance, and use your sense to tell how someone is feeling.

clairgustant
someone who has clear taste

You experience the sensation of taste without anything entering your mouth, taste things that remind you of loved ones who have passed, receive communication from angels or spirit guides from taste, and love cooking or taste-testing different foods.

clairsentient
someone who has clear feeling

You are sensitive to your environment and energy around you, get goosebumps for no reason, sense others' intentions, struggle to buy old things because of the energy residue left behind, recharge during alone time, prefer to experience things rather than discuss or read about them, and have gut feelings.

Personally, I am claircognizant and clairsentient. I use these gifts to help me further understand what my physical, emotional, or spiritual body needs in terms of healing. I further my gift by allowing my intuition to guide me on which crystals are needed to put my body back into alignment. If this information is new to you, it will take some practice to understand your gift. We all have a gift, and it's time you honor and listen to yours!

tuning in

Tuning in is the first step to understanding your energy, the crystals' energy, and how to strengthen your intuition.

how to tune into your energy

1. Keep a journal next to you. Begin by quickly and firmly rubbing your palms together for 20 to 30 seconds, or until you feel a sense of heat rising.

2. Slowly pull your hands apart 6 to 8 inches (15 to 20 cm), with your palms facing one another. Make sure your gaze is at your hands the entire time, but you can close your eyes if you want to.

3. Slowly close your hands back together.

4. Repeat, keeping this motion going.

5. Write down your observations from the energy you felt. Did it feel expansive, magnetic, blocked, static, or light?

how to tune into your crystals' energy

1. Keep a journal next you. Begin by holding a clear quartz point between the palms of your hands.

2. Rub the clear quartz firmly for 20 to 30 seconds, or until you feel a sense of heat rising.

3. Once you have stopped, keep the clear quartz in between your hands.

4. Close your eyes and gaze at your hands.

5. Observe the energy and sensations you feel coming from the clear quartz.

6. Write down your observations from the energy you felt. Did it feel expansive, heightened, blocked, stagnant, or light? Clear quartz amplifies your energy, so you may notice a completely different sensation than you did in the previous exercise.

strengthening your intuition

You can use your intuition as a guide for which crystals are best for you or even a loved one. Here are seven ways to strengthen your intuition.

meditation or breathwork

Spend at least 11 minutes of your day in a quiet space alone. Our intuition is heard the loudest when we go within. You can enhance this alone time with breathwork exercises and meditation.

connect with mother nature

Take at least 10 minutes out of every day to spend time in nature, perhaps walking barefoot or even hugging a tree. Nature helps you connect to your energy and guides, grounds you, quiets the mind, and calms the nervous system. When you can become present in the moment, you are strengthening that little voice inside of you, *your intuition*.

use oracle cards

Oracle cards can provide guidance and clarity when you are trying to understand what your intuition is telling you. They help you strengthen your intuition by giving you confirmation of what you already know.

yoga

Yoga connects us with our body through postures, calms our mind through meditation, and provides connection to our mind, body, and soul through controlled breathing. When we can let go of all outer world distractions and go within, we are strengthening our intuition.

reiki or any energy work

Reiki or any other kind of energy work draws universal energy from the source to promote overall well-being. This is a fantastic method for improving your intuition by connecting to your inner guidance, whether you are a Reiki energy healer or receiving a session.

ignite your creativity or imagination

When you constantly obsess over the need to control everything that happens in your life, you restrict the energy of flow. By engaging in creative and imaginative activities such as painting, writing, daydreaming, or journaling, you are strengthening your intuition by allowing yourself to be in the present moment and in flow instead of structure.

feel more into your body

One of the best ways to tell whether you are receiving a message from your intuition is to determine whether it's coming from a place of love. Intuitive guidance is never fear-based; that is only your mind making up an illusion of what it believes it needs for protection or to be safe. Intuition is a feeling solely based in love. When you go within and listen to what your body wants or needs from a place of love, you are strengthening your intuition.

understanding when your energy
is out of alignment

When our energy centers (chakras, meridians, and aura) are out of harmony for a time, physical symptoms, illnesses, or diseases may arise. Crystal healing is one of the best methods for restoring energy balance. Before you begin our crystal healing session, it's important to first understand where your energy is out of alignment. You can do so using a pendulum, an energy scan, muscle testing, or an aura scan.

crystal pendulum method

A pendulum is a weighted object, typically a crystal, that is hung from a single chain or cord. It is a spiritual tool that is used to help you tune into your intuition and find guided answers to specific questions or concerns you may have. Here's how to use one.

1. Keep a journal next to you. Before you begin, make sure you cleanse and charge your crystal pendulum.

2. Hold the pendulum chain between your thumb and pointer finger.

3. Start at your root chakra and ask the pendulum to show you whether the chakra is overactive, underactive, blocked, or balanced. You can also use a pendulum mat that has the seven chakras on it as a representation of your own. Take note of the following pendulum movements:
   Overactive: chaotic motion
   Underactive: counterclockwise
   Blocked: no motion
   Balanced: clockwise or front to back motion

4. Repeat for each chakra, going from the root chakra up to the crown chakra.

5. Write down your observations from the pendulum's answers.

If you want to use this method to receive a yes or no answer about your energy, you can use a pendulum chart or mat that has a predefined area representing the topics you want answers to or just a simple yes or no mat. The pendulum will swing front to back if the answer is yes or side to side if the answer is no.

Sometimes your thoughts and intentions have the power to influence the movement of the pendulum. To be sure, repeat this step three times. You can also have a loved one do a pendulum reading for you for even more confirmation.

This is the best method for getting the most accurate and direct answers.

energy scan method

1. Keep a journal next to you. Begin by firmly rubbing your palms together for 20 to 30 seconds, or until you feel a sense of heat rising.

2. Gently pull your hands apart and place them either hovering around or touching your crown chakra.

3. Close your eyes and ask for energetic feedback on whether the chakra is overactive, underactive, blocked, or balanced.
   Overactive: extreme heat or chaotic energy
   Underactive: cold or empty energy
   Blocked: heavy, dense, or sticky energy
   Balanced: smooth and peaceful energy

4. Repeat for each chakra, going from the crown chakra down to the root chakra.

5. Write down your observations from the channeled guidance.

Everyone feels energy differently, so this may vary slightly for you and your readings of your energy. Through practice, you will get to understand your energy and intuition on a deeper level, and you will begin to understand the sensations you feel when your, a loved one's, or your crystals' energy is out of balance.

muscle testing method

1. Stand straight up with your feet shoulder-width apart and your hands by your sides.

2. Take a few moments to go within, breathe, and ground yourself. This will allow you to tap into your subconscious mind.

3. Once you feel aligned, ask your body to show you yes. Typically, you will sway slightly forward.

4. Then ask your body to show you no. Typically, you will sway slightly backward.

5. To be sure you are getting accurate answers before you begin, ask yourself to show you love and then ask yourself to show you hate. If you sway forward for yes, you will sway forward when you feel love. If you sway backward for no, you will sway backward for hate.

6. Now you can ask yourself specific questions and get answers from your subconscious mind. If you don't know where to begin, start with the chakras. "Is my root chakra out of balance?" Then continue these questions all the way to your crown chakra.

You can ask as specific or generic question as you want. Your subconscious mind never lies. Just make sure you're not giving yourself false positive results by consciously swaying forward or backward. Allow your subconscious mind to take over. You can have someone else ask you the questions, to keep yourself in a deeper conscious state of mind.

aura scanning method

1. Keep a journal nearby, if you would like. Start by getting into a meditative state; this may take a couple of minutes.

2. Quickly and firmly rub your palms together for 20 to 30 seconds, or until you feel a sense of heat rising.

3. Begin your aura scan by placing the palms of your hands 2 to 3 inches (5 to 7.5 cm) away, facing your body.

4. Start above the crown chakra at the top of your head and work all the way to your root chakra below the bottom of your feet.

surprise crystal choices

Crystals don't always have to go on the exact chakra that is recommended. Sometimes you may be guided to place a rose quartz on your root chakra, for example. This is because your energies are trying to go back into alignment. Or, if you have an overactive root chakra, you may be intuitively guided to place a blue lace agate and a black tourmaline at your root chakra. I cannot tell you how many times I have come out of a session with my energy healer, Lisa Toney, to find that she had felt intuitively called to place a crystal in an atypical spot on my body. Next time you are doing a crystal layout or meditation, ask your intuition to guide you to where to put your crystal. It may surprise you.

5. Spend about 30 seconds to a minute in each chakra.

6. As you move down the body, make mental notes or write down any points in the energy field where you felt a sense of disruption or blockage in the flow of energy.

You can also do this scan using a selenite wand. The selenite wand will not only help detect energy disruptions or blockages, but it will also protect and clear out your auric field.

Understanding your energy is a very important part of crystal healing. Once you start adding crystals to your energy field, you will have a deeper understanding and intuitive sense of how each crystal is affecting your energy. It will help you decide whether you need to add more crystals, take away certain crystals, or end your crystal healing session.

Understanding your energy is one of the greatest forms of self-love. At the end of the day, only you can heal yourself. You are in charge of everything you do, feel, and say. By tuning into your energy frequently, you will be able to discover yourself on such a deep level and begin uncovering deep healing that needs to be done.

how to tell which
crystal is right for you

As I mentioned at the beginning of this chapter, everything that I have taught you about crystals is only a guide, but your greatest guide is the one within. You can know the exact crystal(s) you need to use solely based on your intuition. All the remedies I have given you in this book are just guides to begin your journey. They have worked amazingly for me and my clients, but that doesn't necessarily mean they are the perfect layout or crystal that you need. Here is a great way to let your intuition guide you to which crystal(s) you want to carry with you, meditate with, create a crystal grid for, or use in another way.

Intuitive guidance for choosing your crystals:

1. Cleanse and charge all your crystals.

2. Lay them all out in front of you.

3. Ground yourself and get into a meditative state; this may take a couple of minutes.

4. Quickly and firmly rub your palms together for 20 to 30 seconds, or until you feel a sense of heat rising.

5. Scan your crystals by placing the palms of your hands 1 to 2 inches (2.5 to 5 cm) away from the crystals, facing them.

6. Allow your intuition to lead you to the crystals whose energy you are drawn to. You can do this with your eyes opened or closed.

7. Pick as many crystals as you feel called to. You may feel a tingling sensation, warmth, or a guided yes to know which crystals are meant for you that day.

8. If you don't know each crystal's benefits just yet, this is a fun way to learn; you can come back to this book, check the healing properties of your chosen crystal, and see how on point your intuition was.

11 crystal healing remedies

physical, mental, emotional, spiritual, and other remedies using crystal layouts or crystals pairs

I HAVE ALWAYS BEEN highly intuitive and energy sensitive, but it wasn't until I went deep into my crystal healing journey that I began to understand my overall well-being on a deeper level. I want you to be able to do the same. There are many ways to use crystals. This chapter includes some exact remedies that I have noticed for physical, mental, emotional, and spiritual imbalances.

For best results, make sure that the crystal you use is in contact with the skin. If this is not an option, placing the crystals on top of your clothes or a blanket works as well. Make sure that your crystal is fully cleansed and charged—you don't want any lingering negative energy from a past usage or someone else. If you have several imbalances that you'd like to work on, be sure to address one issue at a time.

Once you have decided on what you want to work on, make sure to set your intentions and attune to the crystal's energy. Use your intuition and how your body responds to the crystal. Your body may be done processing the energy when the crystal comes off your body, your energy starts to cool down or vibrate at a gentler level, or the area that your crystal is in makes a twitching movement. Please use the following as a guide and seek professional medical help if needed.

health remedies

pain (method 1)

Crystals: black tourmaline, selenite, amber

Meditation: Hover your black tourmaline over your body starting at the crown chakra and moving down to the root. Imagine any stuck energy being pulled out of your body and pushed to the ground, then under the earth, into an energy "trash can." Keep this motion going for 1 to 3 minutes, until you intuitively feel you have released any stuck energy. Once you're done, place the black tourmaline at the bottom of your feet. You can begin your meditation. Lie down, sit down, or if you're in extreme pain and want something else to focus on (such as the TV), you can do that as well. Place the selenite and amber on the localized area where you're experiencing pain. Place both hands on top of the area in pain, breathe into that area, and show it love. You can be in this meditation for as long as you'd like, but I would highly suggest a minimum of 30 minutes.

Daily Remedy: Keep a piece of selenite or amber on you at all times. When you feel any tension or pain, hold the crystal on the localized area and breathe with ease and love.

pain (method 2)

Crystals: two clear quartz points

Meditation: To relieve energetic causes of pain, you can use two clear quartz points. Direct one point toward the localized area of pain and the other point outward from the body. Lie in this meditation for 3 to 15 minutes, or until you intuitively feel your body has released the stuck energy.

accelerated healing after an injury

Crystals: two lemurian wands

Meditation: Get into a comfortable position lying down or sitting straight up. Hold one lemurian wand in each hand. Visualize the localized area that needs healing as already healed. For instance, if you broke your ankle, imagine each bone that is broken back to its healthy state. This will accelerate the body's natural healing process. Stay in this meditation for a minimum of 30 minutes.

Daily Remedy: Before you go to bed, place a lemurian in the localized area that needs healing. If you can, wrap a bandage around it to keep it in place. When we are asleep, we do the most healing, so this process will accelerate your body's natural healing process even further.

anxiety or stress

Crystals: raw lepidolite and raw hematite

Meditation: Get into a comfortable position lying down or sitting straight up. Hold the lepidolite in your receptive (nondominant) hand facing upward and the hematite in your sending (dominant) hand facing downward. This will allow the vibrations of peace, serenity, and tranquility to be pulled in from the universe and support your emotional well-being, while simultaneously releasing excess negative energy (such as anxiety or stress) to bring you back into balance and the present moment. Stay in this meditation for a minimum of 11 minutes. The longer you stay in this meditation, the calmer and more at peace you will begin to feel.

Daily Remedy: Keep one lepidolite and one hematite in a crystal pouch, a pocket, or your bra daily to continue to release any stress or anxiety and bring in the vibrations of peace and harmony. You can also wear these crystals as bracelets: lepidolite on your receptive hand and hematite on your sending hand.

stomach imbalances

Crystals: citrine and bumblebee jasper

Meditation: Get into a comfortable position lying down or sitting straight up. Hold the citrine in one hand and the bumblebee jasper in the other hand. Or lie flat on the ground and place them both on your solar plexus chakra. This will soothe any stomach issues or imbalances and strengthen your solar plexus chakra. Stay in this meditation for a minimum of 11 minutes and ask the universe to show you what brings you joy, confidence, and personal power. You may find your inner sense of gratitude for what is.

Daily Remedy: Keep one citrine and one bumblebee jasper in a crystal pouch, in a pocket, as jewelry, or in your bra daily to continue to ease any stomach issues or imbalances.

headache or migraine

Crystal: amethyst

Meditation: Get into a comfortable position lying down or sitting straight up. Gently place your amethyst on your third-eye chakra or as close to the pain as possible. Imagine a beautiful purple light expanding from your third-eye chakra to the rest of your body. You are a beautiful, pure soul who is free of all pain, worry, and fears. Allow yourself to be in this meditation for 3 to 15 minutes, or until the pain subsides.

Daily Remedy: Keep one amethyst in a crystal pouch, in a pocket, as jewelry, or in your bra daily and pull it out to provide relief if need be.

fertility

Crystals: carnelian heart, two shiva lingam

Meditation: Get into a comfortable position lying down. Gently place the carnelian heart on your womb and hold a shiva lingam in each hand. Focus on your womb and imagine your beautiful baby in your belly. You can even give it a gender and name, if you feel called to. If you'd like to deepen this meditation even further, have your significant other join you by placing their hands on the carnelian and also imagining your beautiful baby in your womb. Do this meditation for at least 15 minutes.

Daily Remedy: Before you go to bed every night, place the carnelian heart on your womb.

energy and vitality

Crystals: citrine, four clear quartz points

Meditation: Lie flat on your back and place the citrine on your belly. Then place all four clear quartz points facing toward you at the four corners of your body (head, feet, left side of chest, right side of chest). This will draw energy into your body and fill up your solar plexus chakra, where the core of our energy and vitality is held. Imagine a beautiful bright yellow light bathing you in infinite light starting from your auric field and all the way into your solar plexus. You may feel a new glow to you when this meditation is done. I would highly recommend staying in this meditation for 11 minutes.

Daily Remedy: Keep one citrine and one clear quartz in a crystal pouch, in a pocket, or in your bra daily to continue to bring in energy.

hormonal balance

Crystals: rainbow moonstone and chrysocolla

Meditation: Get into a comfortable position lying down or sitting straight up. Hold the rainbow moonstone in one hand and the chrysocolla in the other hand. This will have a gentle vibration that slowly brings your hormones back into balance. Stay in this peaceful meditation for a minimum of 30 minutes and repeat the affirmation: *I bring balance and light to my hormones.*

Daily Remedy: Keep one rainbow moonstone and one chrysocolla tumble in a crystal pouch, in a pocket, as jewelry, or in your bra daily to continue to bring balance to your hormones.

immune system balance

Crystals: four double-terminated herkimer diamonds, one orange calcite, four mookaite jasper tumbles.

Meditation: Lie flat on your back and place all nine crystals near the center of your solar plexus chakra. Start with the orange calcite in the center of your belly, then surround the orange calcite with alternating crystals, mookaite jasper then herkimer diamond. Place your left hand on the orange calcite and then the right hand on top of your left. Imagine a beautiful bright orange light coming from the orange calcite, slowly filling up your entire solar plexus chakra, and then expanding to the rest of your body. Stay in this crystal layout for as long as you desire; I would recommend at least 15 to 20 minutes.

Daily Remedy: Wear the crystal combination of orange calcite, herkimer diamond, and mookaite jasper throughout your day for additional immune support and balance.

premenstrual syndrome (pms)

Crystals: one rainbow moonstone, two hematite, one rose quartz

Meditation: This crystal layout will calm the ovaries and release any negative energy tied to them. Place the rainbow moonstone and rose quartz on your womb area or lower back and a hematite below each foot. You can either lie flat

on your back or sit straight up for this meditation, whatever is most comfortable for you. Sometimes my PMS symptoms will get really bad, and the fetal position is the only position I find comfort in—that works too. Take slow and controlled deep breaths. Really focus on your breath and let the crystals do the rest. Stay in this calming meditation for as long as you desire, or until the symptoms have subsided.

Daily Remedy: You can keep this crystal combination (hematite, rainbow moonstone, rose quartz) in a daily crystal pouch or in your bra to bring you relief throughout your time of the month.

sleep

Crystals: lepidolite and shungite

Meditation: Get into a comfortable position lying down in your bed. Hold the lepidolite in your receptive (nondominant) hand and the shungite in your sending (dominant) hand. This will allow the vibrations of peace, serenity, and tranquility to be pulled in from the universe and support your emotional well-being, while simultaneously releasing excess or stuck negative energy. Allow your body to just be. If your mind begins to wonder, repeat this affirmation: *With these breaths, I welcome a restful sleep.* When you use this meditation, you may notice that you wake up the next morning with the crystals still in your bed because you fell asleep with them in your hands!

Daily Remedy: You can place a lepidolite, howlite, shungite, or amethyst under your pillow at night to help you fall asleep and stay asleep. If you struggle with consistently waking up in the middle of the night, hold a rose quartz near your heart to help bring your circadian rhythm back into balance.

libido

Crystals: carnelian and ruby

Meditation: Get into a comfortable position lying

down or sitting up. Gently place the carnelian and the ruby on your sacral chakra. This will allow the vibrations of pleasure and passion to be pulled in from the universe and into your sacral chakra to boost your libido. Ask the universe to show you what brings you joy in your sexual relationship. Do this meditation for at least 3 to 11 minutes.

Daily Remedy: Keep a carnelian and a ruby by your bedside to increase your libido.

nervous system balance

Crystals: black onyx, ocean jasper, kunzite, and blue sapphire

Meditation: Get into a comfortable position lying down. Place the black onyx on your root chakra in between your feet, the ocean jasper on your solar plexus chakra, the kunzite on your heart chakra, and the blue sapphire on your third-eye chakra in between your eyebrows. Imagine the energy vibrating from the black onyx, through the ocean jasper and kunzite, and up to the blue sapphire all together as one. This will help you release any stuck or unwanted energy that is putting your nervous system out of balance, and it will help you bring the vibrations of peace and love to calm and realign your nervous system. Stay in this crystal layout for as long as you desire; I recommend at least 11 to 20 minutes.

Daily Remedy: Keep one kunzite, one ocean jasper, one black onyx, and one blue sapphire in a crystal pouch, in a pocket, or in your bra daily to continue to bring your nervous system back into balance and to a place of peace and harmony.

pregnancy bond with baby

Crystals: two rose quartz palms or tumbled stones

Meditation: Get into a comfortable position lying down, sitting straight up, or in whatever position feels most comfortable to you at this time in your pregnancy. Hold one rose quartz stone in each hand and begin to meditate. During your meditation, imagine giving your baby a hug. As you are hugging him or her, a beautiful bright pink light is connecting you two, bringing in the most abundant feelings of unconditional love, support, gratitude, and connection. Enjoy this deep, loving meditation for as long as you please. This meditation will also give your baby comfort and the knowledge that it is safe to come out into the world when they are ready.

Daily Remedy: Rose quartz has a very gentle energy; keep a rose quartz tumble in your bra, in a pocket, in a pouch, or as jewelry all day long to strengthen the love between you and your child.

Note: If you are pregnant, go light with crystals in general because it can be a lot for the baby.

weight loss

Crystals: carnelian, blue apatite, and kyanite

Meditation: Get into a comfortable position lying down. Then place all three crystals near your belly, starting with carnelian closer to your sacral chakra, the blue apatite near your belly button, and the kyanite right above the blue apatite on your solar plexus chakra. During your meditation, connect to positive affirmations of how you want to view your body. For instance, repeat affirmations such as: *I love my body, I am comfortable in my own skin*, and *My body deserves my love and respect*. Allow yourself to feel whatever emotions may arise. They may be stuck, so it's important to let them flow and not block them out. I would highly recommend staying in this deep meditation for at least 11 minutes.

Daily Remedy: Wear this crystal combination (carnelian, blue apatite, and kyanite) in a crystal pouch, in a pocket, as jewelry, or in your bra daily to continue your successful weight loss journey.

healing remedies

self-love

Crystals: one rose quartz heart, four raw morganite, four clear quartz points

Meditation: Lie flat on your back and place all nine crystals near the center of your heart. Start by placing the rose quartz heart on your heart. Then surround the heart with alternating crystals, morganite and then clear quartz. Make sure all the points are facing inward toward the heart to draw in unconditional love for yourself from the universe. Place your left hand over your heart and then your right hand on top of your left. Imagine a beautiful pink light coming from the rose quartz heart and slowly filling up your entire heart chakra and then expanding to the rest of your body. Stay in this crystal layout for as long as you desire; I would recommend at least 15 to 20 minutes.

Note: If this is too much energy, reduce the crystal layout to just a rose quartz heart in the center of your chest.

Daily Remedy: Keep one rose quartz heart, a raw morganite, and a clear quartz in a crystal pouch, in a pocket, or in your bra daily to continue to bring feelings of unconditional love toward yourself.

overwhelming emotions

Crystals: blue lace agate and black tourmaline

Meditation: Get into a comfortable position lying down or sitting straight up. Hold the blue lace agate in your receptive (nondominant) hand facing upward and the black tourmaline in your sending (dominant) hand facing downward. This will allow the vibrations of peace, serenity, and tranquility to be pulled in from the universe and support your emotional well-being, while simultaneously releasing excess negative energy to bring

you back into balance and the present moment. Stay in this meditation for a minimum of 3 minutes. The longer you stay in it, the calmer and more at peace you will begin to feel. Sometimes I use this to help me fall asleep at night when my brain is on overload.

Daily Remedy: Keep one blue lace agate and one black tourmaline tumble in a crystal pouch, in a pocket, or in your bra daily to continue to release any negative energy and bring in the vibration of peace and harmony.

grief

Crystals: one morganite, one rhodochrosite, two rose quartz

Meditation: This crystal layout will help resolve emotional trauma and open your heart to forgiveness and unconditional love. Lie flat on your back and place all four crystals near the center of your heart. Start by placing the morganite on your heart chakra. Then use the other crystals to surround the heart chakra in a Y shape, with the morganite being the center of the Y, the rhodochrosite being the stem of the Y pointing down toward your belly, and a rose quartz on each side of your chest for the branches of the Y. During your meditation, focus on your heart center and ask your body to allow feelings to come and then be released when you're ready. This meditation should make you feel much lighter and filled with a new sense of love. How long you meditate depends upon how deep you want to go and for how long your body is ready to accept this healing. Three minutes may be your maximum.

Daily Remedy: Keep one rose quartz, a morganite, and a rhodochrosite in a crystal pouch, in a pocket, or in your bra daily to continue to bring feelings of emotional release, forgiveness, and unconditional love.

confidence

Crystals: sunstone, citrine, and rose quartz

Meditation: Get into a comfortable position lying down. Place the sunstone on your sacral chakra, the citrine on your solar plexus chakra, and the rose quartz on your heart chakra. Place your hand on top of the sunstone and your other hand on top of the rose quartz. Imagine the energy from the crystals vibrating together as one. This will fill you with unconditional love for all that you are and allow you to feel confident in not only who you are but how you show yourself to the world. Stay in this crystal layout for as long as you desire; I would recommend at least 15 to 20 minutes.

Daily Remedy: Keep a rose quartz, a citrine, and a sunstone in a crystal pouch, in a pocket, or in your bra daily to continue to bring you feelings of confidence, courage, kindness, and unconditional love for exactly who you are.

joy

Crystals: ocean jasper and sunstone

Meditation: Get into a comfortable position lying down or sitting straight up. Hold the ocean jasper in one hand and the sunstone in your other hand. This will allow the vibrations of pleasure, happiness, and gratitude to be pulled in from the universe and support your emotional well-being. Stay in this meditation for a minimum of 11 minutes and ask the universe to show you what brings you joy. You may find that happiness is not external, but an internal feeling of what you've been searching for. The longer you stay in this meditation, the more joy you will begin to feel. You can also use this meditation as a mood lifter or to help combat depression.

Daily Remedy: Keep one ocean jasper and one sunstone tumble in a crystal pouch, in a pocket, as jewelry, or in your bra daily to continue to bring feelings of joy, gratitude, pleasure, and happiness.

releasing trapped emotions

Crystal: selenite wand

Meditation: Before you begin, decide on one specific trapped emotion that you want to release. This could be anxiety, fear, overwhelm, anger, hatred, or anything else that you are ready to release so you can feel fully aligned with your best self. Then stand straight up with your feet shoulder-width apart and your hands by your sides. Take a few moments to go within, breathe, and ground. This will allow you to tap into your subconscious mind. Once you feel relaxed and centered, hold your selenite wand 2 to 3 inches (5 to 7.5 cm) away from your third-eye chakra (in between your eyebrows) and ask your sub-conscious mind to release your trapped emotion. Move the wand over the top of your head and down the back of your neck as far as you can reach. Repeat this motion three times. This medi-tation is powerful, so only do this once a day.

Releasing trapped emotions can be very energetically moving. I wouldn't suggest keep-ing crystals with you daily with the intention of consistently releasing trapped emotions. This can put your system on overload. A daily meditation is plenty. You may even notice after one medi-tation that you aren't emotionally ready to do it again right away. That is totally fine! Listen to your body.

positive relationships

Crystals: one amazonite, two carnelian, and one pink opal

Meditation: Get into a comfortable position lying down. Place the carnelian on your sacral chakra, the pink opal on your heart chakra, and the ama-zonite gently on your throat chakra. Imagine the energy from the carnelian, the pink opal, and the amazonite vibrating together as one. This will fill you up with confidence about your relationship, your ability to speak your truth, and your ability to open your heart to receiving love. Stay in this crystal layout for as long as you desire; I would recommend at least 10 to 15 minutes.

Daily Remedy: Keep one amazonite, one carnelian, and one pink opal in a crystal pouch, in a pocket, or in your bra daily to continue to bring feelings of confidence, trust, honor, and love into your relationship(s).

love

Crystals: one rose quartz heart and four herkimer diamonds, preferably double-terminated

Meditation: This crystal layout will draw in unconditional love for yourself and others from the universe and support your emotional well-being. Lie flat on your back and place all five crystals near the center of your heart. Start by placing the rose quartz heart on your heart. Then place the four herkimer diamonds on your body in the north, south, east, and west directions of the heart. Place your left hand on the heart and then your right hand on top of your left. Imagine a beautiful pink light coming from the rose quartz heart, slowly filling up your entire heart chakra, and then expanding to the rest of your body. Stay in this crystal layout for as long as you desire; I would recommend at least 15 to 20 minutes.

Daily Remedy: Keep a rose quartz heart in a daily crystal pouch or in your bra over your heart chakra to continue to bring feelings of unconditional love and open your heart up to love again. Wearing a rose quartz bracelet or necklace is also an amazing way to attract unconditional love into your life.

addiction

Crystals: hematite, rhodochrosite, kyanite, and amethyst

Meditation: Get into a comfortable position lying down. Place the hematite between your feet on your root chakra, the rhodochrosite on your heart chakra, the kyanite on your throat chakra, and the amethyst gently on your third-eye chakra. Allow your body to just be. Allow any negative thought patterns or feelings that come up to come in so they can then be released through the hematite and out of your body. This may feel uncomfortable at first, but sometimes we need the stuck energies to rise before they can be released. As you allow your body to be, the crystals will fill you up with emotional support, release, and self-love. Stay in this crystal layout for as long as you desire; I would recommend at least 20 to 30 minutes.

Daily Remedy: Keep one amethyst and one kyanite in a crystal pouch, in a pocket, or in your bra daily to continue to help you conquer your addiction(s).

anger

Crystals: howlite and smoky quartz

Meditation: Get into a comfortable position lying down or sitting straight up. Hold the howlite in your receptive (nondominant) hand facing upward and the smoky quartz in your sending (dominant) hand facing downward. This will allow the vibrations of peace and serenity to be pulled in from the universe and support your emotional well-being, while simultaneously releasing trapped energy that has been built up over time. Stay in this meditation for a minimum of 10 minutes. You should begin to feel a huge sense of relief and a cooling sensation once your body has released the anger and is ready to be done with the meditation.

Daily Remedy: Keep one howlite and one smoky quartz tumble in a crystal pouch, in a pocket, or in your bra, or wear both as bracelets daily to continue to release anger and bring feelings of peace and harmony into the emotional body.

compassion

Crystals: one emerald, one kunzite, one morganite, and two rose quartz

Meditation: This crystal layout will open your heart up to forgiveness, love, and care for others from a place of unconditional love. Lie flat on your back and place all five crystals near the center of your heart. Start by placing the emerald on your heart. Then place the kunzite below the emerald (toward your belly), the morganite above the emerald, and the rose quartz on the left and right sides of the emerald. During this meditation, imagine a beautiful green light coming from the emerald and then connecting to the energy of the kunzite, morganite, and rose quartz. Through this connection and expansion, you slowly allow yourself to fill up your entire heart chakra and then expand this vibrant green energy to the rest of your body. If this meditation makes you emotional, that is a great sign of release! Allow what is to be. Stay in this crystal layout for as long as you desire; I would recommend at least 15 to 20 minutes.

Daily Remedy: Keep this crystal combination (emerald, kunzite, morganite, and rose quartz) in a crystal pouch or in your bra over your heart chakra daily to continue to bring you emotional support during this gradual process.

forgiveness

Crystals: eudialyte, rhodochrosite, and sugilite

Meditation: Get into a comfortable position lying down. Place the eudialyte in between your feet at the root chakra, rhodochrosite on your heart chakra, and sugilite above your head on the crown chakra. Allow your body to just be. This is a very deep healing that can be a lot at first, so be kind to yourself and allow any emotions or feelings that arise to come and be released through your root chakra. As you allow your body to be, the crystals will fill you up with emotional support, compassion, release, and unconditional love. Stay in this crystal layout for as long

as you desire; I would recommend at least 11 to 15 minutes.

Daily Remedy: Keep one sugilite, one rhodochrosite, and one eudialyte in a crystal pouch, in a pocket, or in your bra daily to continue to forgive yourself and others.

peace

Crystals: four howlite, four lepidolite, and two blue chalcedony

Meditation: This crystal layout will help you bring your body back into the present moment and help you feel at peace. Before your meditation, surround your aura with the four howlite and four lepidolite crystals. Alternate them, starting with the howlite at your right shoulder, the lepidolite near your neck, and so on until you get to the left shoulder. Once you have finished, get into a comfortable position lying down. Hold your blue chalcedony crystals in each hand and begin your meditation. Imagine a beautiful white light starting at your crown chakra and filling your body up completely, from the third-eye chakra all the way down to the root chakra. Stay in this meditation for a minimum of 11 minutes. The longer you stay in it, the calmer and more at peace you will begin to feel.

Daily Remedy: Place a howlite, a blue chalcedony, and a lepidolite crystal in a pouch under your pillow at night to help you fall asleep and bring you feelings of peace and harmony.

focus and concentration

Crystals: two fluorite and one blue sapphire

Meditation: Get into a comfortable position lying down. Place the blue sapphire on your third eye and hold one fluorite in each hand. Focus on your third-eye chakra and repeat this affirmation: *I am focused on becoming the best version of myself.* This crystal layout and meditation will help you stay focused and concentrate on being present in the moment, and this energetic positive vibration will stay with you throughout your day. Stay in this meditation for a minimum of 3 minutes.

Daily Remedy: Keep this crystal combination (fluorite and a blue sapphire tumble) in a crystal pouch, in a pocket, or in your bra daily to continue to bring direct focus, concentration, and determination with little distraction throughout your work or school day.

self-acceptance

Crystals: rose quartz, kunzite, and rhodochrosite

Meditation: Get into a comfortable position lying down. Place all three crystals near the center of your heart chakra, starting with rose quartz at the heart, then rhodochrosite at your sternum, and finally kunzite at your upper chest. Place your left hand over the rose quartz and the right hand over the kunzite. Allow your body to just be and repeat the affirmation: *I love and accept myself for exactly as I am.* As you allow your body to be in the moment, the crystals will fill you up with the vibration of self-acceptance to help you fully love yourself unconditionally, exactly as you are. Stay in this crystal layout for as long as you desire; I would recommend at least 11 to 15 minutes.

Daily Remedy: Keep one rose quartz, one rhodochrosite, and one kunzite in a crystal pouch, in a pocket, or in your bra daily to continue to accept yourself or what happened to you from a place of unconditional love and understanding.

positive thoughts

Crystals: blue calcite and black tourmaline

Meditation: Get into a comfortable position lying down or sitting straight up. Hold the blue calcite in your receptive (nondominant) hand facing upward and the black tourmaline in your sending (dominant) hand facing downward. This allows the vibrations of positive thoughts and optimism to be pulled in from the universe and support your emotional well-being, while simultaneously releasing limiting beliefs, low expectations of yourself, and any negative energy blocks or barriers you may have built up. Stay in this meditation for a minimum of 3 minutes. The longer you stay in it, the more positive you will begin to feel.

Daily Remedy: Keep one blue calcite and one black tourmaline raw or tumble in a crystal pouch, in a pocket, or in your bra daily to continue to release any negative thoughts and bring in the vibration of positivity and optimism. You can also wear them as bracelets, with blue calcite on your receptive hand and black tourmaline on your sending hand.

speaking your truth

Crystals: aquamarine palm stone, kyanite palm stone, and blue lace agate palm stone

Meditation: This crystal layout will help you find the courage to speak your authentic truth and articulate your thoughts more clearly. Before your meditation, lie down and place the kyanite either under or on top of your throat (whichever is more comfortable for you). Hold the aquamarine in one hand and the blue lace agate in the other. During your meditation, allow the crystal to fill your entire throat chakra with gentle blue light. Move this beautiful blue energy with the flow of your breath. Allow yourself to soak in this energy and continue the meditation for as long as your body needs. I highly recommend a minimum of 3 minutes; 11 minutes is ideal. You can also do this layout before bed and ask the universe to show you in your dreams how to articulate your words with authenticity, love, and truth.

Daily Remedy: Carry an aquamarine, a kyanite, and a blue lace agate crystal in a pouch, in your pocket, or in your bra to strengthen your ability to speak your truth throughout your day.

self-worth

Crystals: carnelian, citrine, and garnierite

Meditation: Get into a comfortable position lying down. Place the carnelian on your sacral chakra, the citrine on your solar plexus chakra, and lastly the garnierite on your heart chakra. Place your left hand over the carnelian and your right hand over the garnierite. Allow your body to just be and repeat the affirmation: *I am worthy of love and happiness.* As you allow your body to be in the moment, the crystals will fill you up with the vibration of greater love, respect, and appreciation for your own value. Stay in this crystal layout for as long as you desire; I would recommend at least 15 to 20 minutes.

Daily Remedy: Carry one or all of the crystals (carnelian, citrine, and garnierite) with you in your pocket, in your bra, or in a crystal pouch daily. This will continue to bring reminders of your worthiness.

releasing fears

Crystals: blue chalcedony palm stone and gold sheen obsidian palm stone

Meditation: Before your meditation, write down in your journal or on a piece of paper all the unwanted fears that push you away from the highest vibration of love. Once you have finished, safely burn the paper, and watch how the energy begins to feel released from those fears. Once you have finished, begin your meditation, sitting up or lying down comfortably. Hold the blue chalcedony in your receptive (nondominant) hand facing upward and the gold sheen obsidian in your sending (dominant) hand facing downward. This will allow the vibrations of fear to be released in a healthy way that results in feeling light and free. Get yourself grounded and present. Focus your attention on your root chakra and ooze that red energy from your root chakra down into mother nature. Once you feel present and grounded, with every breath out, repeat the affirmation: *I breathe out negative energy.* See

this negative energy leaving your body, just like the smoke left the paper before you began your meditation. Continue this meditation for 5 to 10 minutes, or until you feel energetically at a place of peace and love.

Daily Remedy: Wear the crystal combination of a small gold sheen obsidian and a blue chalcedony in a crystal pouch, in a pocket, or in your bra daily to continue the healing process of releasing your fears and filling you up with love, grounding, grace, peace, and courage.

setting boundaries

Crystals: amazonite and sunstone

Meditation: Get into a comfortable position lying down or sitting straight up. Hold the amazonite in your receptive (nondominant) hand facing upward and the sunstone in your sending (dominant) hand facing downward. This will allow the vibrations of support, guidance, and awareness to be heightened in helping you set boundaries with others. During your meditation, imagine your auric field providing a huge shield of white light surrounding and protecting you. Allow this light to expand past your aura and out to the rest of the world. Stay in this meditation for as long as it takes for you to feel protected, enlightened, and empowered. I would suggest at least 11 minutes for this meditation.

Daily Remedy: You can carry one or two of the following crystals daily to empower you to set boundaries with others: amazonite, sunstone, ruby, red jasper, carnelian, amber, charoite, garnierite, and Libyan desert glass.

manifestation

Crystals: moldavite and three hematite. If you want to add even higher vibrations to this meditation, include six double-terminated herkimer diamonds.

Meditation: Set your specific intentions for what you want to manifest (see chapter 2). Then place the three hematites below your root chakra. This will help you keep grounded, as moldavite is highly vibrational. Then place the moldavite on your heart or third-eye chakra, whichever you intuitively feel called to. Lastly, if you'd like to add even higher vibrations, place six herkimer diamonds surrounding your crown chakra, from the left shoulder around to the right, with the points facing toward and away from you. Once your crystals are laid out, begin your meditation by focusing on the specific manifestation you'd like to call in from the universe. See it and feel it like it's already happened. You can stay in this meditation for as long as you feel called to; I would highly recommend 11 minutes. Repeat this crystal layout daily until you have achieved your manifestation.

Daily Remedy: Keep one moldavite and one hematite in a crystal pouch, in a pocket, or in your bra daily to continue to bring forth your manifestations into reality.

Note: If you are an empath or sensitive soul, moldavite may be too powerful for you and can even take you out of your body, giving you feelings of anxiety or imbalance. A gentler substitute is Libyan desert glass or citrine. If you are new to moldavite, slowly allow your body to adjust to its energy by introducing it daily for a minute and adding more time as you feel more comfortable with its energy.

strengthening intuition

Crystals: four clear quartz points, spirit quartz, and azurite

Meditation: Before your meditation, surround your aura with the four clear quartz points facing inward toward you, with the spirit quartz in the middle of them, above your head on your crown chakra. Once you have finished, get into a comfortable position lying down, and gently place the azurite on your third-eye chakra in between your eyebrows. During your meditation, direct your focus to your third-eye chakra. Imagine a deep indigo blue light shining from your third eye out into the universe. Allow this light to transcend into a portal that leads you to answers that you have been asking for from the universe. Stay in this meditation for as long as you feel guided to; I would recommend 11 minutes. By opening your intuition, you are also calming the nervous system, reducing or eliminating brain fog, and lessening anxious feelings.

Daily Remedy: Carry a small spirit quartz, an azurite, and a clear quartz in a pouch, in a pocket, or in your bra to stimulate your third-eye chakra and awaken your intuition throughout your day.

spiritual connection and awakening

Crystals: raw smoky quartz, sugilite tumble, gold rutile, amethyst palm stone, and smoky quartz palm stone

Meditation: Get into a comfortable position lying down. Place the raw smoky quartz in between your feet on your root chakra. Then place the sugilite tumble on your third-eye chakra and then the golden rutile above your head on your crown chakra. Hold the amethyst palm stone in your receptive (nondominant) hand facing upward and the smoky quartz palm stone in your sending hand (dominant) facing downward. This will allow the vibrations of spiritual expansiveness and awakening to be pulled in from the universe, while simultaneously rooting your body down so you don't lose control or your sense of physical being. Allow your body to just be and become aware of your spiritual consciousness. Stay in this meditation for at least 11 minutes, but no longer than an hour.

Daily Remedy: Wear a golden rutile and smoky quartz bracelet daily, or place a sugilite, a smoky quartz, and an amethyst tumble in a pouch, in a pocket, or in your bra daily to continue to help you become more spiritually connected and aware.

grounding

Crystals: hematite, red jasper, and bloodstone

Meditation: Before your meditation, place the hematite underneath your right foot and the red jasper underneath your left foot. Then lie down in a comfortable position and place the bloodstone over your heart. Once you are present and relaxed, imagine yourself as a tree. Trees are always grounded, but sway with the wind (*flow of life*). Imagine your feet as roots of the tree, grounded into the earth. Then imagine your legs up to your chest as the trunk of the tree. Then imagine your arms, neck, and head as the branches. Lastly, imagine your connection to the world around you as the leaves of the tree. As you begin to sink into this deep connection to yourself and mother nature, direct your focus to the bloodstone at your heart chakra. Create a dark green expansion of light that travels down into your root chakra and down into mother nature. Allow its energy to bring you back into the present moment. Continue this meditation for as long as your body needs. I highly recommend a minimum of 3 minutes; 11 minutes is ideal.

Natural cubic pyrite for attracting wealth

Daily Remedy: Wear a hematite, bloodstone, or red jasper bracelet daily to keep you feeling grounded, uplifted, confident, and present in the moment.

protection

Crystals: six selenite, six clear quartz points, one amethyst, and one black tourmaline

Meditation: Before your meditation, lay out the six selenite crystals and six clear quartz points (facing outward from your body), alternating around your auric field. Then lie down in a comfortable position and hold the amethyst in your receptive (nondominant) hand facing upward and the black tourmaline in your sending (dominant) hand facing downward. Once you are present and relaxed, imagine a bright white light surrounding your entire aura like a shield. Stay in this spiritual protection for at least 11 minutes.

Daily Remedy: Keep a selenite stick on the top of a doorframe in each room of your house for spiritual protection from the negative energy from others. You can also keep one amethyst and one black tourmaline in a crystal pouch, in a pocket or purse, in your car, or in your bra daily for constant protection wherever you go.

creativity

Crystals: two carnelian

Meditation: Keep a journal nearby. Get into a comfortable position lying down. Place the carnelian on your sacral chakra, one on each hip. Then gently place your hands on top of them. Once you are relaxed and calm, focus your attention on your sacral chakra and see swirls of orange energy. As this energy is stirring up, allow your body to open up to its creative flow. This will help spark new ideas, invite creative visions, expand your thinking, and come up with out-of-the-box ideas. Write down any visions or ideas that come up during your meditation. You can do this meditation for as long as you need to; I would allow for at least 3 minutes.

Daily Remedy: Keep two carnelian tumbles, one in each pocket, on you daily to allow for creativity to flow and new ideas to spark.

abundance

Crystals: citrine sphere and golden healer sphere

Meditation: This crystal layout will help you radiate abundance and expansion, allowing you to find your personal power and manifest your greatest desires. Get into a comfortable position lying down. Hold the citrine sphere in one hand and the golden healer sphere in the other.

Focus on your solar plexus chakra and repeat the affirmation: *I radiate abundance and universal light*. Stay in this meditation for a minimum of 3 minutes.

Daily Remedy: Keep this crystal combination (citrine and golden healer) in a crystal pouch, in a pocket, or in your bra daily to continue to bring abundance, light, manifestation, prosperity, and energy throughout your day.

chakra balancing

Crystals: red jasper (root chakra), sunstone (sacral chakra), citrine (solar plexus chakra), rose quartz (heart chakra), angelite (throat chakra), lapis lazuli (third-eye chakra), and amethyst (crown chakra)

Meditation: Get in a comfortable position lying down. Set each crystal on the corresponding chakra layout on your body, starting at the root chakra and working up to the crown chakra. Then close your eyes, placing your hands on the crystal for the root chakra. Then visualize your crown chakra opening as you inhale white light from the universe. Allow this light to flow through to your root chakra and fill up your crystal with this beautiful white universal light. Expand into this energy for 3 minutes. Repeat this process for all seven chakras, going in order from the root to the crown. Try to allow yourself to be in this chakra-balancing layout for at least 20 minutes. Allow your intuition to guide you if you need more or less time in each chakra. Once you are finished, remove all the crystals, starting from the crown chakra and moving down to the root chakra. This order will help ease your energy back down gently. You should notice that you feel much more centered, balanced, and aligned.

Daily Remedy: Wear a seven-chakra beaded bracelet daily to keep your chakras balanced and aligned at all times.

aura clearing, strengthening, and protecting

Crystals: one smoky quartz, two citrine, two green tourmaline, and one selenite

Meditation: Before your meditation, place all six crystals surrounding your auric field: Place the smoky quartz below your root chakra to dissolve any negative energy encased in the aura. Place the citrines on both sides of your belly to help cleanse, align, and fill any holes in your aura. Place the green tourmalines on both sides of your heart to help fill in any holes in the auric field, especially those surrounding your heart. Lastly, lay the selenite above your crown chakra to protect your aura. Once your crystals have been placed, begin your meditation. Imagine a bright white light surrounding your entire aura like a shield, filling in any holes, and then finding that extra strength. Stay in this aura crystal layout for at least 11 minutes.

Daily Remedy: Wear a smoky quartz bracelet on your sending (dominant) hand and a selenite bracelet on your receptive (nondominant) hand daily to keep a constant flow of glowing white light surrounding the auric field. You can also create a small crystal pouch for your pocket or purse with the crystal combination of smoky quartz, green tourmaline, citrine, and selenite and keep it on you daily.

release, protection, and refill for empaths

Crystals: malachite, citrine, and black tourmaline

Meditation: Get into a comfortable position lying down or sitting straight up. Hold the malachite with both hands and imagine the energy blockages that are not yours being pulled out of you, pushing out your belly button. Then hold the citrine in your receptive (nondominant) hand facing upward and the black tourmaline in your sending (dominant) hand facing downward. This will allow the vibrations of purified energy to be pulled in from the universe and into your solar plexus power, while simultaneously releasing excess negative energy that is not yours or doesn't serve your highest good. Stay in this meditation for a minimum of 11 minutes.

Daily Remedy: Keep one black tourmaline and one citrine in a crystal pouch, in a pocket, or in your bra daily to continue to provide energetic protection, refill, and release.

angelic guidance

Crystals: three (or up to six) double-terminated herkimer diamonds, kunzite, angelite, and celestite

Meditation: Before your meditation, place a journal or a piece of paper and pen near you so you can jot down any messages you receive from your angel(s). Place the herkimer diamond crystals with the points facing toward your body in the shape of a crown surrounding your crown chakra. Lie down flat on your back and place the kunzite on your heart chakra, the angelite on your throat chakra, and the celestite on your third-eye chakra. Close your eyes and begin your meditation with a two-part breath, inhaling through the mouth the entire time: Inhale through your belly, then your heart, and exhale the energy out through your arms while you breathe out through your mouth. Repeat this breathing in this crystal layout for 11 minutes. During this meditation, ask your angels for guidance.

Daily Remedy: Sleep with an angelite and a celestite tumble under your pillow at night. Before you go to bed, ask your angels to guide you in your dreams.

other crystal layouts

attracting wealth

Crystals: green aventurine and pyrite

Meditation: Get into a comfortable position lying down or sitting up. Hold the green aventurine in one hand and the pyrite in the other. Focus on the exact wealth you want to manifest and repeat the affirmation: *Money comes to me easily and effortlessly.* This crystal layout with meditation will help you radiate abundance to help you manifest wealth into your life and release any fears tied to your illusion of what money is. Stay in this meditation for at least 3 to 11 minutes.

Daily Remedy: Carry one or all of the following crystals daily to help attract wealth in abundance into your life: citrine, green aventurine, pyrite, and moldavite. You can place a piece of pyrite in your wallet next to your money or on top of a check to attract more wealth as well.

finding a better job

Crystals: tiger's eye, eudialyte, and green aventurine. You can also add moldavite to increase the speed of finding a better job.

Meditation: Before your meditation, place the tiger's eye on your sacral chakra, the eudialyte on your heart, and the green aventurine on your chest. Then lie down in a comfortable position and begin. Once you are present and relaxed, imagine yourself at the job of your dreams. Ask your body to show you how it would feel to have this job. Ask your mind to show you how it would make you thrive. And ask your spirit how this job would align with your highest self. Allow this positive energy to be a magnet to the universe that aligns you with the most perfect job; you may already have one in mind, or you may receive the guidance to the right one. Continue this meditation for as long as you feel guided to. I highly recommend 11 minutes.

Daily Remedy: Keep this crystal combination (eudialyte, green aventurine, and tiger's eye) in a crystal pouch, in a pocket, or in your bra daily to attract the best job for your highest self.

success

Crystals: golden healer and jet

Meditation: Get into a comfortable position lying down or sitting straight up. Hold the golden healer in your receptive (nondominant) hand facing upward and the jet in your sending (dominant) hand facing downward. This will allow the vibrations of guidance, inner knowledge, visions, potential, and accomplishment to be pulled in from the universe and into your awareness while simultaneously releasing any excess negative thoughts or limiting beliefs that are tied to what successes you believe you are capable of. During your meditation repeat this affirmation with every exhale: *I am capable of living and achieving my wildest dreams.* Stay in this meditation for a minimum of 3 minutes; the longer you stay in it, the more connected and aware you will feel about the true meaning of your success and how to get there.

Daily Remedy: Keep one golden healer and jet, raw or tumble, in a crystal pouch, in a pocket, or in your bra daily to continue to release any negative thoughts or limiting beliefs and bring in the vibration of success. You can also wear them as bracelets, with a golden healer on your receptive hand and a jet on your sending hand.

air travel protection

Crystals: black obsidian and amethyst

Meditation: Do this meditation before you head to the airport and while the plane is taking off. Hold the black obsidian in one hand and the

Rose quartz is perfect for using in healing remedies, such as self-love, grief, and compassion.

amethyst in the other. During your meditation, fill up your entire body with a beautiful white light, and then expand that white light to your auric field. This huge shield of white light surrounds and protects you. Allow this light to expand past your aura and out into the rest of the world. Stay in this meditation for as long as you need; airports can be especially draining for empaths or sensitive souls. I would recommend doing this meditation for at least 15 to 30 minutes before you head to the airport.

Daily Remedy: Keep as many of the following crystals on you as a shield from negative energy or potentially harmful situations: black obsidian, amethyst, super 7, blue apatite, lepidolite, labradorite, and blue kyanite.

visual glossary

Bowl (Sunstone)

Cabochon (Serpentine)

Carved Animal
(Labradorite Turtle)

Carved Diety
(Larimar Buddha)

Carved Symbol
(Lepidolite Angel)

Cube (Copper)

Double Terminated
(Black Obsidian)

Egg (Pink Tourmaline)

Flame (Amazonite)

Freeform (Green Opal)

Merkaba (Sunstone)

Obelisk (Charoite)

Palm (Amazonite)

Point (Mookaite)

Pyramid (Rhodochrosite)

Raw (Pyrite)

Sphere (Charoite)

Tumble (Amazonite)

Vogel (Rose Quartz)

Worry Stone (Sodalite)

Asterate Star (Rose Quartz)

Cluster (Vera Cruz Amethyst)

Druzy (Malachite)

Elestial (Smoky Quartz)

Etched (Smoky Quartz)

Geode (Amethyst)

Inclusion (Dendritic Quartz)

Key/Imprint (Lemurian)

Manifestation (Clear Quartz)

*Phantom Quartz
(Chlorite Phantom)*

Rainbow (Smoky Quartz)

Record Keeper (Lemurian)

*Record Keeper
(Lemurian Quartz)*

*Self-Healed
(Himalayan Quartz)*

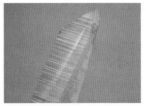

Striations (Lemurian)

Window (Tiger's Eye)

INDEX OF CRYSTALS

about the author

Rachel Hancock is a Certified Advanced Crystal Practitioner, Reiki Master, and holds a bachelor's degree in Physical and Health Science with a minor in Psychology. She, along with her husband Joel, is the founder of LovingThyselfRocks, one the top crystal purveyors and crystal education sites on Instagram. Founded in 2018, LovingThyselfRocks has sold hundreds of thousands of crystals to customers around the world and is located in Winter Park, Florida, as well as online. Rachel's mission is to promote the power of self-love and healing crystals.

acknowledgments

To my husband and soulmate, Joel Hancock, thank you deeply for being my rock through everything. You have always reminded me in my darkest days that there was a greater purpose out there for me, I just have to move through the darkness and into the light to see it. I am so beyond grateful to have you by my side through it all. You have helped make this dream of mine come to life in so many ways. Thank you for helping me with the book photography, loving support, and guidance. I love you so very much. Together, we are able to help the lives of so many through our crystal company Lovingthyselfrocks, and I hope to do the same with this book.

To my Lovingthyselfrocks team (friends and family), Mom, Hannah (sister), Kelsey, Billy, Mark, and Marco, thank you for believing in me since day 1. The love and passion you have to help change people's lives through crystals and love, inspires me daily. Your support, love, kindness, and hard work is deeply appreciated from the bottom of my heart. Our company wouldn't be possible without each and every one of you. You all mean the world to me, and I am forever grateful to not only have you as part of the LTR team, but as my family.

To Lisa Toney, I am beyond grateful to have been blessed by the guidance of the Universe that led me to you. You were the first person who introduced me to my spiritual journey, energy work, and crystals. This book wouldn't have been possible without you. I am so grateful to have you as a friend and spiritual mentor.

To Diane Pilatovsky, I am so blessed that the Universe led me to you. You have helped me through the darkness moments of my life and helped me learn so much about my own spiritual journey, energy work, personal growth, and unconditional love for self. Thank you from the bottom of my heart, writing this book wouldn't have been possible without you.

To my Lovingthyselfrocks community, I am forever grateful for all of your love and support. You have made this book opportunity possible. Thank you for your loving, kind, and caring messages daily that have allowed me to strengthen my knowledge and understanding on how crystals have helped heal you in ways that I could share with readers in this book. Your healing has made a ripple effect on not only your life, my life, but anyone who reads this book. Thank you deeply.

To Ashley Leavy from Love and Light School of Crystal Therapy, thank you for your deep love and passion for sharing your knowledge and healing about crystals. I am forever grateful to have gotten my Advanced Crystals Practitioner Certification from your program. You're such a light to this world.

To Jill and the entire Quarto Publishing Team, thank you for this incredible opportunity to write and publish *The Ultimate Guide to Crystals*. Each and every one of you have made this book possible and I am forever grateful for your kindness, hard work, guidance, and passion.

To all my guides and mentors, thank you for guiding me into the light of who I really am. I am forever grateful to have found and love who I am and share my life's purpose with the world. Each and every one of you has a special place in my heart and I am so blessed that the Universe led me to you.

To all of my friends and family, it's been such a joy seeing all of you step into the love and light that you are. Thank you for your loving support for my husband and I's crystal company Lovingthyselfrocks and the writing of this book. I love each and every one of you.

index